The pasta bible

The pasta bible

The definitive guide to choosing, making, cooking and enjoying Italian pasta

Jeni Wright

southwater

Dedication

I would like to dedicate this book to my very dear friend Elisa, who has inspired and delighted me with her wonderful Italian cooking, especially her home-made pasta.

This edition is published by Southwater
an imprint of Anness Publishing Ltd
www.annesspublishing.com

If you like the images in this book and would like to investigate using them for publishing, promotions or advertising, please visit our website www.practicalpictures.com for more information.

Publisher: Joanna Lorenz
Executive Editor: Linda Fraser
Editor: Joy Wotton
Copy Editors: Jenni Fleetwood and Jay Thundercliffe
Production Controller: Ben Worley
Designer: Patrick McLeavey
Photography: William Lingwood (recipes) and Janine Hosegood (techniques and cut-outs)
Food for Photography: Lucy McKelvie and Kate Jay (recipes) and Annabel Ford (techniques)

Front cover shows Spaghetti with Salmon and Prawns – for recipe, see page 132

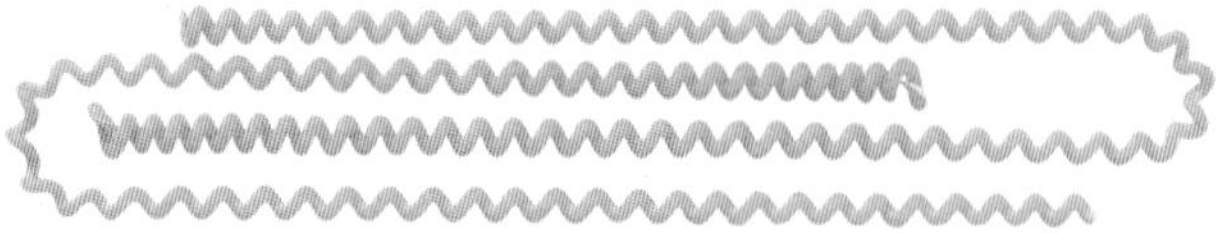

Cook's Notes

Bracketed terms are intended for American readers.

For all recipes, quantities are given in both metric and imperial measures and, where appropriate, in standard cups and spoons. Follow one set of measures, but not a mixture, because they are not interchangeable.

Standard spoon and cup measures are level. 1 tsp = 5ml, 1 tbsp = 15ml, 1 cup = 250ml/8fl oz.

Australian standard tablespoons are 20ml. Australian readers should use 3 tsp in place of 1 tbsp for measuring small quantities.

American pints are 16fl oz/2 cups. American readers should use 20fl oz/2.5 cups in place of 1 pint when measuring liquids.

Electric oven temperatures in this book are for conventional ovens. When using a fan oven, the temperature will probably need to be reduced by about 10–20°C/20–40°F. Since ovens vary, you should check with your manufacturer's instruction book for guidance.

Medium (US large) eggs are used unless otherwise stated.

CONTENTS

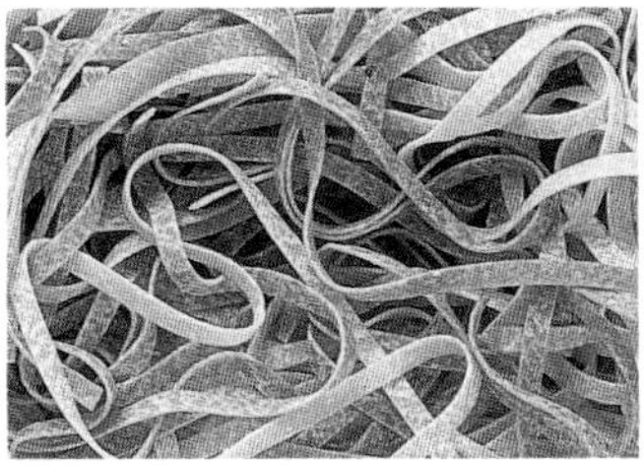

Introduction

Pasta is one of the most popular foods in the world today. Available in an amazing range of shapes and flavours, it is incredibly versatile, and can be served in scores of different ways. Students love it for the energy it gives them at low cost, chefs delight in introducing light and healthy sauces for modern palates, families favour bakes that can be cooked ahead and which will stretch to serve extra guests. Simple or sophisticated, quick and easy to cook, it is the perfect choice for everyday and spur-of-the-moment meals.

Introduction

The origin of pasta

There is a great deal of controversy surrounding the origin of pasta. Who invented it? Was it the Chinese, the Italians, or even the Arabs? There is absolutely no doubt that Marco Polo brought noodles back to Italy from China in 1295, but most food historians agree that a kind of pasta was well known in Italy long before this time. Wall paintings in an Etruscan tomb show utensils – a pastry board, rolling pin and wheel – that are remarkably similar to those used today for making pasta. There is also evidence that the Romans made an unleavened dough of flour and water which they fried, cut into pasta-like strips and ate with a sauce. Apicius, the famous Roman gastronome of the 1st century AD, described baked dishes in which a pasta-like dough was layered with other ingredients. A kind of Roman lasagne?

Wherever or whenever pasta was first "invented", it seems to have been the Sicilians who were the first to boil it in water. They learnt irrigation and cultivation from the Arabs who conquered the island in the 9th century, and by the 12th century there is evidence they were eating a long thin type of pasta like spaghetti. Meanwhile, the Calabrians had mastered the art of twisting pasta strips to make tubes that resembled modern-day macaroni.

In a 13th-century Italian cookbook published just before Marco Polo's return from China, there are recipes for making different pasta shapes, including ravioli, vermicelli and tortelli. So one way or another, pasta did exist in Italy before Marco Polo, and the pasta museum in Rome has many writings, paintings and etchings to substantiate this.

By the time of the Renaissance, pasta featured frequently on Italian menus. The rich Florentines teamed it with costly sugar and spices, but the less well-off had to content themselves with eating pasta plain or with humble ingredients, such as garlic, vegetables and cheese.

In those early days, pasta was simple, fresh and hand-made, a far cry from the many different commercially produced dried shapes and flavours that we know today. The credit for inventing these must go to the Neapolitans.

The fertile soil in the region around Naples was found to be ideal for growing durum wheat, which makes the best flour for commercial pasta, and the unique combination of sun and wind in this part of southern Italy was just right for drying out the shapes. Once the Neapolitans discovered this, the pasta-making industry burgeoned around the city of Naples, and by the late 18th century the consumption of pasta in Italy had really taken off. Maccheroni, spaghetti and tagliatelle were among the first shapes to be produced commercially, made with flour and water only.

At this time pasta was regarded as food for the poor, and tended to be served with tomato sauces. Tomatoes loved the growing conditions in the south as much as the durum wheat, and once the Italians fell in love with the tomato there was no looking back.

The egg-enriched pasta that northern Italians favoured was not produced commercially at this time. *Pasta all'uovo* was freshly

There is no doubt that Marco Polo brought back noodles to Italy from China in the late 13th century. However, an Italian cookbook, which was published just before his return, includes recipes for making pasta. His departure from Venice is depicted in this early 14th-century painting, Romance of Alexander.

Workers in the fields at Pitti Palace, Florence, in the late 19th century tending the hard durum wheat, which Italians call grano duro. This type of wheat produces the ideal flour for pasta.

made, often with a meat filling or sauce, and was served to the rich. It was not until the 20th century that improvements in industrial equipment made the manufacture of egg pasta a viable commercial proposition.

Pasta today

Wherever Italians went, they took their pasta with them. Those that emigrated to America and Great Britain adapted pasta shapes and sauces to suit local tastes and ingredients, a tradition which happily continues to this day.

Pasta is becoming more and more popular as a healthy, quick-cooking and versatile food, and Italian manufacturers have quickly responded to the demand, constantly developing new flavours and using the latest technology to create original shapes.

Commercially produced dried pasta has always been highly regarded in Italy. It is in no way inferior to fresh home-made pasta, but is simply a different form of this fabulous food. Italian cooks always keep a few packets of dried pasta in their store cupboards and use it on a daily basis – even in the north of Italy, where the tradition of making fresh pasta at home endured for a lot longer than it did in the south of the country.

The right kind of wheat

The ideal variety of wheat for the flour used in commercial pasta making is durum (Triticum durum), which Italians call *grano duro*. This hard summer wheat produces a flour that is high in gluten. Dough made from durum wheat flour is pliable and easy to knead and shape. The majority of durum wheat for the Italian pasta-making industry is grown in Italy or imported from North America. The flour from durum wheat, called *semola* in Italian, makes a high quality pasta that holds its shape well. Cooked properly until *al dente*; it should be just tender, with a pleasant nutty bite. When you are buying pasta in packets or boxes, always check that it is made from 100 per cent durum wheat. The Italian phrase to look out for is *pasta di semola di grano duro*. This type of pasta may be more expensive than one made with a mixture of durum wheat and soft wheat, but you will get a much better result. Inexpensive pasta made with soft wheat flour tends to stick together during cooking and its texture is often soft and flabby. Generally speaking, the Italian makes are the best. Ask the staff at your local delicatessen which brands they recommend, and spend as much as you can afford. There is a big difference in texture and taste between the higher priced Italian brands and the cheaper types of pasta, and you will quickly find that it pays to buy the best.

The northern preference for egg pasta

In southern Italy the majority of pasta is made with durum wheat and water only, and literally hundreds – if not thousands – of different shapes are manufactured. In northern Italy, the preference is for pasta with added egg, *pasta all'uovo*. The tradition for using this type of pasta began in Emilia, where filled and stuffed pasta shapes originated. Home cooks found that adding a little egg to the dough strengthened it, and helped to keep the filling in during cooking. As Italian housewives began

Above: Healthy ingredients, such as olive oil, tomatoes, garlic and peppers, combine wonderfully well with pasta and are used over and over again by Italian cooks. This may be one of the reasons that the incidence of heart disease in Italy is one of the lowest in the world.

Below: The various sizes and shapes of holes in these commercial pasta dies allow for the production of a wide range of long and short pasta shapes.

Above right: In modern pasta factories sophisticated machines are used to weigh and pack the finished product.

to make less and less fresh pasta at home and turned to buying it from the shops, small factories started making dried egg pasta to meet the demand. Now it is fast becoming a huge industry, although there are fewer fancy shapes made with egg than there are with plain pasta. This is because egg pasta is more difficult to work with. It is not used for making long thin shapes like spaghetti because they would break too easily. Commercially manufactured *pasta all'uovo* may contain as many as 7 eggs to 1kg/2 1/4lb flour, so it has a richer taste than plain pasta and absorbs more water.

If you buy Italian egg pasta, the packet should state that it is 100 per cent durum wheat and egg *(semola di grano duro e uova)*. *Pasta all'uovo* complements the cream and butter sauces that are popular in the north. The tomato and olive oil sauces of the south have always been traditionally served with plain pasta, although *pasta all'uovo* is now catching on in the south, too.

The nutritional value of pasta

Rich in protein, vitamins and minerals, pasta is a complex carbohydrate food. It provides as much energy as a pure protein like steak, but with little or no fat. Of the eight amino acids essential to make up a complete protein, pasta contains six, so it only needs a small quantity of cheese, meat, fish, pulses or eggs – the traditional ingredients for serving with pasta – to make it complete. If you are using *pasta all'uovo*, you need even less additional protein.

The key to healthy eating lies in eating pasta as the Italians do, with only a small amount of extra ingredients. In Italy, it is traditional for pasta to be served as a first course, before the main course of fish or meat. Eaten with a small spoonful of sauce and a light sprinkling of grated cheese, nothing could be more well-balanced and nutritionally sound.

The incidence of heart disease in Italy is one of the lowest in the civilized world, and doctors, nutritionists and scientists agree that the Italian diet plays a large and important role in this. In Italian cooking, healthy ingredients, such as extra virgin olive oil, fresh and canned tomatoes, garlic, onions, olives, red peppers and fresh parsley are used all the time, plus lots of fresh fish, vegetables and salad leaves, fruit, pulses and lemon juice. Most of these ingredients combine wonderfully well with pasta, and they are used over and over again in the recipes in this book.

Pasta is a completely natural food that contains no additives. Pasta with egg contains the most nutrients, while wholewheat pasta has the highest percentage of vitamins and fibre. For coeliacs and those trying to avoid wheat, all kinds of gluten-free pastas are widely available, made from rice, maize and other gluten-free flours. Gluten-free pasta and flour can be used in many of the recipes in this book; but take into account the instructions on the packet.

Pasta is inexpensive, quick and easy to cook, and incredibly versatile. It is the perfect convenience food: in the time it takes to boil the water and cook the pasta, most sauces are ready to serve. *Pasta all'uovo* is especially nutritious and good for children who don't like eggs. Athletes and other sportspeople will appreciate the fact that as a high-energy food, pasta is easy to digest and yet immensely satisfying.

It makes sense, to include pasta in our diets as often as possible, if not every day. People watching their weight may be surprised to know that a 75g/3oz portion of cooked pasta yields only about 100 calories (424kJ) and can therefore be eaten as part of a calorie-controlled diet, as long as it is only lightly sauced.

Pasta as an everyday meal

In Italy pasta is generally eaten as a first course (*primo piatto* or just *primo*) as part of the main meal of the day. This may be at lunchtime or in the evening, depending on family circumstances and whether the meal is served during the week or at the weekend. The meal usually begins with antipasto, which is followed with a *primo piatto* of either soup, pasta, rice or gnocchi. Pasta used to be served as a lunchtime first course when lunch was traditionally the main meal of the day, but now that more and more Italian women are working outside the home, these customs are changing and there are fewer hard-and-fast rules about lunch and dinner. After the *primo piatto*, the second course, *secondo piatto*, is served. This is either fish or meat followed by vegetables or salad, then cheese, fresh fruit and coffee. Desserts are normally reserved for special occasions.

When pasta is served as a first course, the usual amount is 65–90g/2½–3½oz uncooked weight per person. Sauce is added sparingly; this is usually tossed with the freshly drained hot pasta in the kitchen, and the mixture is then brought to the table in one large bowl.

Coloured pasta looks and tastes very good, but always check the label before buying, because some varieties include artificial colourings.

By the time the pasta reaches the dining room it has mingled with the sauce and taken on some of its flavour. In some homes the bowl is passed around the table and everyone helps themselves, while in others one person does the serving. When you are serving pasta directly from the bowl, it looks most attractive if you retain a small ladleful of the sauce to put on top of the pasta after tossing, then sprinkle this with cheese or herbs at the last moment.

If it suits your lifestyle best to serve pasta as a main course for lunch or supper, simply increase the weight of uncooked pasta to 115–175g/4–6oz per person and make more sauce. For convenience, you may prefer to serve pasta in shallow soup plates or bowls or on dinner plates. Warm these beforehand and serve and eat the pasta as soon as possible so that it can be enjoyed at its best. If you accompany your main course with a fresh leafy green salad and follow with some fresh fruit, you will have a tasty, nutritious and supremely satisfying meal. *Buon Appetito!*

Although traditionally served from one large bowl that is passed around the table, you may prefer to serve pasta in shallow soup plates or bowls.

Dried Pasta

The many hundreds of different types of dried pasta are divided into categories. Long, short and flat shapes are the most common, but there are also stuffed shapes, shapes suitable for stuffing and tiny shapes for use in soup. Among these, you will find some less well-known regional shapes and the more unusual and decorative designer shapes.

Only buy dried pasta that is made using 100 per cent durum wheat. If you decant pasta shapes into storage jars, use up any remaining pasta before adding more from a new packet. Older pasta may take longer to cook than that from a fresher packet, and different brands of the same shape may not necessarily have the same cooking time.

Long Pasta / *Pasta Lunga*

Dried long pasta in the form of spaghetti is probably the best-known pasta of all time, and was certainly one of the first types to be exported from Italy. Spaghetti is still very widely used, but nowadays there are many other varieties of long pasta that look and taste just as good. There are no hard-and-fast rules when matching pasta to sauce, so experiment with alternative varieties to add interest to your cooking, always remembering that long pasta is best served with either a thin, clinging sauce or one that is smooth and thick. If too thin and watery, the sauce will simply run off the long strands; if too chunky or heavy, the sauce will fall to the bottom of the bowl and you will be left with a bowl full of chunks and no pasta to eat it with. Clinging sauces made with olive oil, butter, cream, eggs, finely grated cheese and chopped fresh herbs are good with long pasta. When ingredients such as vegetables, fish and meat are added to a smooth thick sauce, they should be very finely chopped.

Bavette

Bucatini

Capelli d'angelo a nidi

Capelli d'angelo

Capellini

Capellini a nidi

Long pasta comes in different lengths, but 30cm/12in is about the average. In specialist food shops, you may see dried pasta that is much longer than this but think twice before buying it because extra-long pasta can be tricky to cook and eat, and often not worth the bother. The width of long pasta varies too; the strands can be flat, hollow, round or square, while other types have the pasta strands coiled up into nests.

Most long shapes are available in plain durum wheat only. The shapes made with egg (*all'uovo*) are very delicate, and are either packed in nests or compressed as waves. Fine long pasta, such as spaghetti, is far too delicate to be made with egg, but a short version from Emilia-Romagna, called capricciosa all'uovo, is available.

Bavette

This type of long pasta is known all over Italy, but is very common in the South. The noodles are narrow and flat, like tagliatelle, only slimmer. Indeed, some southern Italians use the name bavette to describe tagliatelle. Bavettine is a narrower version. Both types can be plain or all'uovo (with egg).

Bucatini
This looks like spaghetti but is slightly chunkier. The strands are hollow (*buco* means hole), like hard, inflexible drinking straws. This type of pasta is best known in the Roman dish, *Bucatini all'Amatriciana*, which has a tomato, bacon and pepper sauce, and in Sicily it is traditionally served with a sauce of fresh sardines. Bucatoni is a fatter version, while perciatelli is bucatini by another name.

Capelli d'angelo
The name means angel's hair, which is an evocative description for this extremely fine pasta. It is used in broths and soups, and is popular with children. You may find it packed in nests, labelled capelli d'angelo a nidi. These nests are easy to handle and cook – one nest per person is the usual serving, so you can use as many nests as you require. Capellini and capel Venere are similar to capelli d'angelo.

Chitarra
Also known as spaghetti alla chitarra, this type of pasta is cut on a special wooden frame strung with wires like guitar strings (*chitarra* is Italian for guitar). It is therefore square-shaped rather than round, but can be used as an alternative to spaghetti.

Fusilli
Spaghetti spirals that look like long opened-out corkscrews. You may see these labelled fusilli lunghi or fusilli col buco, to distinguish them from the more widely known short fusilli and eliche. Fusilli is often used with tomato sauces.

Lasagnette
This flat pasta resembles tagliatelle, but the noodles are slightly wider. There are several types, most of which have frilly edges. Reginette is similar. You can use lasagnette in place of any ribbon pasta.

Linguine
In Italian the name means little tongues and accurately describes a very thin spaghetti-like pasta that has flattened edges. You may also see linguinette and lingue di passera (sparrows' tongues), both of which are even narrower. Wholewheat linguine is also available. All are good with the simple olive oil-based sauces and smooth tomato sauces of southern Italy.

Maccheroni
A very familiar form of pasta. We know a short version of it as macaroni, but in Italy the long thick tubes are widely used for all kinds of sauces – in some regions the word maccheroni is even used as a generic term for pasta and maccheroncini is simply the name given to very thin, long pasta. Maccheroni comes in different lengths and thicknesses, with straight or angled ends, in plain, egg and wholewheat varieties. There is even a square-shaped chitarra version, which comes from Abruzzi. There they call it maccheroni alla chitarra, but it also goes by the name of tonnarelli. Maccheroni is useful because it goes with so many different sauces.

Spaghetti alla chitarra

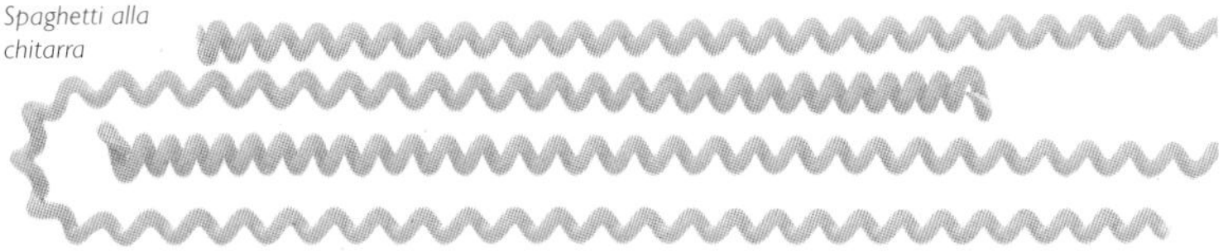
Fusilli lunghi

Lasagnette reginette

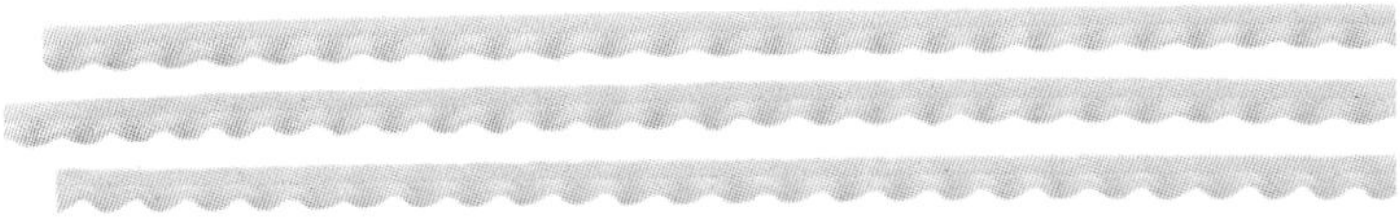
Lasagnette tripolini

Linguinette

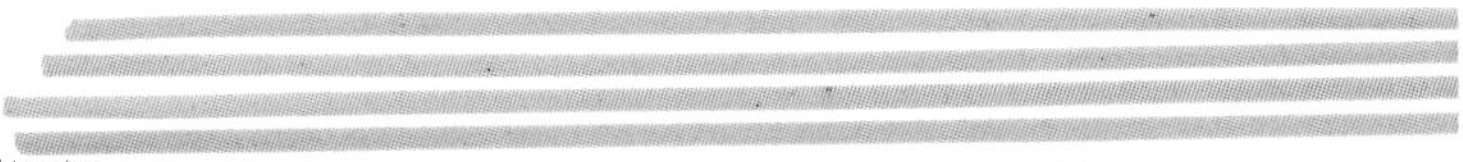
Linguine

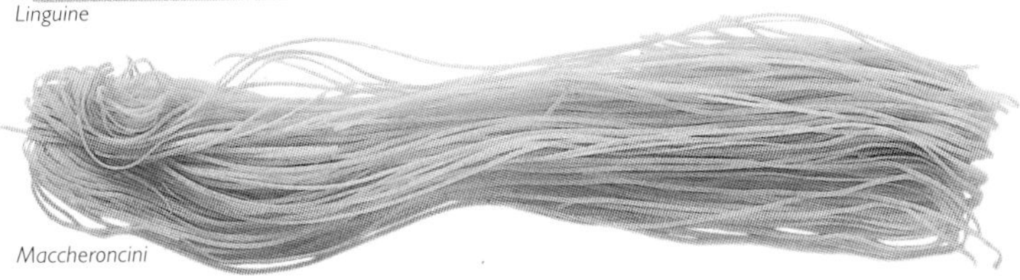
Maccheroncini

Maccheroni

Spaghetti

This familiar type of pasta takes its name from the word *spago*, which means string. Spaghetti means little strings; spaghettini is a thinner variety, and spaghettoni is thicker. Spaghetti originally came from Naples, but today it is made in other parts of Italy too, and the length and width vary from one region to another.

Numerous different brands, flavours and colours are available, including whole-wheat (*integrali*), spinach (*spinaci*) and chilli (*peperoncini*) so the choice is yours, but avoid the inexpensive brands. Long Italian spaghetti tends to be very good; it is graded by number according to the thickness. Good-quality spaghetti made in Italy is still one of the best forms of pasta, despite the ever-increasing range of other shapes. It goes well with many different kinds of sauces.

Tagliatelle

The most common form of ribbon noodles, tagliatelle derives its name from the Italian verb *tagliare* meaning to cut. The noodles are usually about 8mm–1cm/ 1/3–1/2in wide, but there are fine versions called tagliatellina, tagliarini and tagliolini, and an even finer type called tagliolini fini. Traditional tagliatelle comes from Bologna. It is made both with and without egg and with spinach (*verdi*), but new flavours and colours are constantly coming on to the market.

All types of tagliatelle are sold coiled in nests, which conveniently unravel during cooking when given a good stir. Paglia e fieno, which literally means straw and hay, is a mixture consisting of half plain egg and half spinach egg pasta, packed together in separate bundles of each colour. The noodles are usually quite thin, either tagliarini or tagliolini. Both tagliatelle and paglia e fieno are very popular because they go well with most sauces, although strictly speaking, tagliatelle should not be served with a fish sauce. Meat sauce is the classic, as in *Tagliatelle alla Bolognese*.

The Roman version of tagliatelle is called fettuccine. These long, flat noodles are virtually the same as tagliatelle, but slightly thinner.

Spaghetti

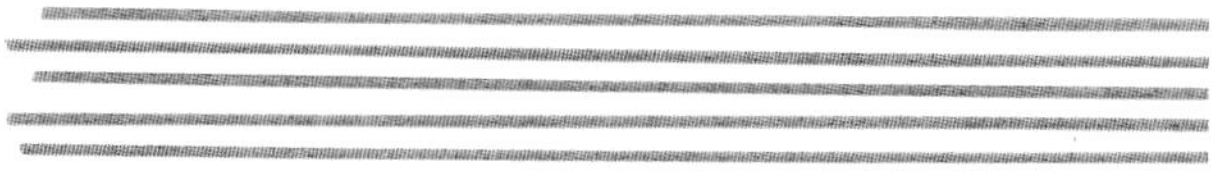

Spaghetti integrali

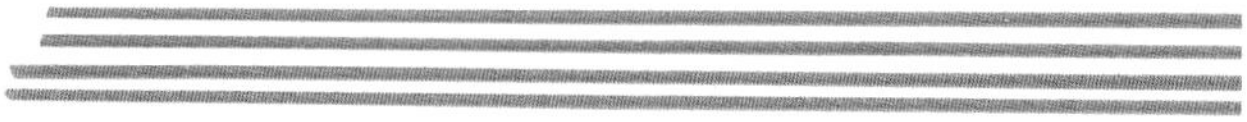

Spaghetti con spinaci

Spaghettoni

Spaghettini

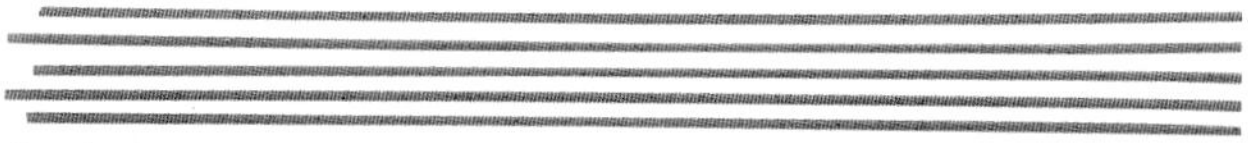

Spaghettini con peperoncini

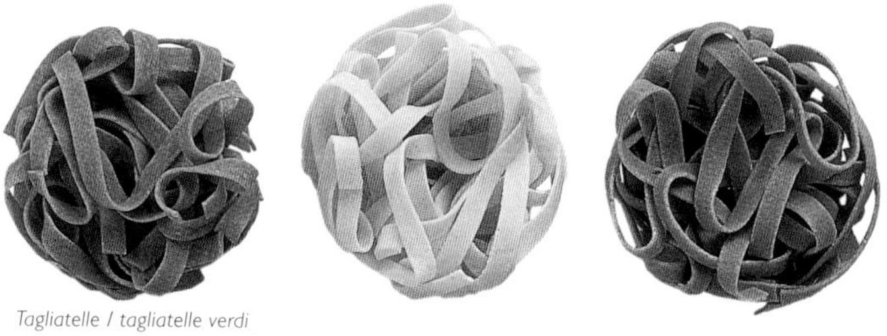

Tagliatelle / tagliatelle verdi

Vermicelli

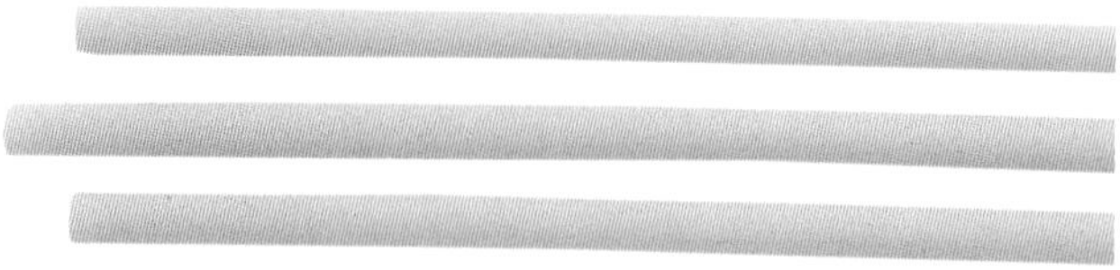

Ziti

Mezza zita

Vermicelli

This sounds appealing, but the name means little worms, which is rather unfortunate. It describes a very fine form of spaghetti – the original Neapolitan name for spaghetti was vermicelli, and southern Italians still sometimes refer to spaghetti as vermicelli, which can be confusing. This type of pasta comes in plain and egg (*all'uovo*) varieties and is very versatile, going well with most light sauces, but especially the light, fresh tomato and seafood sauces for which Naples is famous. There is an even finer version called vermicellini, and a similar noodle called fidelini.

Ziti

This pasta takes its name from the word *zita*, meaning fiancée. In the old days it was traditional in southern Italy to serve ziti at wedding feasts and on other special occasions. Ziti is very long, thick and hollow – like maccheroni – and the custom is to break it into the length required when you cook it. Because of their size, the tubes go well with robust and chunky sauces; they are also sometimes broken into short lengths and baked in a *timballo*, which is a cup-shaped mould. The pasta is used to line the mould, which is then filled with a savoury mixture such as mushrooms, ham or chicken livers combined with a sauce and topped with cheese. Zitoni are fatter than ziti; mezza zita are thinner.

Tagliolini all'uovo

Paglia e fieno

Tagliarini all'uovo

Some Regional Types of Long Dried Pasta

Fettuccine comes from Lazio, and these noodles are used in classic Roman pasta dishes, such as *Fettuccine all'Alfredo*. They are flat ribbons, like tagliatelle but narrower (about 5mm/¼in wide), and always sold coiled into loose nests. The three most common types are plain durum wheat, with egg (*all'uovo*), and with spinach (*verdi*), and you can use them interchangeably with tagliatelle. Fettuccelle is similar, but is straight rather than coiled. Fettuccelle integrali is the wholewheat variety.

Frappe is a type of pasta from Emilia-Romagna. The 2.5–4cm/1–1½in wide noodles are flat, with wavy edges, about halfway in size between tagliatelle and lasagne. Made with egg and very delicate, the noodles are packed by a special machine that presses them into waves.

Pappardelle are broad ribbon noodles (2–2.5cm/¾–1in wide), with wavy edges. They come from Tuscany, where they are still made fresh with egg every day, but dried versions are now becoming more widely available, many of them with only one wavy edge or straight edges. They are good with heavy meat and game sauces. Nastroni are similar straight-sided noodles that are sold coiled into nests.

Trenette are noodles from Liguria, where they are traditionally served with pesto sauce. The Genoese dish, *Trenette alla Genovese*, combines trenette with pesto, potatoes and beans. The noodles are about 3mm/⅛in wide, and are made with egg. They resemble bavette and linguine, which can be substituted for them if you find trenette difficult to find.

Fettuccine al nero

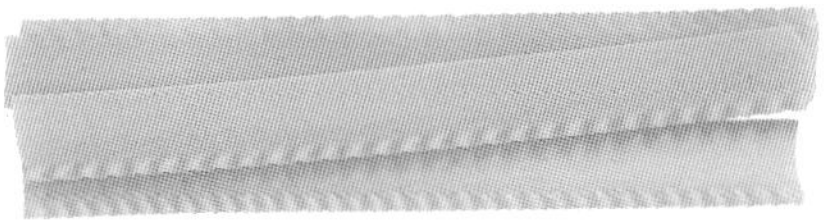

Pappardelle

Trenette

Fettuccelle

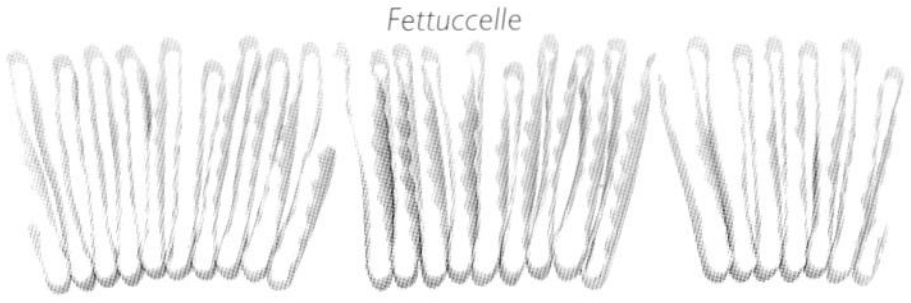

Frappe

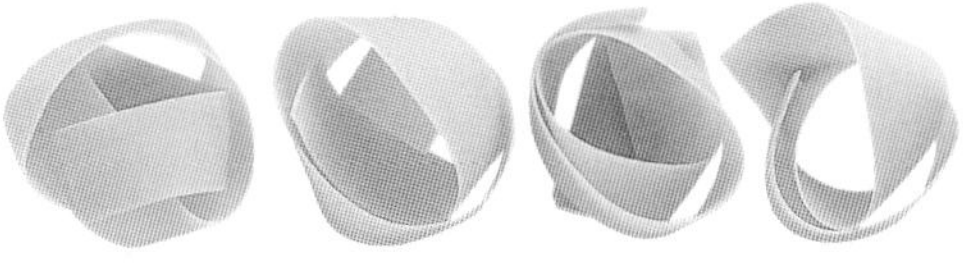

Nastroni

Short Pasta / *Pasta Corta*

There are literally hundreds of different short pasta shapes, and new ones are constantly coming into our shops. Some people prefer short pasta simply because it is easier to cook and eat than long pasta. It also goes well with many different sauces, and in most cases you can choose any shape you fancy, regardless of whether your sauce is a smooth tomato-, cream- or olive oil-based type, or is chunky with large pieces of fish, meat or vegetables. Exceptions are regional dishes that are traditionally cooked with a specific shape, such as *Penne all'Arrabbiata* from Lazio.

Short pasta is divided into two main groups. Pasta secca is factory-made, using durum wheat flour and water. This is by far the largest group, and you will find that most packets of dried pasta list only these two ingredients on the label. *Pasta all'uovo* is made with the addition of eggs. It is naturally a brighter yellow than pasta secca and has more nutritional value. Popular in the north of Italy, especially in Emilia-Romagna, *pasta all'uovo* has different properties from plain pasta and goes especially well with the rich creamy and meaty sauces associated with that part of Italy. It has an advantage over plain durum wheat pasta in that it cooks slightly more quickly and is less likely to become overcooked and soggy. Although it is more expensive than plain pasta, egg pasta is becoming more popular and therefore more widely available, so look out for it in an increasing number of shapes.

New flavours and colours in short pasta shapes are on the increase too. For many years, tomato (*pomodoro*) and spinach (*verde*) were all that was available, but today there seems to be no end to the number of different colour and flavour combinations, ranging from garlic, chillies and herbs to beetroot, salmon, mushroom, squid ink and even chocolate. Often three colours (red, white and green) are packed together and labelled tricolore. Wholewheat pasta, called *pasta integrale*, is made from durum wheat and other cereals. It is higher in fibre than plain durum wheat pasta and takes longer to cook. It has a chewy texture and nutty flavour.

Benfatti

Benfatti

The word *benfatti* means well made and originally described the little offcuts or scraps of pasta left over from making other shapes, such as tagliatelle. Traditionally these were used in soups so they would not be wasted, but they proved so popular that they are now made and marketed as a shape in their own right. Benfatti are available plain and with egg, and are good in salads as well as soups.

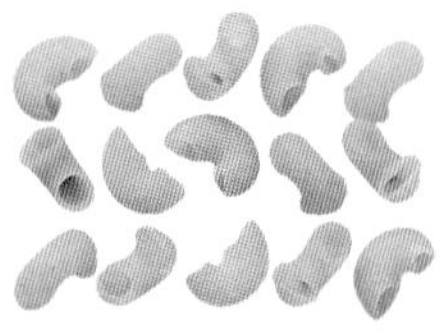

Chifferini rigatini

Chifferini

Also called chifferi, chifferoni and chifferotti, these are small curved tubes like short maccheroni that has been bent. Some versions are ridged (*rigatini*). The holes in the middle fill with sauce, making them an excellent shape for all types of pasta sauces and soups.

Conchigliette rigate

Conchiglie

As the name suggests, these shapes resemble small conch shells. Sometimes they are ridged, in which case they are called conchiglie rigate. They are one of the most useful small shapes because they are concave and trap virtually any sauce. For this reason they are extremely popular and are widely available in many different

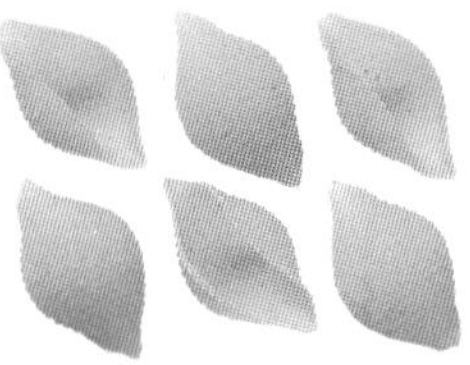

Conchiglie rigate

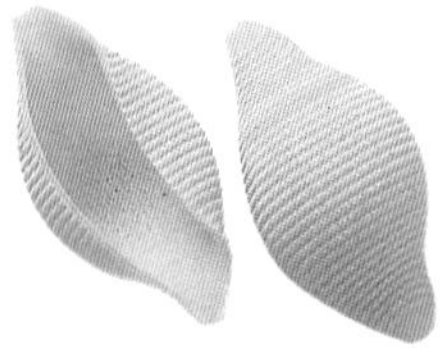

Conchiglioni rigati

colours and flavours. Sizes vary too, from tiny conchigliette for soups to conchiglione, which are jumbo shells for stuffing.

Eliche

The name comes from the Italian word for screws or propellers, which is exactly what these shapes look like. They are often mis-labelled as fusilli, which are similar, but when you see the two side by side there is a marked difference. Eliche are short lengths of pasta, each twisted into a spiral, like the thread of a screw. They are available in different thicknesses, colours and flavours, including wholewheat and tricolore, and are good with most sauces, but especially those that are tomato-based. You may only be able to buy them labelled as fusilli – the two are interchangeable and their names often depend on which part of Italy they come from.

Eliche all'uovo

Eliche tricolori

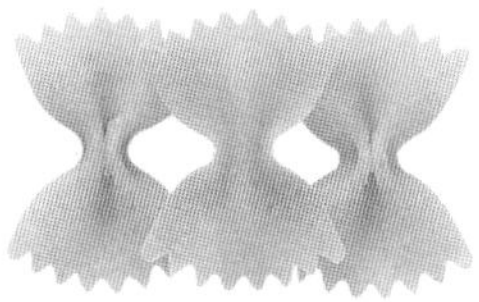

Farfalle

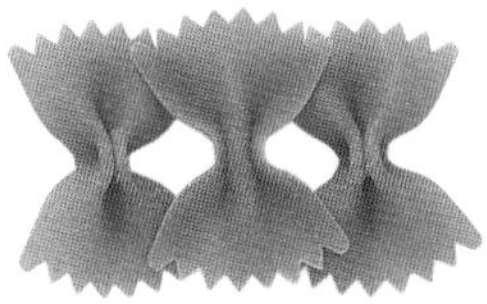

Farfalle verde

Farfalle salmonseppia

Farfalle tricolore

Farfalle

The word means butterflies, but these shapes are sometimes also described as bow-ties – the Italian word for bow-tie is *cravatta a farfalla*. They are very pretty, with crinkled edges, and are sometimes ridged. Due to their popularity, farfalle are available in a wide variety of colours and flavours, including plain, with egg and tricolore (plain, tomato and spinach flavours, which are sold together in mixed packets). Farfalle can be served with any sauce, but they are particularly good with cream and tomato sauces. Children love them. In Modena, farfalle are known as strichetti.

Fusilli

These spirals of thin pasta look like tight coils or springs and are formed by winding fresh dough around a thin rod. The spiral opens out, rather than remaining solid as it does in the case of eliche, for which fusilli are often mistaken. Check when buying, because most packets of fusilli are in fact eliche. Genuine fusilli is likely to be plain, neither made with egg nor coloured. The shapes go well with thin sauces.

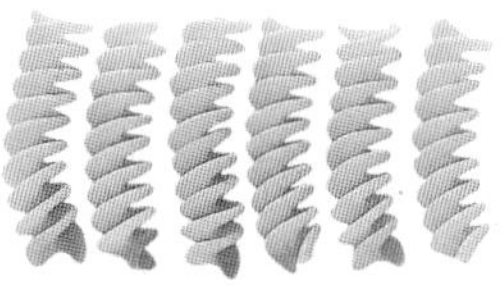

Fusilli

Fusilli con spinaci

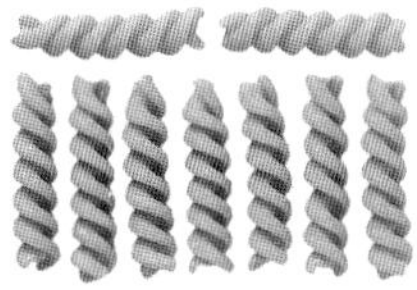

Fusilli all'uovo

Lumache rigate

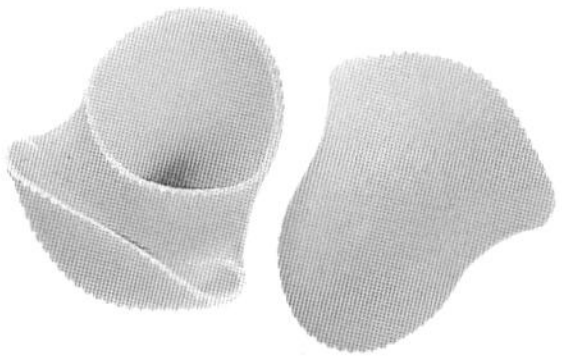

Lumachoni rigati

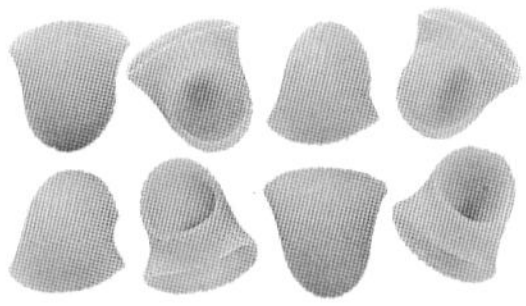

Gomiti rigati

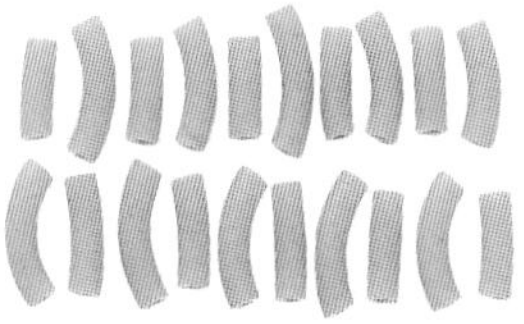

Maccheroni

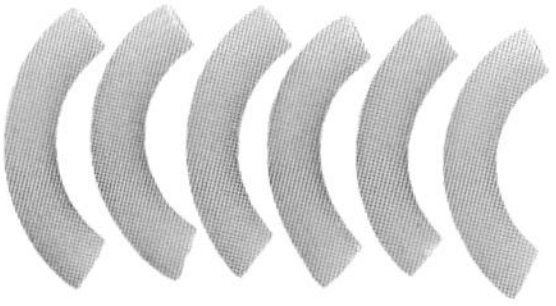

Maccheroncelli

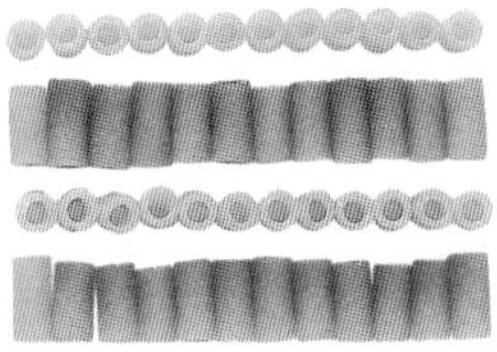

Tubetti

Lumache

Snail shells were the inspiration for this attractively shaped pasta. Unlike conchiglie, they are not shaped like conch shells, but resemble a larger version of pipe, because they are fashioned out of hollow pasta. Lumache are excellent for trapping sauces. The most common type available is lumache rigate (ridged), and there is also a large version called lumaconi. Gomiti is a similar conch shell shape.

Maccheroni

When cooks in the south of Italy speak of maccheroni, they usually mean long pasta, but in the north of the country they prefer it short. It is the short type that is generally exported as macaroni (sometimes labelled "elbow macaroni" although some brands are straighter than others). This used to be the most common short pasta shape outside Italy, but other more interesting shapes now rival its popularity. Being hollow, it is a good shape for most sauces and baked dishes, so will always remain popular. Both plain and egg maccheroni are available, and there are also many different sizes, including a thin, quick-cooking variety. Tubetti is the name given to a miniature version that is often used in soups.

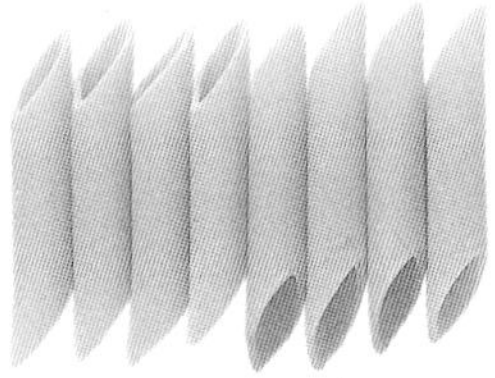

Penne lisce

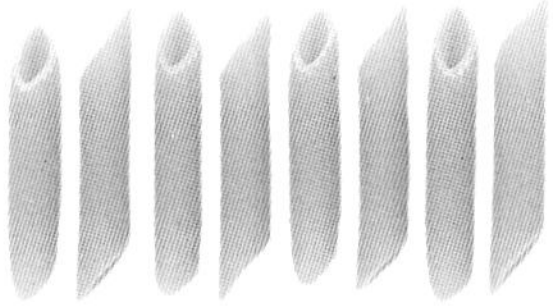

Penne rigate

Penne rigate con spinaci

Penne mezzanine

Mezze penne tricolori

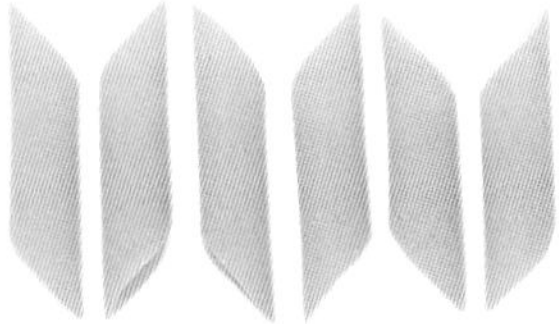

Pennoni

Penne

Like maccheroni, penne are hollow tubes, but their ends are cut diagonally so they are pointed like quills (*penne* means feather or quill pen). In the popularity stakes, they seem to have taken over from maccheroni, possibly because of their more interesting shape. They go well with virtually every sauce and are particularly good with chunky sauces as their sturdiness means that they hold the weight well. Penne lisce are smooth; penne rigate are ridged. Other less common varieties include the small and thin pennette and even thinner pennini and penne mezzanine, the short and stubby mezze penne or "half penne", and the large pennoni. Penne made with egg and flavoured penne are very common.

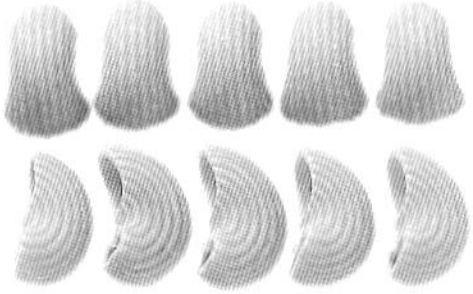

Pipe rigate

Pipe

These shapes look like a cross between conchiglie and lumache. They are curved and hollow (the name means pipes) and more often than not ridged (pipe rigate). As short pasta shapes go, they are quite small. They are excellent for catching sauce and make an interesting change from other more common hollow varieties. Plain and wholewheat types are available, and there is also a smaller version called pipette.

Rigatoni

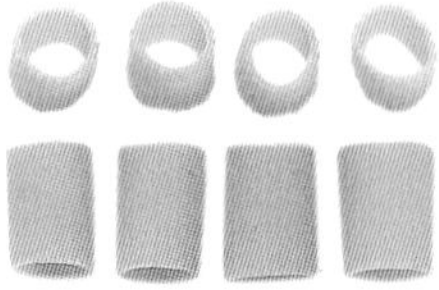

Mezzi rigatoni

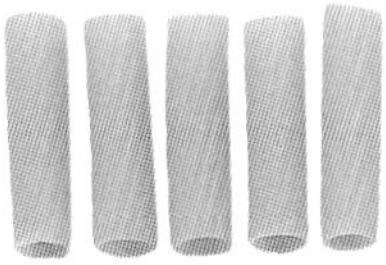

Elicoidali

Elicoidali con basilico

Rigatoni

From the maccheroni family, these are ridged, hollow, chunky-looking shapes. They are very popular because they are sturdy enough to hold chunky sauces, and they come in many flavours. There is a short version called mezzi rigatoni and a straight, stubby version called millerighe. The texture of rigatoni always seems slightly chewier than that of other short pasta. Similar in shape but slightly narrower are elicoidali, which have curved ridges (their name means helixes). Elicoidali can be plain or flavoured with ingredients such as basil.

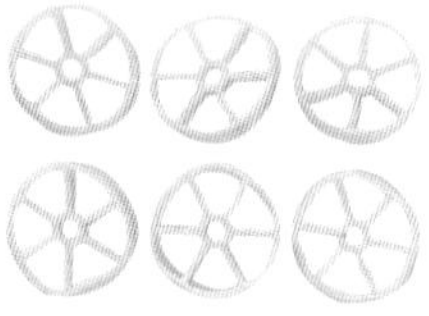

Rotelle

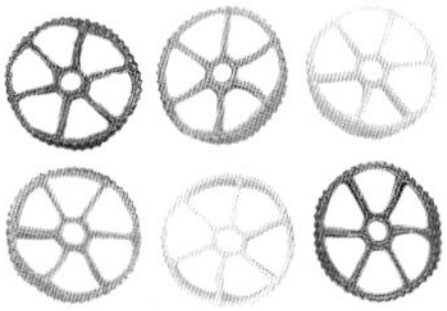

Rotelle tricolore

Rotelle

These are cartwheel shapes. There is a ridged variety, rotelle rigate, and sometimes this shape goes under other names such as ruote, ruote di carro and trulli. Although not a classic Italian shape, the spokes of the wheels are very good for holding chunky sauces. Children like them, and most supermarkets sell them in different colours and flavours. The plain Italian brands taste very good.

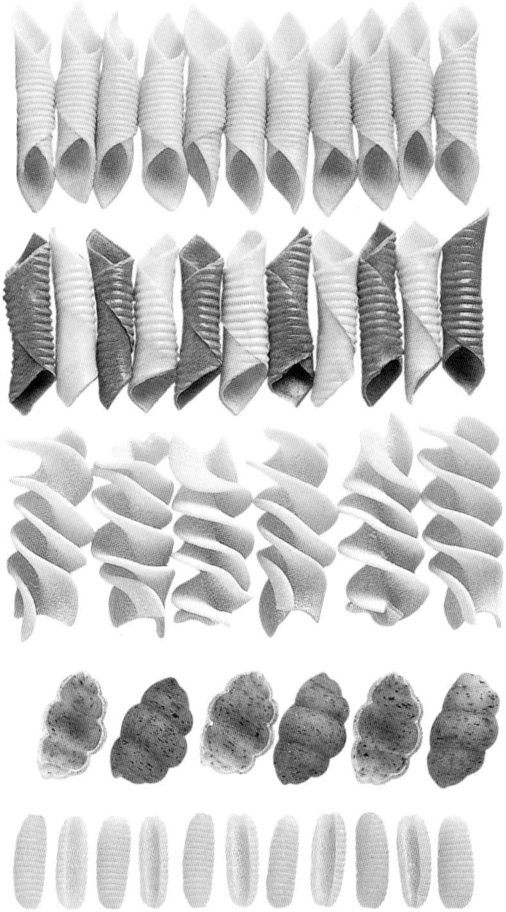

Above from the top: Garganelli all'uovo, garganelli paglia e fieno, girondole di Puglia, gnocchi sardi integrali and gnocchetti sardi

Some Regional Types of Short Dried Pasta

Garganelli come from Emilia-Romagna. They are tubular egg pasta shapes that resemble penne, but which look more like scrolls than quills because you can clearly see how they have been rolled. This is done on a special tool, called *il pettine*, that looks like a large comb.

Gnocchi sardi are from Sardinia. They are named after the gnocchi potato dumplings, but are smaller, like little razor shells. Gnocchetti sardi are smaller still, and are mostly used for soups. Malloreddus is another Sardinian name for gnocchi. These shapes are often flavoured with saffron, and served with traditional meat and vegetable sauces. They are quite chewy in texture.

Orecchiette, or little ears, are from Puglia in the south-east of Italy. Always made with durum wheat, they have a chewy texture and are served with the traditional sauces of the region, especially those made with broccoli.

Pizzoccheri are buckwheat noodles from Valtellina in Lombardy, not far from the border with Switzerland. They are thin and flat and usually sold in nests (*a nidi*) like fettuccine, but they are about half the length. Pizzoccheri are also sometimes cut to make short noodles. Their flavour is nutty, and they go well with the robust flavours of northern Italian cuisine, most famously with cabbage, potatoes and cheese in the baked dish of the same name.

Strozzapreti, which literally translated means priest stranglers, come from Modena. They are said to derive their name from the story of a priest who liked them so much he ate too many – and nearly choked to death. In fact, strozzapreti consist of two pieces of pasta twisted or "strangled" together. Other similar twisted shapes are caserecce, fileia and gemelli. The Genoese trofie, although not twisted, are similar, and can be substituted for strozzapreti.

Trofie are from the Ligurian port of Genoa, where it is traditional to serve them with pesto sauce. They are rolls of solid pasta with pointed ends, quite small and dainty. At one time you could only get home-made trofie, but now they are available dried in Italian delicatessens, in which case the shapes are sometimes open along one side rather than solid. They are well worth buying if you want to make an authentic *Genoese Trofie al Pesto*.

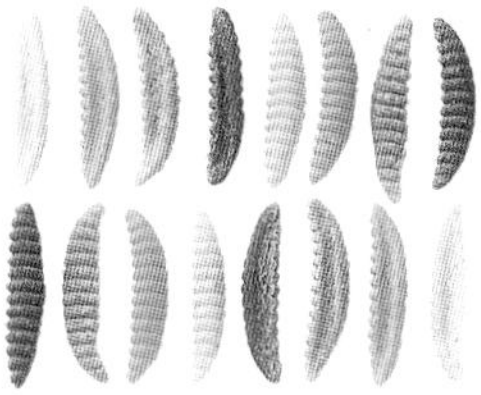

Gnocchetti sardi

Pizzocheri a nidi

Strozzapreti

Orecchiette

Short-cut pizzocheri

Trofie

Flat Pasta

Although there are many kinds of long flat ribbon pasta, such as fettuccine and tagliatelle, there is really only one broad, flat pasta used for baking in the oven (*al forno*), and that is lasagne. Thin sheets of lasagne are designed to be baked between layers of sauce in the oven, or cooked in boiling water until *al dente*, rolled around a filling to make cannelloni, then baked. All types of lasagne are designed to be used in this way, and are never served with a separate sauce.

Plain lasagne

Made from durum wheat and water, this type of lasagne comes flat-packed in boxes. There are three different colours – yellow (plain), green (*verdi*), which is made with spinach, and brown or wholewheat (*integrali*). The shape varies according to the manufacturer, from narrow or broad rectangles to squares. Most sheets are completely flat, but some are wavy all over. Others have crimped or curly edges, which help to trap the sauce and look attractive too. Get to know the different brands and their sizes and choose the ones that fit your baking dish, to avoid having to cut them to fit. This makes light work of assembling the layers before baking. Check the cooking instructions on the box because regular plain lasagne needs to be pre-cooked before being layered or rolled. The usual method is to plunge about four sheets at a time into a large pan of salted boiling water, boil for about 8 minutes until *al dente*, then carefully remove each sheet with a large slotted spoon and/or tongs and lay it flat on a damp cloth to drain. The sheets need to be drained in a single layer or they will stick to each other. This method is fairly time-consuming and messy, but once it has been completed and the lasagne has been assembled, the cooking time in the oven is usually about 30 minutes.

Lasagnette are long, narrow strips of flat pasta, which are crimped on one or two sides. They are used in the same way as lasagne, layered with sauces, then topped with grated cheese and baked in the oven. Festonelle are small squares of lasagnette,

Lasagne verdi

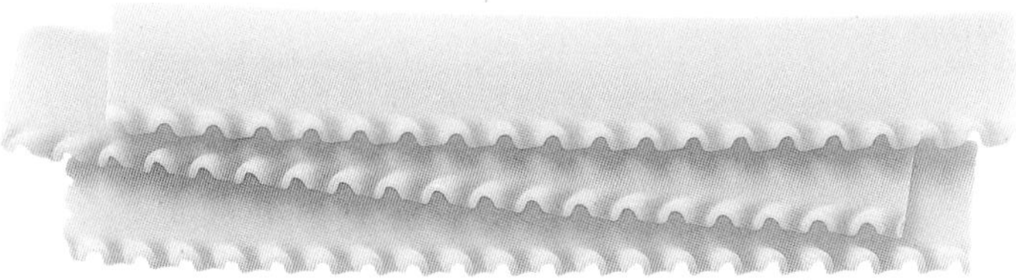

Lasagnette

Lasagnette

Festonelle

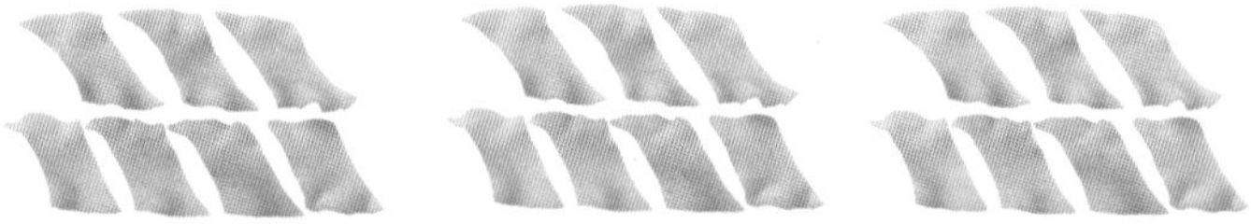

Pantacce

Lasagne

Lasagne

Lasagne verdi

Lasagne verdi all'uovo

which are also used in baked dishes. Pantacce are tiny diagonal pieces cut from lasagnette. They are similar to the hand-cut quadrucci and can be used in baked dishes, but are more often added to soups.

Lasagne all'uovo

This type of lasagne is made with durum wheat and water like plain lasagne, but with the addition of egg. This makes it a brighter yellow than plain lasagne, and richer in flavour and nutrients. It is available as plain egg (lasagne all'uovo) and egg and spinach (lasagne verdi all'uovo). Like the plain lasagne, it comes in different shapes and sizes with a variety of different edgings.

Lasagne

Lasagne all'uovo

Easy-cook Lasagne

Although a relatively recent innovation, easy-cook lasagne is fast becoming the number one favourite. Sometimes labelled "no pre-cooking required", it does not need to be boiled first, but is layered in the baking dish straight from the packet, so saving lots of time and mess. As with the plain and egg lasagne, it comes in all sorts of different shapes, sizes and colours, with straight or fancy edges. It is easiest to use if it is the right shape to fit neatly into your baking dish, although it can be broken to fit. Baking time is slightly longer than with the pre-boiled varieties, so allow at least 40 minutes. Make sure that the sauce you use is runnier than usual because this type of lasagne absorbs liquid during baking and needs extra sauce to keep it moist.

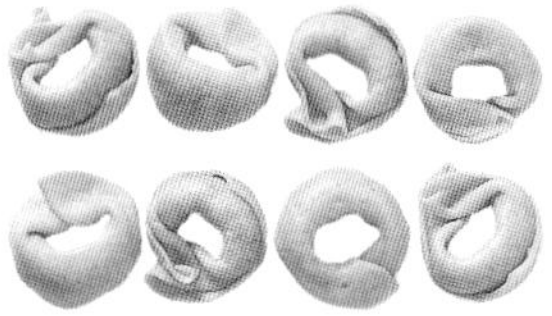

Tortellini all'uovo

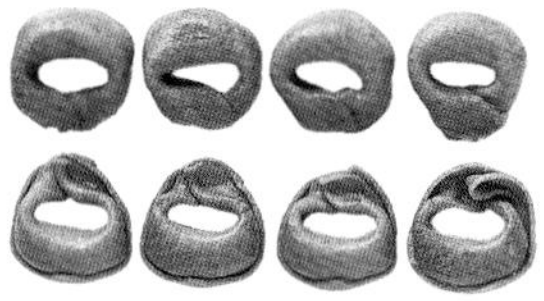

Tortellini verdi

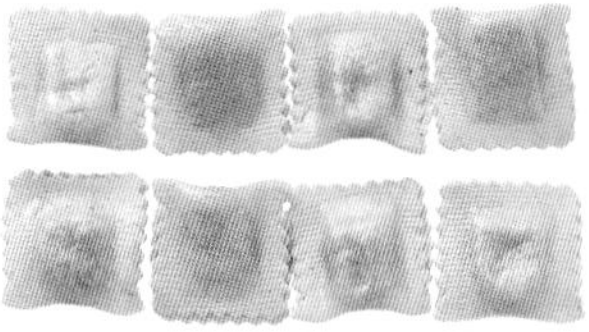

Ravioli all'uovo

Agnolotti all'uovo

Dried Stuffed Pasta / *Pasta Ripiena*

The most common dried stuffed pasta shapes are tortellini (little pies), a speciality of Bologna said to be modelled on the shape of Venus's navel. They are made from rounds or circles of pasta, so they look like little plump rings; another name for them is anolini. Some Italian delicatessens also sell dried cappelletti (little hats), which resemble tortellini but are made from squares of pasta so have little peaks. Cappelletti are more likely to be sold fresh than dried. The same goes for ravioli and agnolotti, although you may find them in larger supermarkets. Tortellini are popular dried because they are traditionally used *in brodo* – simmered in a clear beef or chicken stock until they swell and plump up to make a satisfying soup. Most Italian cooks keep a packet or two of tortellini in the store cupboard for just this purpose, and *Tortellini in Brodo* is often served for an evening meal when the main meal of the day has been at lunchtime. You can also be sure that *Tortellini in Brodo* will be served as a pick-me-up if ever a member of the family is unwell. They are also traditionally served on New Year's Eve in Bologna, perhaps as an antidote to the excesses of Christmas.

Dried tortellini are generally available with a choice of fillings – with meat (*alla carne*) or cheese (*ai formaggi*). The pasta is made with egg and may be plain and yellow in colour, green if flavoured with spinach, or red if flavoured with tomato. All types of tortellini need to be cooked for at least 15 minutes to allow time for the pasta to swell and the ingredients in the filling to develop their flavour. Meat fillings are a mixture of pork sausage and beef with breadcrumbs, Parmesan cheese and spices. Cheese fillings usually consist of a minimum of 35 per cent cheese mixed with breadcrumbs and spices.

Dried tortellini are a useful store-cupboard item as they will keep for up to 12 months (but always check the use-by date on the packet). For a soup, only a handful of the filled shapes are needed and the packet can be resealed. Tortellini are also good boiled, then drained and tossed in melted butter and herbs or a cream, tomato or meat sauce, and served with grated Parmesan. Children like their shape, and they provide a good way of persuading them to eat meat and cheese. A 250g/9oz packet will serve four people.

Dried Pasta for Stuffing / *Pasta da Ripieno*

Large pasta shapes are made commercially for stuffing and baking in the oven. Fillings vary, from meat and poultry to spinach, mushrooms and cheese, and the pasta can be baked in either a béchamel or a tomato sauce. Keep the filling moist and the sauce runny to ensure that the finished dish will not be dry. Dried shapes make an interesting change from lasagne, especially for children's meals, and they are attractive as a first course for a dinner party. They do not need to be boiled before being stuffed.

Cannelloni

Cannelloni

These large pasta tubes (their name means large reeds) are about 10cm/4in long. Plain, spinach and wholewheat versions are available. In Italy, cannelloni is traditionally made from fresh sheets of lasagne rolled around a filling, but the ready-made dried tubes are convenient and less time-consuming to use. They are easy to stuff, using either a teaspoon or a piping bag.

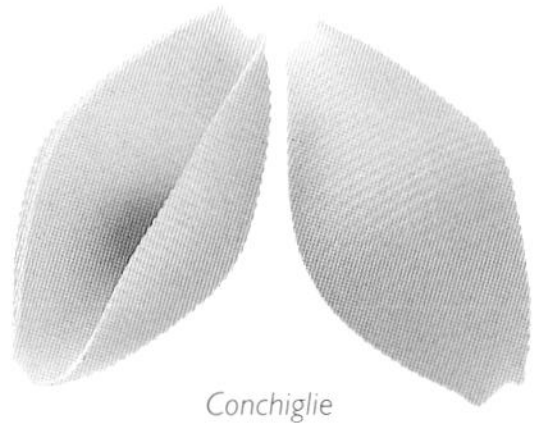

Conchiglie

Conchiglie

Sometimes also called conchiglioni, these jumbo conch shells are available in plain, spinach and tomato flavours, both smooth and ridged. There are often two sizes – medium and large – both of which are suitable for stuffing, although you will probably find the larger ones less fiddly.

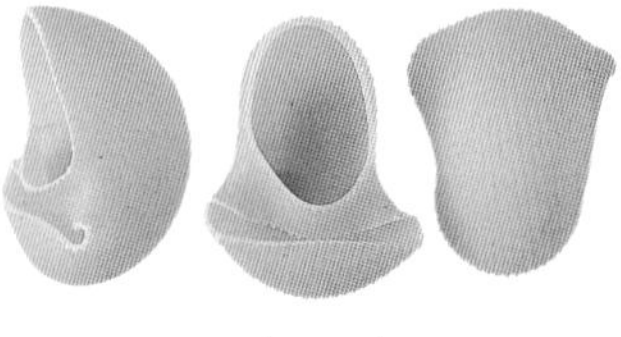

Lumaconi

Lumaconi

These are like conchiglie, but are elbow-shaped – like large snail shells – with an opening at either end. The ones most commonly available are plain and ridged, but you may find different colours in specialist delicatessens. You may also come across similar shapes called chiocciolon, gorzettoni, manicotti and tuffolini.

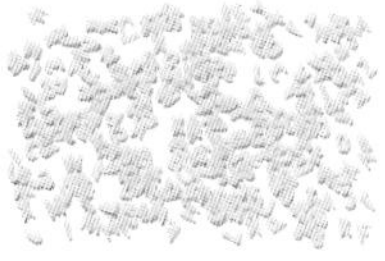
Alfabetini

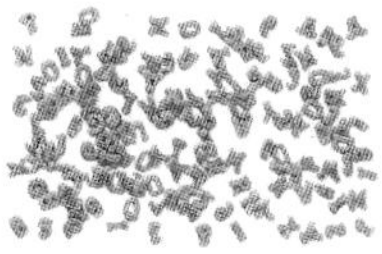
Alfabetini integrali

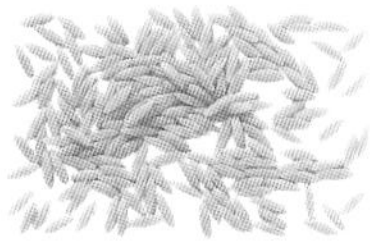
Risoni

Risoni all'uovo

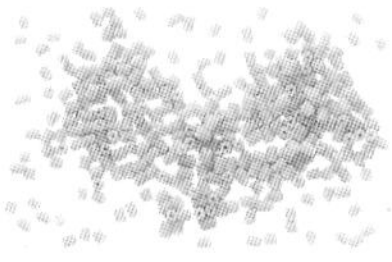
Tubettini

Quadretti

Anellini

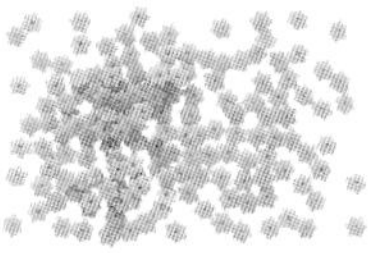
Stelline

Farfalline all'uovo

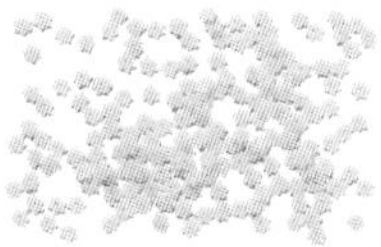
Stellette

Ditalini rigati

Conchigliette

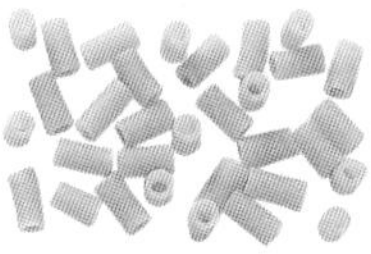
Tubetti

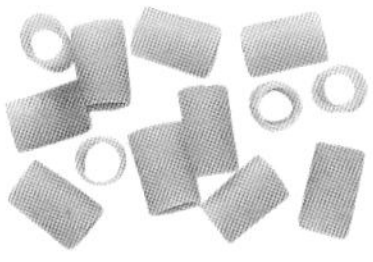
Occhi di lupo

Mezzi tubetti

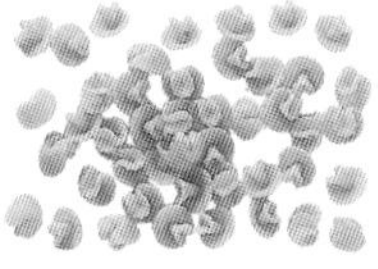
Funghetti all'uovo

Dried Pasta for Soup / *Pastina*

Teeny-weeny pasta shapes are called pastina in Italian, and there are literally hundreds of different ones to choose from. They are mostly made from plain durum wheat, although you may find them with egg and even flavoured with carrot or spinach. In Italy they are always served in broths and clear soups, and are regarded almost as nursery food because they are so often served for children's meals (many Italian babies are weaned on them) or as a pick-me-up for adults who are not feeling well. If you stay in an Italian hospital, you are likely to be served *Pastina in Brodo*.

Shapes of pastina vary enormously, and seem to get more and more fanciful as the market demands.

The smallest and most plain pasta per minestre (pasta for soups) are like tiny grains. Some look like rice and are in fact called risi or risoni, while others are more like barley and are called orzi. Fregola, from Sardinia, look like couscous, and have a similar nutty texture and flavour. Semi di melone are like melon seeds, as their name suggests, while acini de pepe or peperini are named after peppercorns, which they resemble in shape and size if not in colour. Coralline, grattini and occhi are three more very popular tiny shapes.

The next size up are the ones that are most popular with children. These include alfabeti and alfabetini (alphabet shapes), stelline and stellette (stars), rotellini (tiny wagon wheels) and anellini, which can be tiny rings, sometimes with ridges that make them look very pretty, or larger hoops. Ditali are similar to anellini but slightly thicker, while tubettini are thicker still.

Another category of pasta per minestre consists of slightly larger shapes, more like miniature versions of familiar types of short pasta. Their names end in "ine", "ette" or "etti", denoting that they are the diminutive forms. These include conchigliette (little shells), farfalline and farfallette (little bows), funghetti (little mushrooms), lumachine

Peperini

(little snails), quadretti and quadrettini (little squares), orecchiettini (little ears), renette (like baby penne) and tubetti (little tubes). The size of these varies: the smaller ones are for use in clear broths, while the larger ones are more often used in thicker soups, such as minestrone.

Designer Pasta

Relative newcomers to the market are the pasta shapes that bear little or no resemblance to the traditional or regional Italian varieties. Many of these are made outside Italy in any case, while the ones made in Italy are often for export only. It seems that the majority of Italians are happy enough with the pasta they know and love.

Supermarkets and food halls, gourmet food shops, specialist delicatessens and even interior design shops are the best places to find these new shapes. Quality varies enormously, and some of them are nothing more than a gimmick, with very disappointing textures and flavours. Others are more successful, especially the ones made by long-established Italian firms. They make a change from the more usual shapes and are often an interesting talking point, especially when you are entertaining. As a general rule, flavoured pasta is best served with very simple sauces based on olive oil or butter, otherwise the flavours of the pasta and sauce tend to fight one another.

Long Shapes and Noodles

Spaghetti and tagliatelle are often flavoured and coloured. These shapes are either dramatically long or coiled in nests (*a nidi*), and you can even buy a type of pasta called spagliatelle, which is like a cross between the two. You can choose from a single flavour in one packet, or up to five different flavours mixed together, and they can be either plain durum wheat pasta or made with the addition of egg and labelled "all'uovo". Spinach, tomato, mushroom, beetroot, saffron and smoked salmon are all popular flavours, but there are also other stronger flavours, such as chilli and garlic (singly and together) and black squid ink (*nero di seppia*).

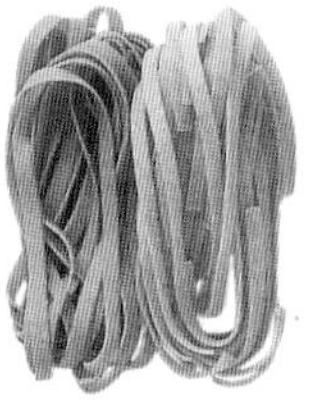

Tagliatelle flavoured with red and green chillies

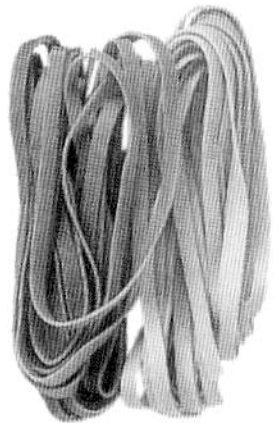

Egg and smoked salmon-flavoured tagliatelle

Three-colour tagliatelle

Garlic- and chilli-flavoured spaghetti

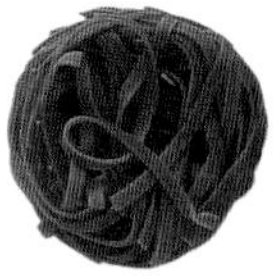

Porcini-flavoured tagliatelle

Tagliatelle flavoured with squid ink and bottarga (mullet roe)

Porcini-flavoured tagliatelle

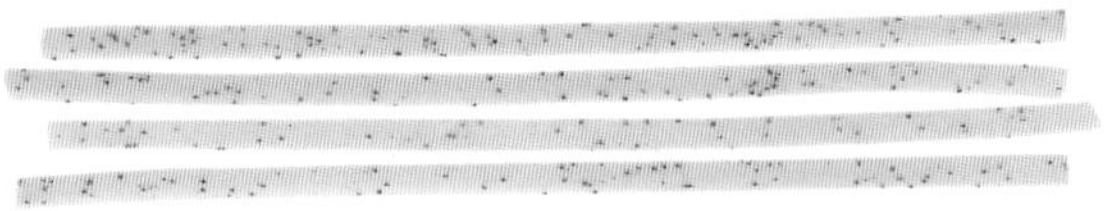

Poppy seed tagliatelle

Porcini-flavoured bavette

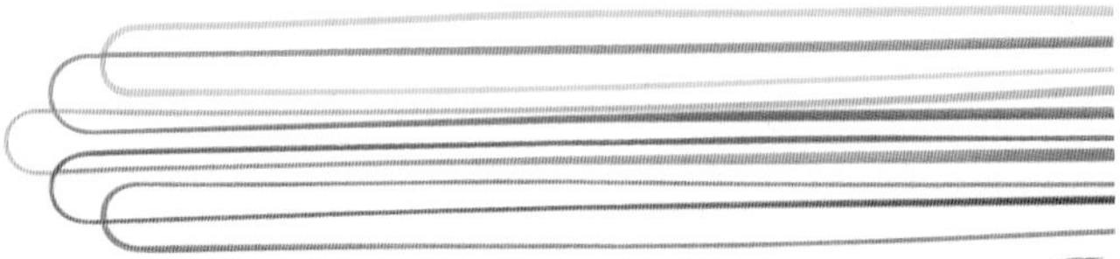

Five-colour spagliatelle

Multi-coloured arlecchino

Basil-flavoured strangozzi

One of the most fanciful combinations comes from Venice. Called arlecchino (harlequin), it is a mixture of black (squid ink), green (spinach and herbs), red (tomato and beetroot) and blue (blueberry and blue Curaçao liqueur). More common and perhaps most successful is tagliatelle speckled with herbs or seeds or, if it comes from Tuscany, flavoured with wild mushrooms (porcini). A broad variety of tagliatelle called bavette from Puglia is also flavoured with porcini. Strangozzi is an unusual thin noodle from Umbria. It comes plain and flavoured with spinach, basil or tomato. It is sometimes sold twisted into a long, thick plait, which looks pretty in the packet, but is best broken into short lengths to cook.

Short Shapes

The most inventive and unusual designer shapes fall into this category. Short pasta is the easiest pasta to eat and so it's the most popular. Manufacturers, ever on the lookout to make and sell more, quickly realised that new short shapes had the most appeal and so developed this sector of the market more than any other. Ever since the 19th century competition in the pasta industry has thrived on the "design" of different short shapes, with some more successful at holding sauces than others. Among these are the frilly ballerine, fiorelli, gigli del gargano, rocchetti rigati and spaccatella, all of which trap sauces quite well but somehow give a strange sensation in the mouth. Shapes such as banane, coralli rigati, creste di gallo, radiatori and riccioli are perhaps too gimmicky for their own good; so too are the mixed bags of highly coloured pasta shapes, such as the seven-colour orecchiette (little ears) and five-colour chioccioloni (snails), which includes chocolate-flavoured pasta along with the more run-of-the-mill plain, tomato, squid ink and wild mushroom (porcini) varieties.

These coloured designer pasta shapes are often labelled *lavorazione artigianale* or *prodotto artigianale*, to indicate that they are made by artisans or local craftsmen, but they are too often disappointing, and they rarely match up to the more traditional shapes that have been tried and tested over very many years.

Five-colour chioccioloni are made from plain pasta and pasta flavoured with squid ink, chocolate, tomato and porcini

Spinach, plain and tomato conchiglie (hand-crafted shells)

Spaccatella

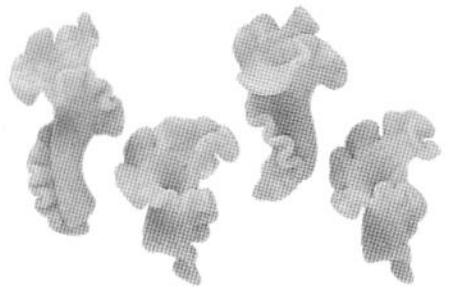

Gigli del gargano

Seven-colour orecchiette are made from plain pasta and pasta flavoured with spinach, tomato, saffron, squid ink, beetroot and porcini

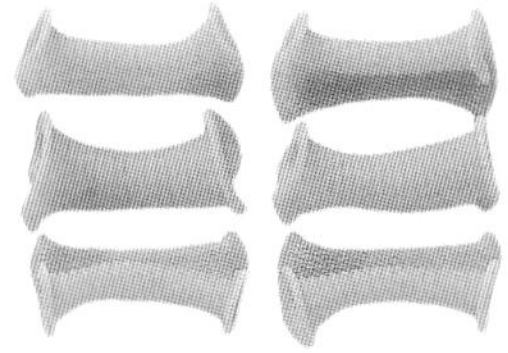

Rocchetti rigati

Fiorelli tricolori

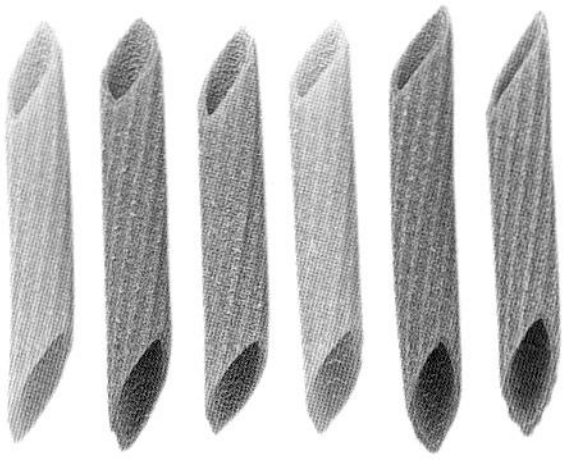

Three-colour pennoti rigati

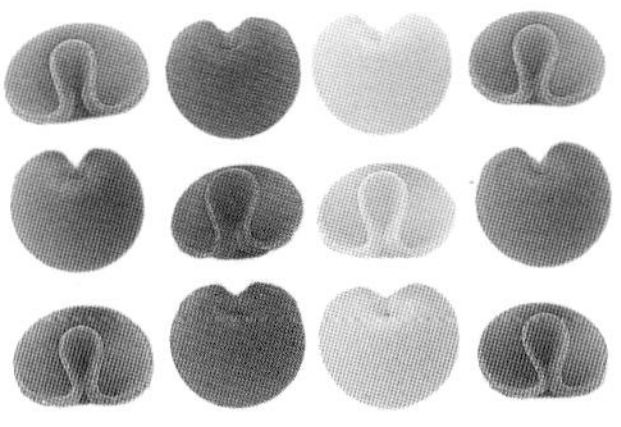

Three-colour cappelletti

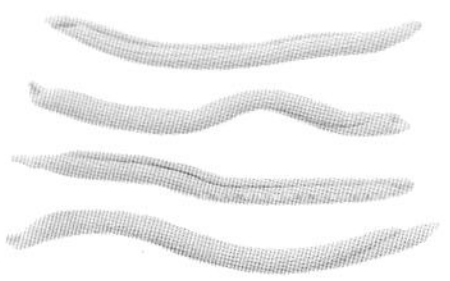

Coralli rigati

Fresh Pasta

In Italy there has long been a tradition for buying fresh pasta, and now the custom has caught on in other countries too. Italians buy from their local *pastificio* or baker, where the beautiful window displays are such a tempting feast for the eye, while we have to content ourselves with delicatessens, supermarkets and food halls. Yet here too, creative talent is running wild when it comes to making fresh pasta, and the choice of different shapes, flavours and fillings is continually increasing – by popular demand. It seems that everybody loves fresh pasta, and we simply can't get enough of it. Quality is excellent, especially with the loose kinds sold in Italian delicatessens. Pre-packaged brands, although labelled fresh, are obviously not as "just-made" and silky-textured as the pasta made on a daily basis in an Italian delicatessen, but they are quite good nevertheless. Flavours vary, but the usual ingredients are spinach, tomato, chestnut, mushroom, beetroot juice, saffron, herbs, garlic, chillies and squid ink.

Buy freshly made pasta on the day you need it or you defeat the object of buying it; otherwise keep it in its wrapping and use it within 1–2 days of purchase (or according to the storage time given on the packet). If you buy fresh pasta loose from an Italian delicatessen, ask the shopkeeper for advice on storage. Fresh pasta is made with egg, which shortens its storage time, but on the plus side this increases its nutritional value and flavour, and gives the plain varieties a lovely sunshine yellow colour.

Fresh pasta takes far less time to cook than dried pasta, but the cooking technique is generally the same for each type. Most plain shapes will be *al dente* in 2–4 minutes, while stuffed shapes take 5–7 minutes, but always ask advice in the shop where it is made (or check the label).

The same rules apply for matching sauces to shapes as with dried pasta – long shapes are best with smooth sauces, while chunky sauces go better with short shapes.

Long and Flat Shapes

These were the first forms of fresh pasta to be available commercially, and were generally made in the local Italian delicatessen by the proprietor or his wife. The choice used to be between plain egg tagliatelle and fettuccine, possibly flavoured with spinach, but now there are far more exciting varieties. Pre-packaged long fresh pasta comes in standard shapes and sizes, but Italian delicatessens sometimes have weekend specials when they offer different flavours and colours according to the seasonal availability of ingredients. This is often the case when a delicatessen supplies a local restaurant with fresh pasta. If a special order is made for a restaurant, the delicatessen may make extra to sell to customers in the shop. These occasional treats are well worth looking out for, as are regional specialities. If the owners of your local delicatessen are from Lazio you may find fresh home-made fettuccine on sale. Ligurians are more likely to make trenette, whereas pappardelle indicates that the owners of the shop probably have family ties with Tuscany or Bologna.

Fettuccine

These long, flat ribbon noodles are the narrow Roman version of tagliatelle, traditionally made about 5mm/¼in wide. Fettuccine are readily available, made with egg and flavoured with spinach. You may also see similar noodles called fettuccelle. The two are interchangeable, and are at their best served very simply with butter and cream.

Fettuccine all'uovo

Fettuccine al nero

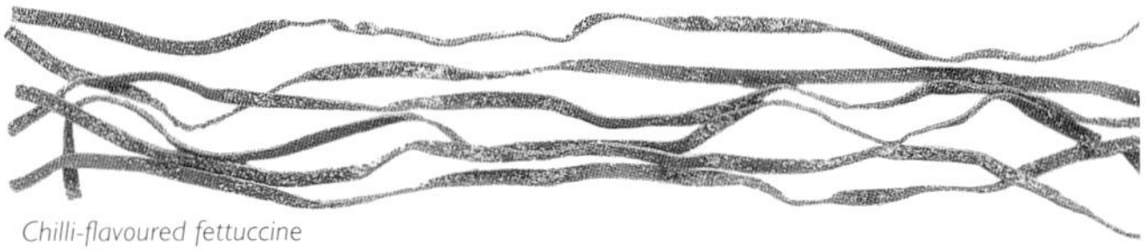

Chilli-flavoured fettuccine

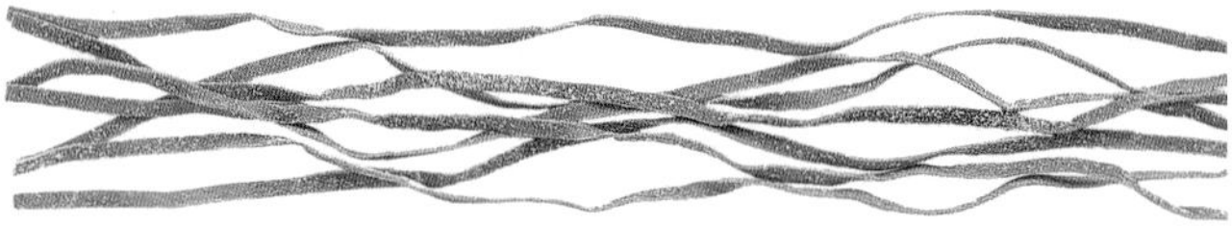

Fettuccine verdi

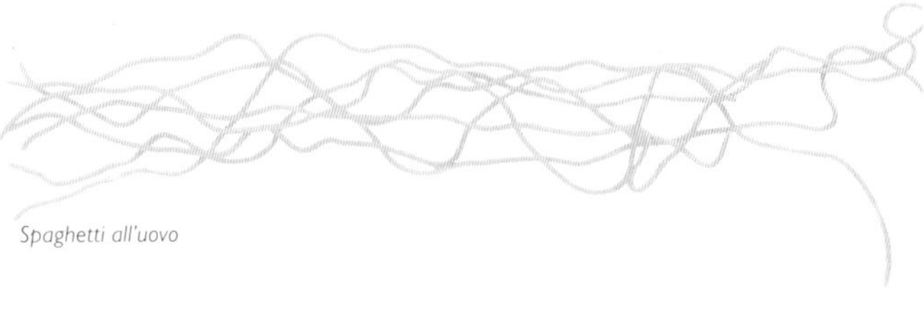

Spaghetti all'uovo

Spinach-flavoured lasagne

Tomato-flavoured lasagne

Lasagne all'uovo

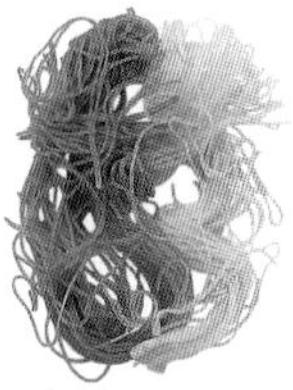

Egg and spinach-flavoured capelli d'angelo

Egg and spinach-flavoured linguine

Pappardelle

Spaghetti

This pasta is widely available, in various widths. A narrow version, spaghettini, is popular, and can be found in some delicatessens. Serve fresh spaghetti or spaghettini Neapolitan style with sauces based on olive oil and tomatoes. Both spaghetti and spaghettini are also good with fish and shellfish, as long as the pieces are cut small. Capelli d'angelo, plain or flavoured with spinach, is also available.

Lasagne

Sheets of lasagne can be found plain, with egg, and flavoured with spinach or tomato. Depending on the manufacturer, they may be rectangles, squares or strips with plain or frilly edges. *Lasagne al forno* (baked lasagne) made with fresh sheets of pasta tastes much better than that made with dried pasta, so the fresh sheets are well worth buying.

Linguine

These look like strands of flattened spaghetti and are very narrow and thin. They are made with egg (*all'uovo*), and go well with a simple dressing of olive oil and flavourings such as finely chopped garlic, chillies or freshly ground black pepper. Linguine are also good with fish and shellfish sauces.

Pappardelle

Flat egg noodles, these vary in width from 2–2.5cm/¾–1in wide. Traditional pappardelle have wavy edges, but you may see them with plain edges – the main thing is that they are wider than any of the other ribbon noodles. They originated in Tuscany, but are also popular in the city of Bologna in Emilia-Romagna. In both these regions, pasta is often served with a rich meat or game sauce, and pappardelle are the perfect choice because the noodles are wide and strong enough to support the chunkiest mixtures. Pappardelle are available plain and flavoured, sometimes with sun-dried tomatoes or porcini.

Squid ink tagliolini

Tagliolini all'uovo

Salmon-flavoured tagliolini

Spinach-flavoured tagliolini

Tagliatelle all'uovo

Spinach-flavoured tagliatelle

Tagliatelle

This is probably the best-known form of fresh pasta. The noodles are long and straight, about 1cm/½in wide. They are available everywhere, in a wide variety of flavours and colours. After plain egg tagliatelle, spinach is the most popular, but it is often flecked and flavoured with fresh herbs, garlic, porcini, sun-dried tomatoes, pepper, chillies and other spices, or beautifully coloured with saffron or tomato. When made with squid ink, it is black and dramatic. Tagliatelle comes from Bologna, where it is always served with Bolognese sauce, but it goes well with any meat sauce. Tagliarini and tagliolini are very thin versions of tagliatelle, about 3mm/⅛in wide, sold either as plain egg (all'uovo) or as paglia e fieno – half white and half green. Mixed packs are versatile and attractive because you can cook the different colours together or keep them separate, depending on the visual effect required. They go well with tomato and cream sauces.

Short Shapes

Supermarkets and other large outlets sell fresh short shapes, but the range is limited. Italian delicatessens sometimes sell a few simple home-made shapes, but because many short shapes need special machines for cutting and shaping there is seldom a wide range in small outlets, and making them by hand would be too time-consuming to be commercially viable. Short shapes tend to stick together, so in supermarkets they are kept in plastic bags in the chilled cabinets; these packs are useful in that they can be stored in the freezer. In some small shops excess moisture is removed by briefly fan-drying the shapes straight after they are made. These are then described as semi-dried and must be sold within 24–48 hours. Shapes vary widely, depending on whether they come from large manufacturers or individual shops. Conchiglie, fusilli and penne are easy to find, while other shapes, such as garganelli and ballerine, are less widely available.

Conchiglie

These shell shapes come in different sizes and colours, and conchiglie tricolore (red, white and green) are popular. They are one of the best shapes for trapping chunky sauces. If they are ridged, so much the better. Conchiglie are also good in salads because they hold dressings well.

Fusilli

Resembling the threads of screws, these should correctly be called eliche, but they are almost always labelled fusilli. Plain, spinach and tomato flavours, either sold separately or mixed together, are easy to obtain. Squid ink fusilli are made in some shops. The versatile shape of this type of pasta means that it goes well with most sauces and is also good in salads.

Garganelli

Sold in some specialist delicatessens, these are made from a very special type of egg pasta from Emilia-Romagna, and look like ridged scrolls. Garganelli need to be made

Ballerine

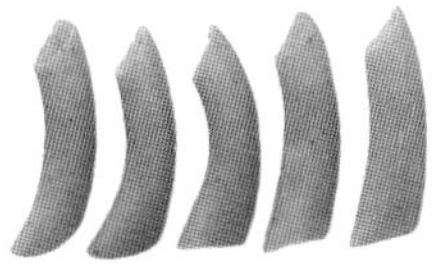

Penne rigate

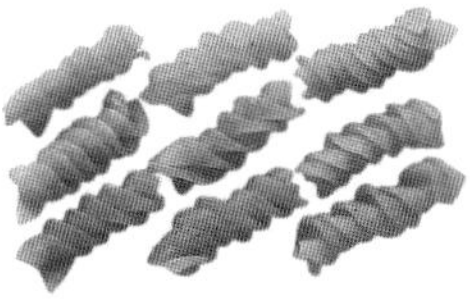

Eliche all'uovo

Conchiglie

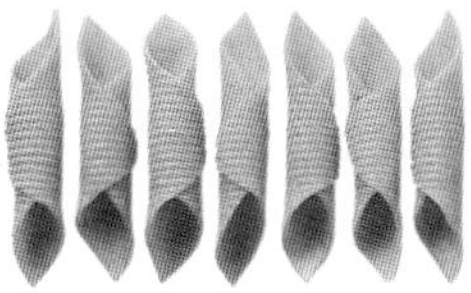

Semi-dried garganelli

with a special tool, called *il pettine* in Italian. Squares of fresh dough are rolled around a rod and against the *pettine*, which has teeth like a comb. The teeth produce the characteristic fine ridges on the outside of the pasta. Plain and spinach flavours are available, either sold separately or mixed together. In Emilia-Romagna, garganelli are traditionally served with a rich meat sauce, but you can use them in any recipe that calls for short maccheroni or penne. They are especially good with rich, creamy sauces.

Penne

Sometimes called quills, these come in a variety of sizes and colours, both smooth and ribbed, just like their dried counterpart. In Rome, fresh penne are served with the chilli-hot arrabbiata sauce, but they go with just about any sauce.

Stuffed Shapes

Until recent years, the only stuffed fresh pasta shapes available were the classic ones traditionally associated with specific regions of Italy. Ravioli was the best known shape, followed by tortellini. These regional specialities are still popular, but nowadays the traditional shapes and fillings are often varied, whether they are being made by a large-scale manufacturer or a single cook working for a local delicatessen. Individual interpretations on the basic shapes, a wide variety of fresh seasonal ingredients for the fillings, plus eye-catching colour combinations for both the pasta and the fillings make variations on the theme seemingly endless. New ideas are being developed all of the time, some more successful than others, so experiment with different kinds of stuffed shapes to find the ones you like the best. Listed here are the most popular and widely available shapes, following the regional tradition.

Agnolotti

These filled pasta shapes come from northern Italy and are a speciality of Piedmont in particular. Traditionally they were shaped like plump little half moons and stuffed with meat, but this is no longer the case: nowadays you will see round and square shapes with vegetable fillings labelled as agnolotti. Square agnolotti with a pleat in the centre are called *dal plin* (with a pleat). One characteristic that all agnolotti should share is a crinkled edge, made by cutting the dough around the filling with a fluted pasta wheel.

Cappelletti

These take their name from the Italian word for little hats. In Emilia-Romagna, small squares of dough are filled and folded to make triangular shapes, then two of the ends are wrapped around

Semi-dried agnolotti all'uovo

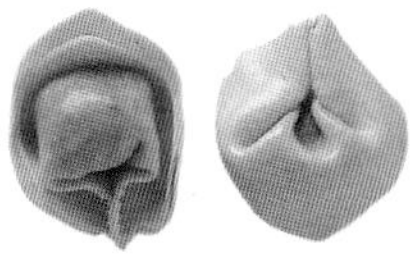

Semi-dried cappelletti all'uovo

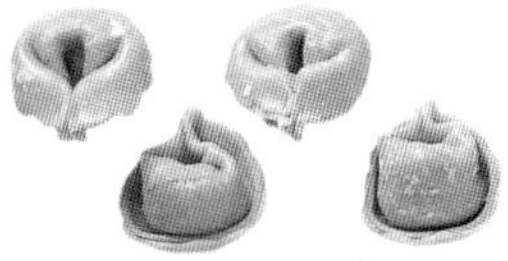

Cappelletti all'uovo stuffed with mushroom filling

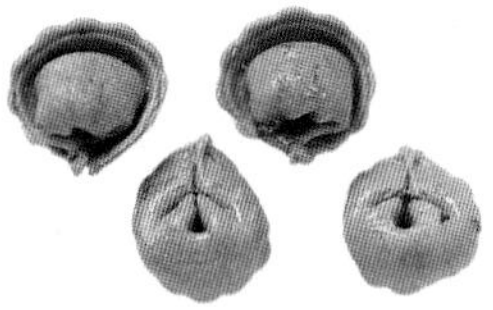

Semi-dried tomato-flavoured cappelletti stuffed with sun-dried tomato filling

and the bottom edge turned up to make a party hat shape with a brim. In some central regions of Italy, however, cappelletti are made with either plain or fluted rounds of dough instead of squares. The dough for cappelletti can be plain or egg (*all'uovo*), or flavoured with tomato or spinach. Cappelletti are traditionally filled with minced meat and cheese and are eaten in northern and central regions of Italy at Christmas and New Year, especially in clear broth – *Cappelletti in Brodo*. You can use them in this way or serve them as a pasta course with a little melted butter and freshly grated Parmesan cheese or, alternatively, toss the cappelletti in a tomato or cream sauce.

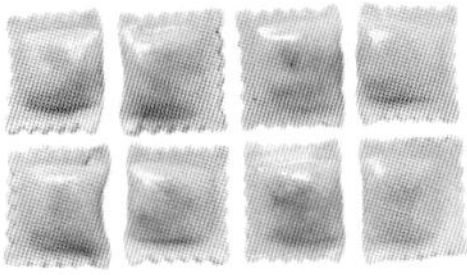

Semi-dried raviolini all'uovo (mini egg ravioli) with a simple minced meat filling

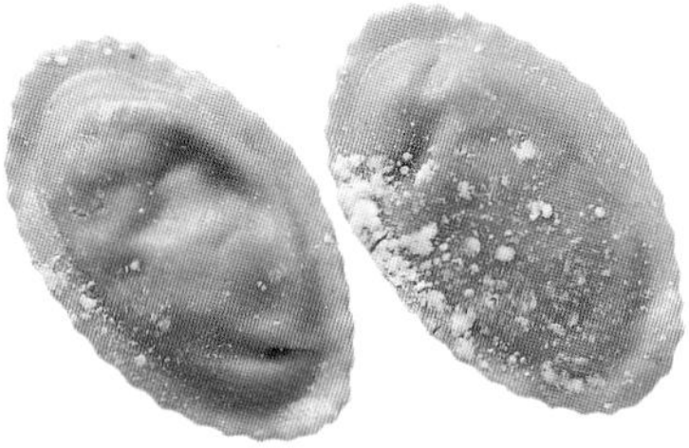

Oval ravioli, which are sometimes called rotondi, stuffed with artichoke filling

Ravioli all'uovo with minced chicken filling

Large rectangular ravioli stuffed with Roquefort cheese

Hand-made plain and spinach-flavoured ravioli

Large ravioli stuffed with minced chicken and asparagus

Plain ravioli stuffed with asparagus filling (left), squid ink-flavoured ravioli stuffed with a herb filling and saffron-flavoured ravioli stuffed with smoked salmon and mascarpone cheese

Pansotti

Sometimes spelled pansoti, these stuffed pasta shapes are Ligurian. The word means chubby, and they are triangular in shape with little pot bellies of filling in the centre. It is traditional to fill pansotti with chopped cooked spinach, chopped hard-boiled eggs and grated Pecorino cheese, then serve them with a walnut sauce. Pansotti are made with small squares of pasta dough and may have straight or fluted edges.

Ravioli

These are usually square with fluted edges, but size and shape vary enormously. Along with tortellini, they are the most widely made of the fresh stuffed pasta shapes, and everyone seems to have their own favourite way of making them. Plain, spinach and tomato doughs are used for the pasta (although other flavours, such as squid ink and saffron, are becoming increasingly available), and the fillings can be anything from vegetables, such as spinach, artichoke and mushroom, to fish and shellfish, and minced veal and chicken. Very tiny ravioli are called raviolini, while the name for ravioli with a pumpkin filling is cappellacci. Tiny round ravioli are sometimes called medaglioni. Large round, oval and rectangular ravioli, stuffed with cheese or vegetable fillings, are occasionally available at Italian delicatessens. Oval ravioli are sometimes called rotondi, while the large rectangular shapes may be called cannelloni rather than ravioli.

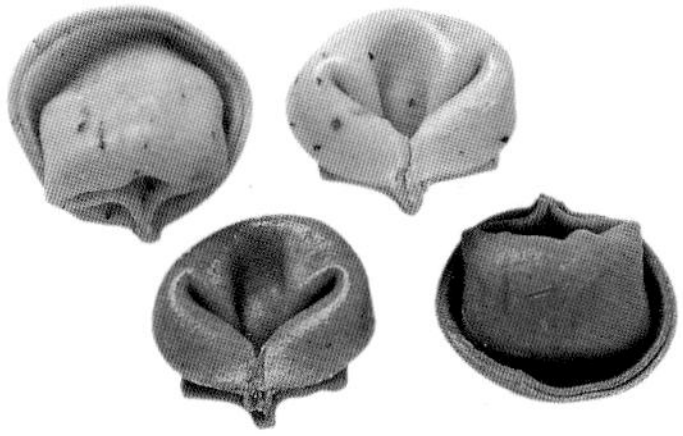

Plain and spinach-flavoured tortellini

Sacchetti filled with a spinach and ricotta filling and tied with thin strips of spring onion

Tortelloni stuffed with an artichoke and truffle oil filling

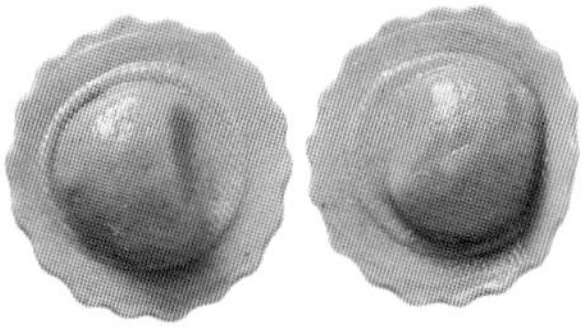

Cappelli all'uovo stuffed with minced salmon

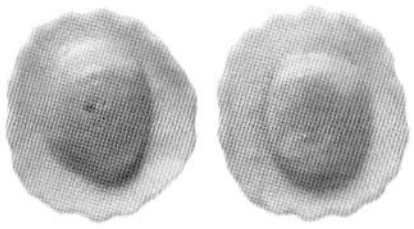

Tomato-flavoured medaglioni all'uovo stuffed with a prawn and trout filling

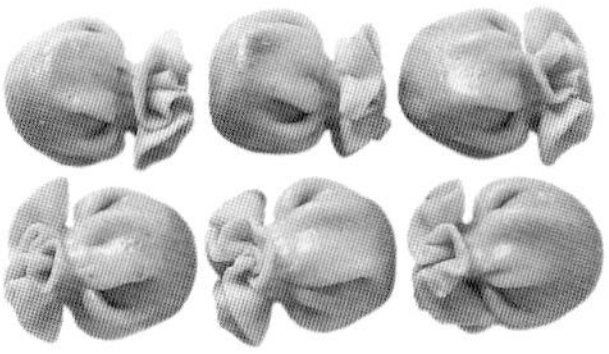

Sacchettini

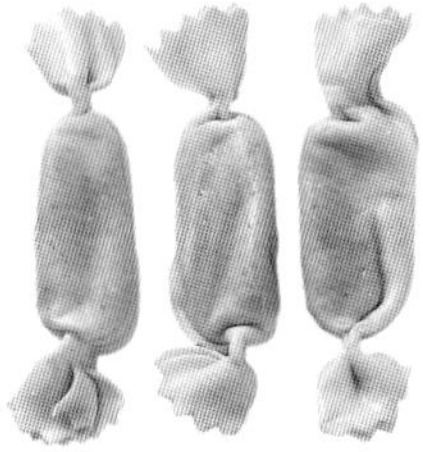

Sweet-shaped caramelle all'uovo stuffed with spinach and ricotta cheese

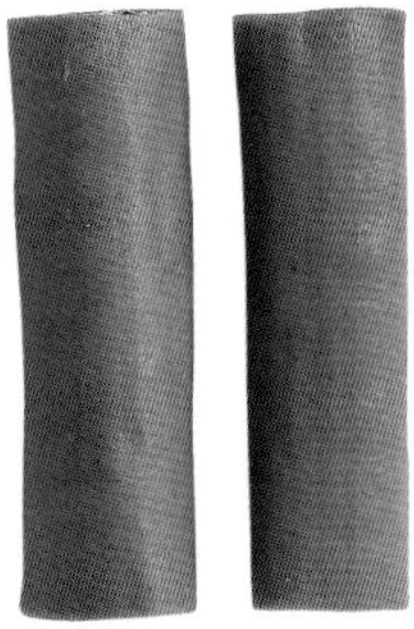

Spinach cannelloni stuffed with a herb and cream cheese filling

Tortellini

Hugely popular, these look more or less the same as cappelletti, but are made from rounds or circles of dough rather than squares so do not have peaks. They are usually slightly larger than cappelletti, while tortelloni and tortelli are larger still. Tortellini are a speciality from the city of Bologna in Emilia-Romagna, where the traditional filling is minced meats and prosciutto (Parma ham). At Christmas it is the local custom to eat *Tortellini in Brodo* as a first course soup before the main course of roast capon or turkey.

Nowadays, tortellini are available everywhere and are eaten all year round. There is a wide variety of colour combinations and fanciful fillings. Black squid ink, garlic, herbs, green olive, spinach and sun-dried tomatoes are among the many ingredients used to flavour the dough, while for the filling you can choose from such delicacies as white crabmeat, pumpkin, ricotta, asparagus, cream cheese, caramelized onions, mushrooms, marinated tuna, aubergines, sweet red peppers, artichokes and even truffles. A mixture of four cheeses is a popular filling.

Other stuffed pasta shapes

Creative cooks have started a trend for making shapes that are not based on regional traditions, so check out your local Italian delicatessen or supermarket for the latest shapes to arrive – you will find new ones appearing all the time. Two very popular pasta shapes are caramelle and sacchetti. *Caramelle* means "caramel", and this pasta shape takes its name from the familiar shape of caramels or toffees with their wrappings twisted at both ends. The filling is encased in the lozenge-shaped centre and is often ricotta-cheese based, while the pasta itself is made with egg and may be plain, spinach or tomato flavoured. Sacchetti are little purses or money bags with scrunched tops. The pasta may be plain or flavoured and the fillings based on cheese or meat. Sacchettini are a tiny version, most often served in soups but also good with smooth, creamy sauces.

Equipment

Pasta demands little in the way of specialist equipment. You are bound to have a large saucepan for cooking the pasta and a colander for draining, while for making sauces you need only a sharp knife and a chopping board for chopping ingredients, a skillet or saucepan for cooking, and a large bowl plus spoons and forks for tossing and serving. There are a few items that will make cooking and serving easier, however, and if you eat pasta frequently you will find them a wise investment. They are all available at good kitchenware shops and department stores.

General Cooking Equipment

You may already have some of these basic items in your kitchen.

Pasta cooking pot

Made of stainless steel, this pan has straight sides with two short handles and an inner perforated draining basket, which also has two short handles. Different sizes are available, so choose the one that suits your needs best. One that will comfortably hold at least 3 litres/5 pints water is adequate if you usually cook for 2–3 people, whereas a 5 litre/8 pint pan is the one you will need if you often have to cook enough pasta for 6–8 servings. Pasta pots are quite expensive as pans go, but they are so practical that if you buy one you will wonder how you ever managed without it. The pasta is boiled in the inner basket, which is lifted out of the water once the pasta is *al dente*, making draining very easy and safe. This kind of pan is also quite versatile: you can use it with the draining basket for cooking or steaming vegetables and puddings, or use the outer pan on its own for cooking stocks, soups, stews – and even preserves. When buying a pasta cooking pot, choose one that is not too heavy or you will find it difficult to manage once it is filled with water.

Skillet

A skillet was originally a cooking pot that stood on three or four legs in the hearth. In the United States, the term came to mean a frying pan. Nowadays, it is used on both sides of the Atlantic to describe a wide, deep pan – like a cross between a wok and a frying pan – with a long handle and a lid. This is the perfect pan for making sauces. Look for one that is at least 23cm/9in in diameter (25–30cm/10–12in is ideal) and 5–7.5cm/ 2–3in deep. If you often cook for a crowd or for varying numbers of people, it is worth buying two of these pans, in different sizes. Choose the best quality you can afford. Some skillets have non-stick surfaces, which is fine as long as they are of good quality.

Left: This purpose-made pasta pan comes complete with an inner perforated basket for draining the pasta.

Above: A wide, deep skillet or frying pan is the ideal pan for making sauces, while a large, deep saucepan will double as a pasta pan if you don't have a purpose-made one.

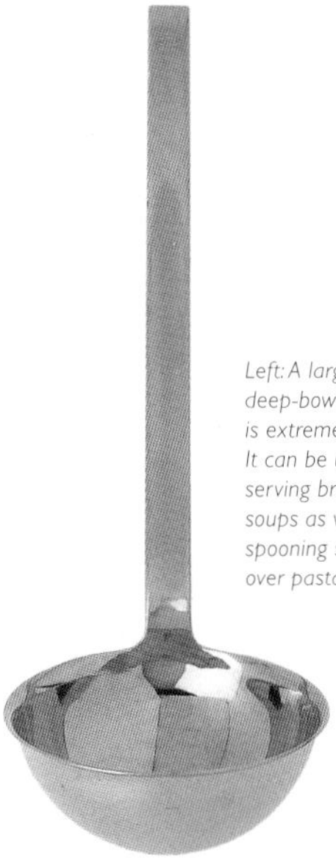

Left: A large, deep-bowled ladle is extremely useful. It can be used for serving broths and soups as well as for spooning sauces over pasta.

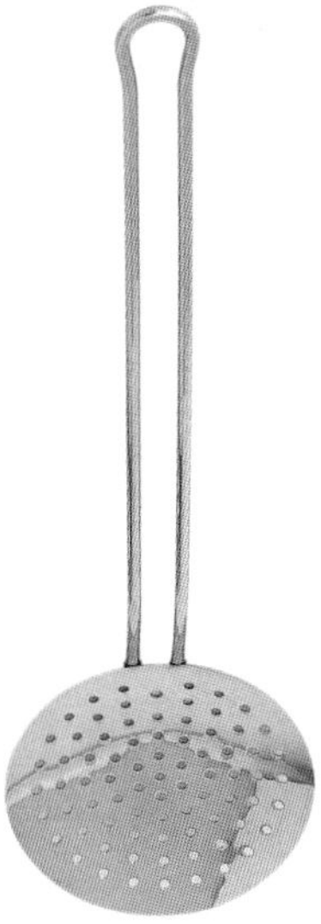

A large perforated ladle (left) or a flatter scoop (right) are ideal for lifting short pasta shapes out of boiling water.

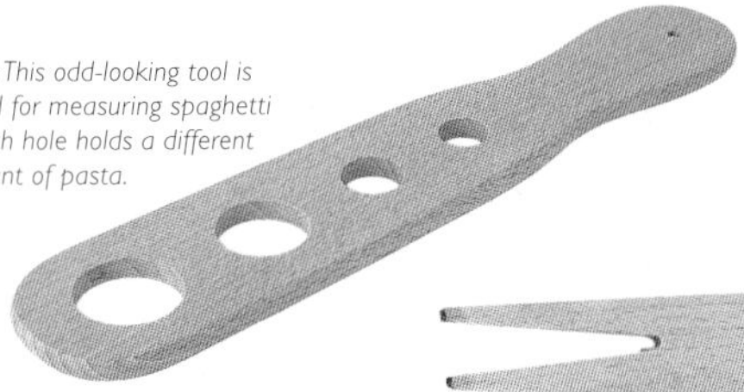

Right: This odd-looking tool is useful for measuring spaghetti – each hole holds a different amount of pasta.

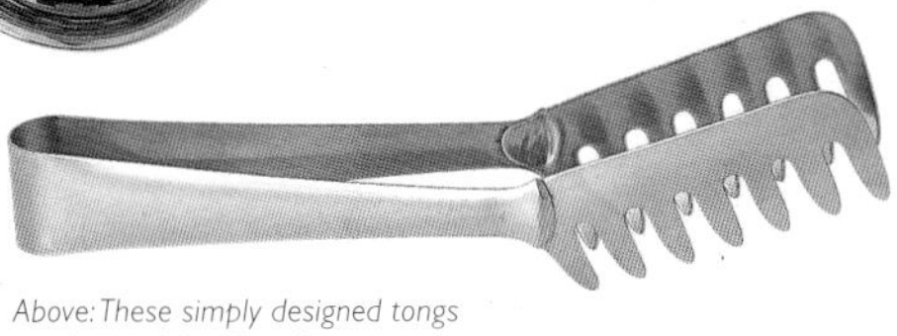

Above: These simply designed tongs can be used for lifting long strands of pasta out of boiling water.

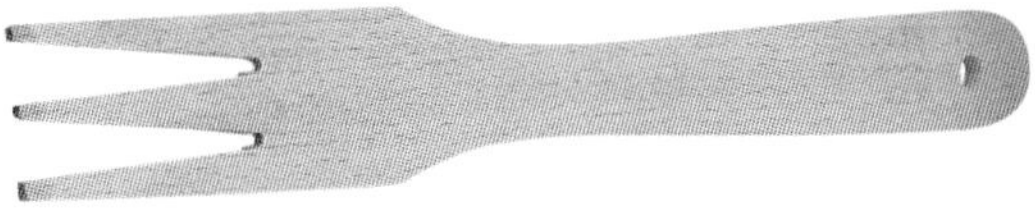

Left: A long-handled wooden fork is the best tool to use for stirring pasta to separate the strands during cooking.

Pasta measurer

Spaghetti is difficult to put on the scales, and measuring by the handful is not always accurate. This wooden gadget has four or five holes, each of which holds enough pasta for a given number of people.

Long-handled fork

This is useful for stirring pasta during cooking to help keep the strands or pieces from sticking together. A wooden fork is better for separating pasta than a solid wooden spoon. There are also wooden pasta rakes or hooks, which look like flat wooden spoons with prongs attached to one side. They do a good job because the pasta does not slip off when it is lifted, but sometimes the teeth come unglued in the boiling water.

Tongs

Nothing is more effective for picking strands of spaghetti and long noodles out of hot water than a good pair of tongs. Sturdy stainless steel tongs are the best, preferably with long handles for safety, but the most important thing is that they feel comfortable in your hand, so check this before buying. Some tongs have awkward mechanisms, springs and hinges – the simpler the design the better. Tongs can be used for lifting out individual strands to check for doneness and for serving.

Scoop or draining spoon

A large, deep perforated, slotted or mesh spoon is the perfect utensil for lifting short pasta shapes out of boiling water. Stainless steel is best.

Ladle

For spooning sauce over pasta and for serving soups, a deep-bowled ladle is the most effective utensil. Sizes vary from small and pointed with a lip for easy pouring, to very large, functional-looking types. Stainless steel is the best material, and it's a good idea to have several ladles in different sizes.

Parmesan knife

This is a short, quite stubby little knife with a shaped handle and a small and sturdy, double-sided blade. It is by no means an essential item, but is quite effective for scraping off shavings of Parmesan cheese from a block. It also looks good if you are serving Parmesan on a cheese board.

Below: The choice of Parmesan graters available includes a small, rotary grater with a storage space for a piece of Parmesan; a standard, stainless steel box grater; and the traditional small, hand-held Parmesan grater, which is ideal for using at the table.

Parmesan graters

There is a huge choice of graters, ranging from the very simple hand grater to electrically operated machines. A simple stainless steel box grater will grate Parmesan and other hard cheeses, such as Pecorino, but it can be cumbersome to use with its choice of different-size teeth. It is possible to buy a small grater especially for Parmesan. This consists of a single rectangular grating plate that is designed specifically for grating hard cheese finely, and has a small handle, which can be grasped firmly. The grater is small and unobtrusive, ideal for using at the table. Mechanical Parmesan mills are also good, as are small, hand-cranked rotary graters, and there are special Parmesan graters available with a box and a lid so that the cheese can be stored after grating. Electric Parmesan cheese graters are only worth buying if you frequently grate a lot of cheese; a less expensive alternative is to use a small electrical chopper, the kind used for chopping herbs.

Equipment for Making Pasta at Home

You can make pasta at home with nothing more sophisticated than a set of scales, some measuring spoons, a work surface and an ordinary rolling pin, but there are a few items of special equipment that will make the job easier. They are all available at specialist kitchenware shops and good department stores.

Tapered rolling pin

The traditional pin used in Italy for rolling out pasta dough is very long – it measures almost 80cm/32in in length. It is about 4cm/1½in wide in the centre and tapers almost to a point at either end. This type of rolling pin is very easy to use and is well worth buying if you enjoy making pasta by hand and don't intend to buy a special machine. A conventional, straight rolling pin can be used instead, but try to get one that is quite slim – no more than 5cm/2in in diameter.

Mechanical pasta machine

The same type of hand-cranked pasta machine has been used in Italian kitchens for many, many years. It has stood the test of time well, because it is still manufactured and used today, with very little modification. Made of stainless steel, it has rollers to press out the dough as thinly as possible and cutters for creating different shapes. The standard cutters usually allow you to make tagliatelle and tagliarini, but you can get attachments and accessories for other shapes including pappardelle, ravioli and cannelloni. The machine is clamped to the edge of a work surface or table and worked by turning the handle. If you make pasta frequently, it is a good buy because it is inexpensive, easy and fun to use, and makes excellent pasta in a very short time. It takes all of the hard work out of making pasta by hand, and you can even get an electric motor attachment so you don't have to turn the handle.

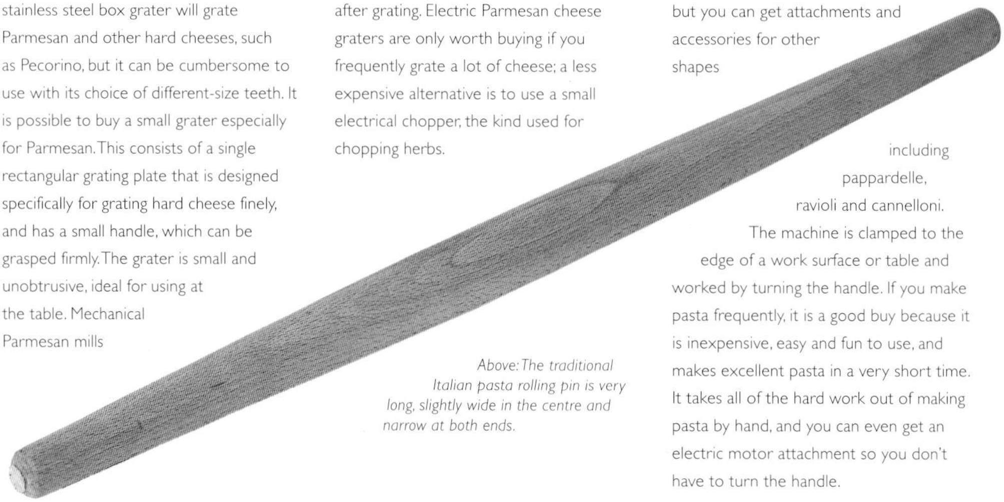

Above: The traditional Italian pasta rolling pin is very long, slightly wide in the centre and narrow at both ends.

Left: The traditional hand-cranked pasta machine with rollers to press out the dough and cutters for tagliatelle and tagliarini is still one of the best ways of making pasta.

Electric Pasta Machines

Tabletop electric pasta machines mix the dough, knead it and then extrude it through cutters, so all you have to do is put the ingredients in the machine and turn it on. You can make more shapes with this type of machine than the mechanical one, but you have less control over the dough because you don't actually handle it at all. Electric pasta machines are only sold in some specialist kitchenware shops. They are expensive to buy, but are a worthwhile investment if you frequently make a lot of pasta – they can make up to 1kg/2¼lb at a time – and have the space to house the machine in a convenient spot.

Left: A stainless steel pasta wheel makes light work of cutting noodles and ravioli.

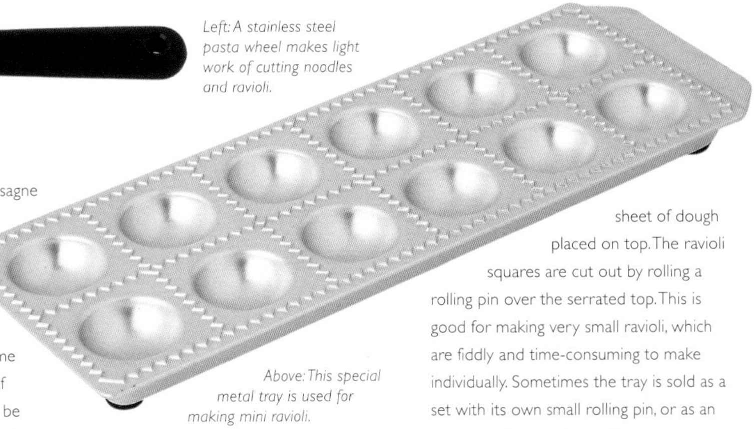

Above: This special metal tray is used for making mini ravioli.

Pasta wheel

This is a useful gadget for cutting lasagne and noodles such as tagliatelle when you don't have a pasta machine, and for cutting out small stuffed shapes such as ravioli. The wheel can be straight or fluted, and there are some types that will cut several lengths of noodle at a time. A sharp knife can be used instead, but a pasta wheel is easier and gives a neater finish. With a pasta wheel, the pasta edges are less likely to be dragged out of shape or torn.

Ravioli cutter

This is virtually the same as a fluted biscuit cutter except that it has a wooden handle and can be square or round. If you want to make square ravioli and cappelletti, you can use a pasta wheel instead of this cutter, so it isn't a vital piece of equipment. For round ravioli, tortellini and anolini you can use a biscuit cutter if you have one. The most useful sizes are 5cm/2in and 7.5cm/3in.

Ravioli tray

You can buy a special metal tray for making ravioli. A sheet of rolled-out dough is laid over the tray, then pressed into the indentations. The filling is then spooned into the indentations and another sheet of dough placed on top. The ravioli squares are cut out by rolling a rolling pin over the serrated top. This is good for making very small ravioli, which are fiddly and time-consuming to make individually. Sometimes the tray is sold as a set with its own small rolling pin, or as an accessory for a pasta machine.

A specially designed ravioli cutter (right), which can be round or square, isn't essential, because fluted and plain biscuit cutters (left) do the same job.

How to Cook and Serve Pasta

It is very easy to cook pasta properly, but without care and attention it is equally easy to cook it badly. A few simple guidelines need to be observed if pasta is to be at its best. Once you have mastered these, you will be able to cook pasta successfully every time, no matter whether it is dried, home-made or bought fresh.

Cooking Pasta in the Microwave

Because of the large amount of water needed to boil pasta, you will not save any time by cooking it in the microwave, but for short shapes and quantities under 225g/8oz, you may find it more convenient than cooking the pasta on top of the stove. The results can be quite successful. Large and long shapes, such as lasagne sheets and spaghetti, need to be cooked in batches, so there seems hardly any point. Where the microwave comes into its own is in reheating pasta sauces, and for reheating previously baked pasta dishes, such as lasagne and cannelloni, especially individual portions of these. The microwave is also useful for thawing and reheating sauces and baked dishes that have been stored in the freezer.

How to microwave short pasta shapes

Put the pasta in a large heatproof bowl with salt to taste and pour over boiling water to cover by 2.5cm/1in. Carefully transfer the bowl to the microwave and cook on High (100 per cent power) for 3–4 minutes for fresh pasta and 8–10 minutes for dried, then leave to stand for 5 minutes before draining.

1 **Synchronize sauce and pasta**
Before starting to cook either sauce or pasta, read through the recipe carefully. It is important to know which needs to be cooked for the longest time – sometimes it is the pasta and sometimes the sauce, so don't always assume one or the other. The sauce can often be made ahead of time and reheated, and it is quite unusual for the timing of a sauce to be crucial, but pasta is almost like a hot soufflé – it waits for no one. This is especially true if you are cooking fresh pasta, for which timing is often only a few minutes, so the sauce needs to be ready and waiting before the pasta hits the water.

3 **Use a large quantity of water**
The recommended amount is 5 litres/8 pints water for every 450g/1lb pasta. If you are cooking less pasta than this, use at least 3 litres/5 pints water. If there is not enough water, the pasta shapes will stick together as they swell and the pan will become overcrowded. This will result in unpleasant, gummy-textured pasta.

WATCHPOINT

It is best not to cook more than 675g/1½lb pasta at a time, even if you have a very large saucepan, because of the danger in handling such a large amount of water. If you are using the microwave to cook pasta it is best not to cook more than 225g/8oz pasta at a time. Use a large heatproof bowl, don't overfill the bowl and transfer it carefully to and from the microwave using heatproof gloves.

2 **Use a big pan**
There needs to be plenty of room for the pasta to move around in the large amount of water it requires, so a big pan is essential. The best type of pan is a tall, lightweight, straight-sided, stainless steel pasta cooking pot with its own in-built draining pan. Both outer and inner pans have two handles each, which ensure easy and safe lifting and draining. If you cook pasta a lot, it is well worth investing in one of these special pans; otherwise use the largest saucepan you have for cooking the pasta and a large stainless steel colander, preferably one with feet for stability, for draining it.

4 **Get the water boiling**
Before adding the pasta, the water should be at a fast rolling boil. The quickest way to do this is to boil water in the kettle, then pour it into the pasta pan, which should be set over a high heat. You may need as much as 2–3 kettlefuls, so keep the water in the pan simmering, covered by the lid, while you boil the kettle again.

5 Add enough salt

Pasta cooked without salt is more or less tasteless, and with insufficient salt it is hardly any better. The recommended amount is 22.5–30ml/1 1/2–2 tbsp salt for every 450g/1lb pasta. There is no need to use sea or rock salt; cooking salt is perfectly acceptable. Add the salt when the water is boiling and just before you are ready to add the pasta. The water will bubble furiously just as the salt is added, which is your cue to shoot in the pasta.

6 Tip in the pasta all at once

Try to get all of the pasta into the boiling water at the same time so that it will cook evenly and be ready at the same time. The quickest and easiest way is literally to shake it out of the packet or the bowl of the scales, covering the surface of the water as much as possible.

7 Return the water quickly to the boil

Once the pasta is submerged in the water, give it a brisk stir with a long-handled fork or spoon and then cover the pan tightly with the lid – this will help to bring the water back to the boil as quickly as possible. Once the water is boiling, lift off the lid, turn down the heat slightly and let the water simmer over a medium to high heat for the required cooking time.

8 Stir the pasta frequently during cooking

To prevent the pasta strands or shapes from sticking together, stir them frequently during cooking so they are kept constantly on the move. Use a long-handled wooden fork or spoon so you can stir right down to the bottom of the pan.

9 Drain carefully and thoroughly

If you have a pasta pot with an inner drainer, lift the draining pan up and out of the water. Shake the draining pan vigorously and stir the pasta well so that any water trapped in pasta shapes can drain out as quickly as possible. It is a good idea to reserve a few ladlefuls of the pasta cooking water in case the pasta needs a little extra moistening when it is tossed with the sauce before serving.

Accurate Timing is Essential for Cooking Pasta

Start timing the pasta from the moment the water returns to the boil after adding the pasta. Always go by the time given on the packet or, in the case of fresh home-made pasta, by the time given in the recipe. For the greatest accuracy, use a kitchen timer with a bell or buzzer because even half a minute of overcooking can ruin pasta, especially if it is freshly made. Dried egg pasta is more difficult to spoil, so if you are new to pasta cooking and nervous about getting it right, start with this type.

For fresh pasta

As a general guide, thin fresh noodles will take only 2–3 minutes, thicker fresh noodles and pasta shapes 3–4 minutes, and stuffed fresh pasta 5–7 minutes.

For dried pasta

The cooking time for dried pasta will vary from 8–20 minutes depending on the type and the manufacturer. Always check the time on the label.

Cooking Fresh Pasta

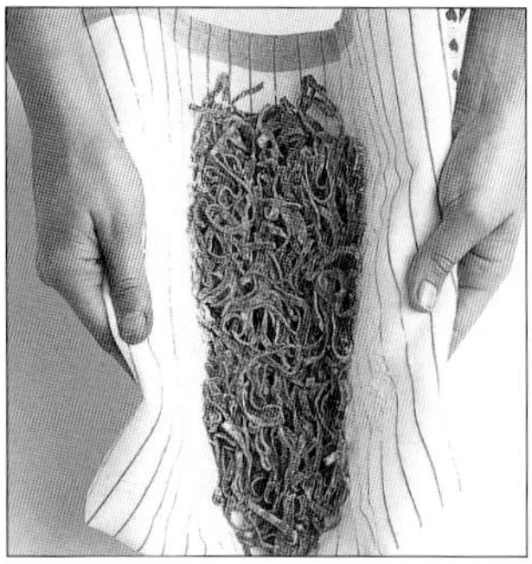

1 For freshly made pasta that has been drying on a dish towel, gather the cloth up around the pasta in a loose cylindrical shape and hold it firmly at both ends.

2 Hold the towel over the water, then let go of the end nearest to the water so that the pasta shoots in.

Cooking Long Dried Pasta

1 For spaghetti you need to coil the pasta into the water as it softens. Take a handful at a time and dip it in the boiling water so that it touches the bottom of the pan.

2 As the spaghetti strands soften, coil them round using a wooden spoon or fork until they are all submerged.

Cooking Stuffed Pasta

1 Stuffed shapes require more gentle handling or they may break open and release their filling into the water, so stir them gently during cooking.

2 The best method of draining stuffed shapes after cooking is to lift them carefully out of the water with a large pasta scoop or slotted spoon (left).

When is it cooked?

The Italian term *al dente* is used to describe pasta that is cooked to perfection. Literally translated this means "to the tooth", meaning that it should be firm to the bite, which is how Italians like their pasta, and therefore how it should be served. Dried pasta, which is made from durum wheat, is always served *al dente*, whereas fresh pasta is made from a softer wheat and so is never as firm as dried, but it should still have some resistance to it. Overcooked pasta is limp and unpalatable and an Italian cook would not serve it.

To check that the pasta is ready, test pasta frequently towards the end of the recommended cooking time by lifting out a piece with tongs, a pasta scoop or a slotted spoon and biting into it. When you are satisfied that it is done to your liking, it is time to stop the cooking.

At-a-glance Quantities

Amounts of pasta given here are intended only as a guide to the number of people they will serve. If you are cooking fresh pasta, you may need a little more than if you are using dried, but the difference is really negligible. What is more significant is whether you are serving a light or substantial sauce with the pasta.

For an Italian-style first course (primo piatto) for 4–6 people, or a main course for 2–3 people:

3 litres/5 pints water
15ml/1 tbsp salt
250–350g/9–12oz fresh or dried pasta

For a first course for 6–8 people, or a main course for 4–6 people:

5 litres/8 pints water
22.5–30ml/1 1/2–2 tbsp salt
300–450g/11oz–1lb fresh or dried pasta

Cook's Tip

If you are using an ordinary saucepan and a colander for cooking and draining pasta, have the colander ready in the sink. Carefully pour the contents of the pan into the colander, then shake the colander vigorously over the sink and stir the pasta to release any trapped water.

Combining the Pasta and Sauce

Recipes vary in the way they combine sauce and pasta. The majority add the sauce to the pasta, but with some it is the other way around. There are no hard-and-fast rules. If you are going to add the sauce to the drained pasta, the most important thing is to have a warmed bowl ready. The larger the bowl the better, because this will allow room for the sauce and pasta to be tossed together easily so that every piece of pasta can be thoroughly coated in sauce.

1 After draining, immediately tip the pasta into the warmed bowl, then pour the sauce over the pasta and quickly toss the two together.

2 If the pasta is not moist enough, add a little of the pasta cooking water. Some recipes call for extra butter or oil to be added at this stage, others have grated Parmesan or Pecorino cheese tossed with the pasta and sauce.

3 Use two large spoons or forks for tossing, or a large spoon and a fork. Lift the pasta and swirl it around, making sure you have scooped it up from the bottom of the bowl. The idea is to coat every piece of pasta evenly in sauce, so keep tossing until you are satisfied that this is done.

4 Occasionally, recipes call for the pasta to be returned to the cooking pan, to be combined with oil or butter and seasonings and tossed over heat until coated. A sauce may be added at this stage too, but care should be taken not to cook the pasta too much in the first place or it may overcook when it is reheated.

Serving and Presentation

Most important of all is to have your family and friends waiting at the table for the pasta, not the other way round. With the exception of baked dishes, all pasta should be eaten as soon as it is cooked and tossed with the sauce, so invite everyone to sit down just before you are ready to drain the pasta.

In most cases, pasta and sauce are tossed together in a large serving bowl in the kitchen, and the bowl is then brought straight to the table. Each person is served straight from the bowl – or the bowl is passed around the table for everyone to help themselves.

To give the pasta a finishing touch, a little Parmesan or Pecorino cheese can be grated on top, or a few chopped fresh herbs, such as parsley or basil, can be sprinkled over. The choice of garnish depends on the dish and the cook, but as a general rule, grated cheese is never served with fish and shellfish sauces. For guidance, follow the garnishing instructions in individual recipes.

Occasionally, the pasta and sauce are divided among individual plates or bowls before serving – as is the practice in restaurants. This is not the traditional custom in Italian homes, but it sometimes helps to get the pasta served quickly. It is an especially good idea when you are entertaining, because each individual serving can have its own attractive garnish.

Matching Sauces to Recipes

Some regional dishes are always made with the same pasta shape. *Bucatini all'Amatriciana*, *Penne all'Arrabbiata* and *Fettuccine all'Alfredo* are all classic Roman recipes, for example, and it is rare to see them served with anything other than the named pasta. The same applies to *Tagliatelle alla Bolognese* from Emilia-Romagna and *Trenette con Pesto* from Genoa. These classics are few and far between, however, and with the ever-increasing number of different shapes on the market it may seem difficult to know which sauces and shapes go well together. Happily, there are no rigid rules, and common sense usually prevails. Heavy sauces with large chunks of meat are unlikely to go well with thin spaghettini or tagliolini, simply because the chunks will slide off, so these sauces and others like them are always served with wide noodles, such as pappardelle, maccheroni and tagliatelle, or with short tubular shapes, such as penne, fusilli, conchiglie and rigatoni.

In the south of Italy, olive oil is used for cooking rather than butter, so sauces tend to be made with olive oil and they are usually served with the dried plain durum wheat pasta such as spaghetti and vermicelli that is also popular in the south. These long, thin shapes are traditionally served with tomato and seafood sauces, most of which are made with olive oil, and with light vegetable sauces. Spaghetti and vermicelli are also ideal vehicles for minimalist sauces like *Aglio e Olio* (garlic and olive oil) from Rome. Grated cheese is not normally used in these sauces, nor is it sprinkled over them.

Classic dishes, such as Fettuccine all'Alfredo (above), Bucatini all'Amatriciana (left), and Penne all'Arrabbiata (below), are almost always served with the named pasta.

Grated cheese is often tossed with pasta and sauce at the last moment, as well as being sprinkled over individual servings at the table.

In the North, butter and cream are used in sauces, and not surprisingly these go well with the egg pasta that is made there, especially fresh home-made egg pasta, which absorbs butter and cream and makes the sauce cling to it. Butter and cream also go well with tomato sauces when these are served with short shapes, especially penne, rigatoni, farfalle and fusilli.

Eating Pasta

Opinions vary as to whether pasta should be eaten from a plate or a bowl. There are no rules, so you can serve it on either. Large, shallow soup plates seem the ideal compromise, and setting each warmed soup plate on a large, cold underplate makes for easy carrying from kitchen to table.

If the recipe recommends extra Parmesan or Pecorino for serving, grate the cheese just before the meal and hand it round in a bowl with a small spoon so that people can help themselves. Salt and pepper mills should also be on the table for those who like to adjust the seasoning.

Pasta is traditionally eaten with a single fork. Spaghetti and other long shapes should not be difficult to manage if they have been well tossed with the sauce. The trick is to twizzle only a small amount around the fork at a time.

Wines to Serve with Pasta

It is impossible to recommend a particular wine to go with every pasta dish, but there are a few guidelines you can follow. If you know where the dish comes from, choose a wine from the same region. If a red or a white wine is used in the cooking of the sauce, select a good-quality wine for cooking and serve the rest with the meal. Otherwise, look at the main ingredient of the sauce and choose a wine that is recommended for that. Many pasta sauces are strong-tasting, garlicky or spiced with chillies, and some are served with mature Parmesan or Pecorino cheese; for these you will need to choose a robust, full-flavoured wine.

Barbaresco
A great red wine from Piedmont. Full-bodied and complex in flavour. Good with poultry and meat sauces.

Barbera
A medium-bodied red from Piedmont, which varies from young and slightly sparkling to rich and concentrated in flavour. Good with meat lasagne.

Bardolino
This fresh-tasting, light and fruity red from Veneto is very good to serve with poultry sauces.

Barolo
A full-bodied red made in Piedmont from Nebbiolo grapes. Good with red meat and game sauces.

Castel del Monte
Full-bodied smooth red and rosé wines from Puglia. Good with poultry and meat.

Chianti
Famous, uncomplicated red from Tuscany. Look for Chianti Classico to serve with red meat, poultry and game sauces.

Cirò
Fresh, zingy white and full-bodied red from Calabria. Drink the white with fish and shellfish sauces, the red with red meat and game sauces.

Est! Est!! Est!!!
A clean-tasting, dry white from the Lazio region. It is good with fish and shellfish sauces.

Frascati
A crisp and fruity dry white from the town of Frascati, which is near Rome in the Lazio region. Good with the very spicy Amatriciana sauce.

Lambrusco
This effervescent red from Emilia-Romagna is good with pork and rich meat sauces.

Orvieto Secco
Dry white, from the town of the same name in Umbria. Serve with fish, shellfish and poultry sauces.

Pinot Grigio
A fresh, fruity dry white from Friuli-Venezia. It is good with any sauce or pasta dish.

Soave
Light, dry white from Veneto made from Garganega grapes. It is good with any sauce or pasta dish, and is reasonably priced.

Valpolicella
Fruity red, sometimes with a bitter aftertaste, from Veneto. The name means valley of many cellars. It is good with red meat sauces.

Valtellina
This perfumed red from Lombardy is made from Nebbiolo grapes. Look for Grumello, Inferno, Sassella and Valgella. It is good with rich meat, poultry and game sauces.

Verdicchio
Crisp, dry white with character from Marche in central Italy. It comes in a carved bottle shaped like a Roman amphora. Good with all kinds of fish and shellfish sauces.

Vernaccia
Rich, nutty red from the island of Sardinia that goes well with fish and shellfish sauces.

How to Make Pasta

Home-made pasta has a wonderfully light, almost silky texture – quite different from the so-called fresh pasta that you buy pre-packaged in some shops. If you use egg in the mixture, which is recommended if you are making pasta at home, the dough is easy to make, either by hand or machine, and the initial process is not that different from making bread. Kneading, rolling and cutting require some patience and practice, but if you invest in an inexpensive mechanical pasta machine, this part of the process will become quick and easy – and great fun too.

Pasta all'Uovo

Pasta with Eggs

The best place to make, knead and roll out pasta dough is on a wooden kitchen table, the larger the better. The surface should be warm, so marble is not suitable.

INGREDIENTS

300g/11oz/2¾ cups flour
3 eggs
5ml/1 tsp salt

Ingredients for Pasta with Eggs

Only three inexpensive ingredients are used for making pasta with eggs: flour, eggs and salt. However, ultimate success depends as much on their quality as on the technique used for making the dough. Olive oil is added to the mixture by some cooks, especially in Tuscany, but it is by no means essential. It gives the pasta a softer texture and a slightly different flavour, and some say it helps make the dough easier to work with, especially if you don't have a pasta machine. For a 3-egg quantity of dough, use 15ml/1 tbsp olive oil and add it with the eggs.

The best flour is called Farina Bianca 00 or Tipo 00, available from Italian delicatessens. Imported from Italy, this is a very fine, soft white wheat flour. If you use ordinary plain flour, you will find the dough quite difficult to knead and roll, especially if you are doing this by hand. If you can't get 00 flour, use a strong plain white bread flour.

Very fresh eggs are essential, and the deeper the yellow of the yolks the better the colour of the pasta. Buy the eggs fresh and use them at room temperature. If they have been stored in the fridge, take them out for about 1 hour before using.

Salt is important for flavour.

1 Mound the flour on a clean work surface and make a large, deep well in the centre with your hands. Keep the sides of the well quite high so that when the eggs are added they will not run out of the well.

2 Crack the eggs into the well, then add the salt. With a table knife or fork, mix the eggs and salt together, then gradually start incorporating the flour from the sides of the well. Try not to break the sides of the well or the runny mixture will escape and quickly spread over the work surface.

3 As soon as the egg mixture is no longer liquid, dip your fingers in the flour and use them to work the ingredients together until they form a rough and sticky dough. Scrape up any dough that sticks to the work surface with a knife, then scrape this off the knife with your fingers. If the dough is too dry, add a few drops of cold water; if it is too moist, sprinkle a little flour over it.

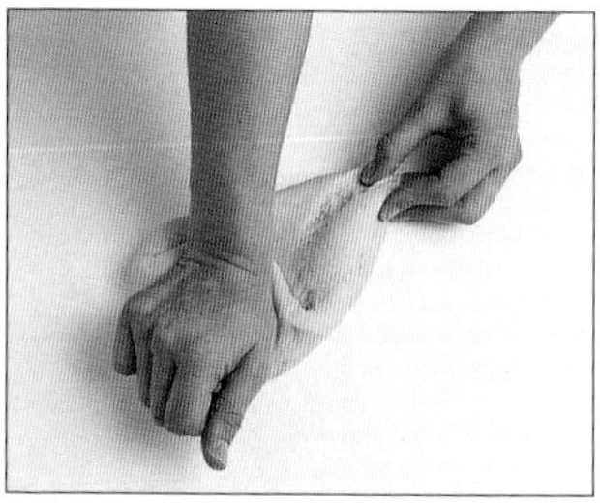

4 Press the dough into a rough ball and knead it as you would bread. Push it away from you with the heel of your hand, then fold the end of the dough back on itself so that it faces towards you and push it out again. Continue folding the dough back a little further each time and pushing it out until you have folded it back all the way towards you and all the dough has been kneaded.

5 Give the dough a quarter turn anti-clockwise, then continue kneading, folding and turning for 5 minutes if you intend using a pasta machine, or for 10 minutes if you will be rolling it out by hand. The dough should be very smooth and elastic. If you are going to roll it out and cut it by hand, thorough kneading is essential.

6 Wrap the dough in clear film and leave to rest for 15–20 minutes at room temperature. It will then be ready to roll out.

COOK'S TIP

Don't skimp on the kneading time or the finished pasta will not be light and silky.

Making Pasta Dough in a Food Processor

If you have a food processor, you can save a little time and effort by using it for making pasta dough. It will not knead the dough adequately, however, so you may find it just as quick and easy to make it by hand, especially if you take into account the washing and drying of the bowl and blade. The ingredients are the same as when making pasta by hand.

1 Put the flour and salt in the bowl of a food processor fitted with the metal blade.

2 Add 1 whole egg and then pulse-blend until the ingredients are mixed.

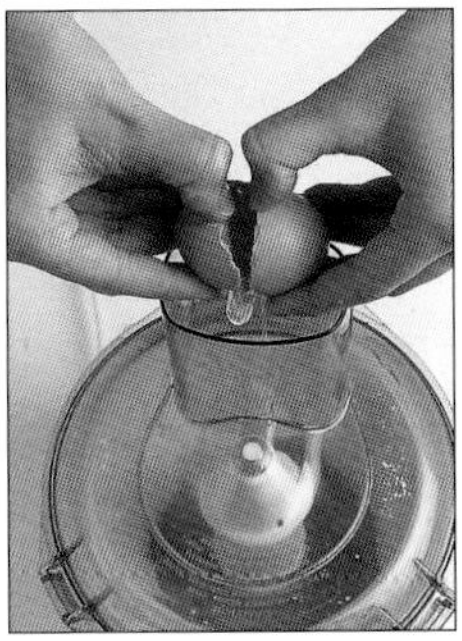

3 Turn the food processor on to full speed and add the remaining whole eggs through the feeder tube. Keep the machine running for just long enough to allow a dough to be formed.

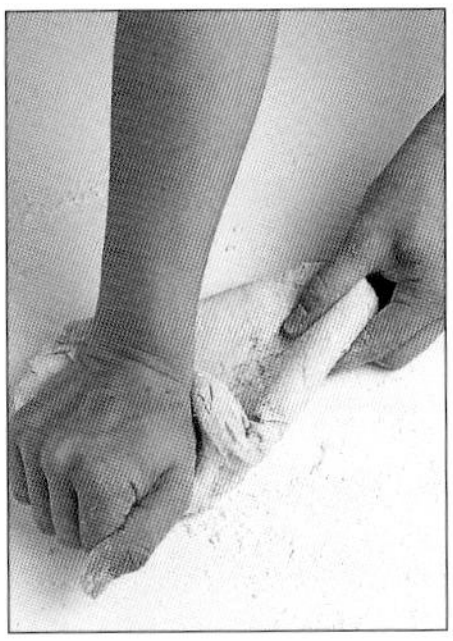

4 Turn the dough out on to a clean work surface. Knead as when making pasta by hand, then wrap in clear film and leave to rest at room temperature for 15–20 minutes.

Making Pasta Shapes by Hand

Once you have made your pasta dough and let it rest, it is ready to be rolled out and cut into various shapes. If you don't have a pasta machine, the following steps show how to do it by hand. The technique is quite hard work and the pasta may not be quite as thin as that made in a machine, but it is equally good nevertheless. If you enjoy making your own pasta and think you would like to make it regularly, it is well worth buying a mechanical pasta machine to save you both time and effort.

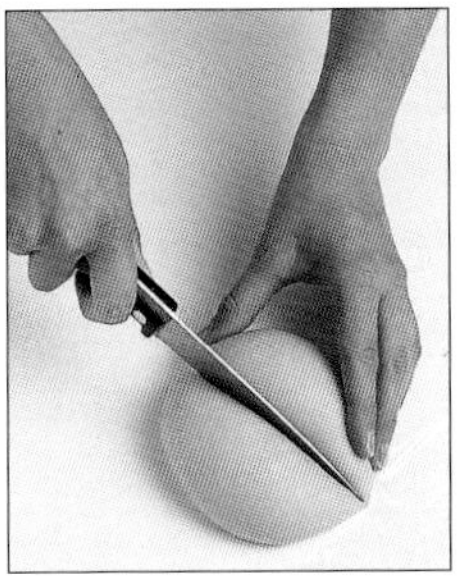

1 Unwrap the ball of dough and cut it in half. Roll and cut one half at a time, keeping the other half wrapped in clear film as before.

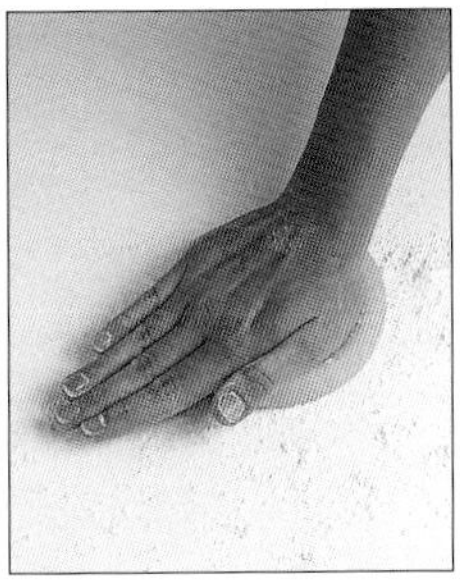

2 Sprinkle a very large, clean work surface lightly with flour. Put the unwrapped dough on the surface, sprinkle it with a little flour and flatten it with the heel of your hand. Turn the dough over and repeat the process to form the dough into a 13cm/5in disc.

3 Using a lightly floured rolling pin, start to roll the dough out. Always roll the dough away from you, stretching it outwards from the centre and moving the dough round a quarter turn after each rolling. If the dough gets sticky, sprinkle the rolling pin, dough and work surface lightly with flour.

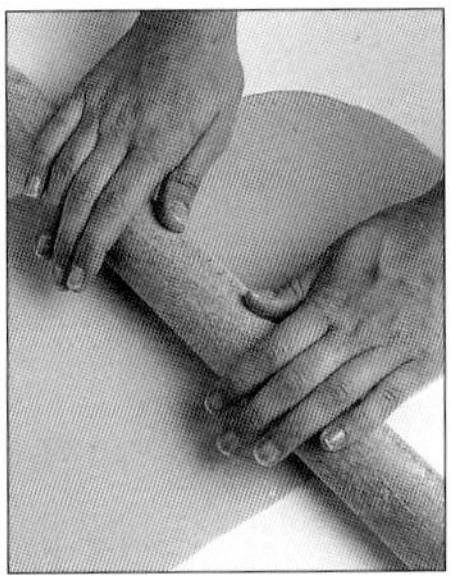

4 Continue rolling, turning and stretching the dough until it is a large oval, as thin as you can possibly get it. Ideally it should be about 3mm/⅛in thick. Try to get it even all over or the shapes will not cook in the same length of time. Don't worry if the edges are not neat; this is not important.

Cutting Ribbon Noodles

1 Before you begin, have ready plenty of clean dish towels lightly dusted with flour; you will need to spread the shapes out on them after cutting. Dust the sheet of pasta (called *la sfoglia* in Italian) lightly with flour. Starting from one long edge, roll up the sheet into a loose cylinder.

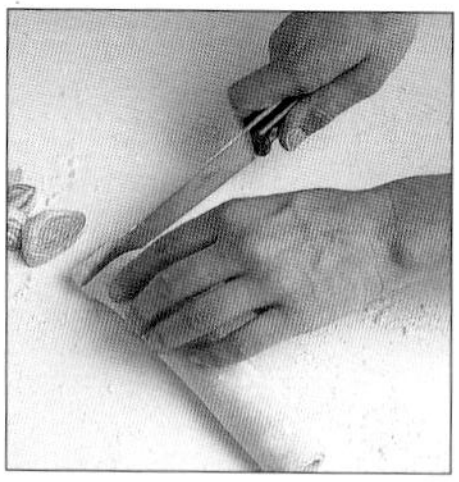

2 With a large sharp knife, cut cleanly across the pasta roll. Cut at 1cm/½in intervals for tagliatelle, slightly narrower (about 5mm/¼in) for fettuccine, and as narrow as you can possibly get for tagliarini or capelli d'angelo. Take care not to drag the knife or the edges of the ribbons will be ragged.

3 With floured fingers, unravel the rolls on the work surface, then toss the noodles lightly together on the floured dish towels, sprinkling them with more flour.

4 Repeat the rolling and cutting with the remaining pasta. Leave the strips to dry on the dish towels for at least 15 minutes before cooking, tossing them from time to time and sprinkling them with a little flour if they become sticky.

Cutting Pappardelle

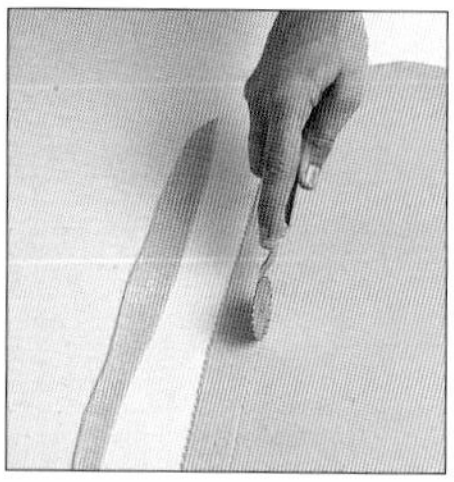

1 Using a fluted pasta wheel, cut the pasta sheet into long strips about 2–2.5cm/¾–1in wide. Try to keep the strips the same width or they will not cook evenly.

2 Spread the pappardelle strips out in a single layer on floured dish towels and sprinkle them with a little more flour. Leave the pappardelle to dry on the towels for at least 15 minutes before cooking.

Cutting Lasagne and Cannelloni

1 With a large sharp knife, cut the pasta sheets into 15–18 x 7.5–10cm/5–6 x 3–4in rectangles or whatever size fits your baking dish best.

2 Spread the rectangles out in a single layer on floured dish towels, sprinkle them with more flour and leave to dry for at least 15 minutes before cooking. They can be used for both lasagne and cannelloni.

Cook's Tip

Don't throw away the trimmings when making pasta shapes, such as tagliatelle and lasagne – cut the trimmings into small pieces and pop them into soup at the last minute. You can cut leftover scraps into any rough shape you like, but there are two shapes that are made especially for soups: quadrucci and maltagliati.

Cutting Quadrucci (for Soups)

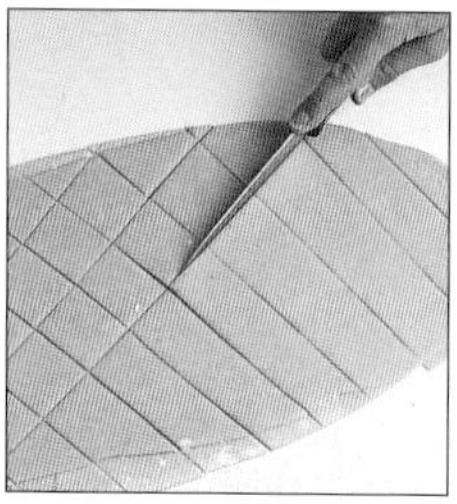

1 Stack two pasta sheets on top of each other, with a light sprinkling of flour in between. With a large sharp knife, cut the pasta diagonally into 4cm/1½in wide strips, then cut across the strips in the opposite direction to make 4cm/1½in squares.

2 Spread the squares out on floured dish towels and sprinkle with more flour. Leave to dry for at least 15 minutes before cooking.

Cutting Maltagliati (for Soups)

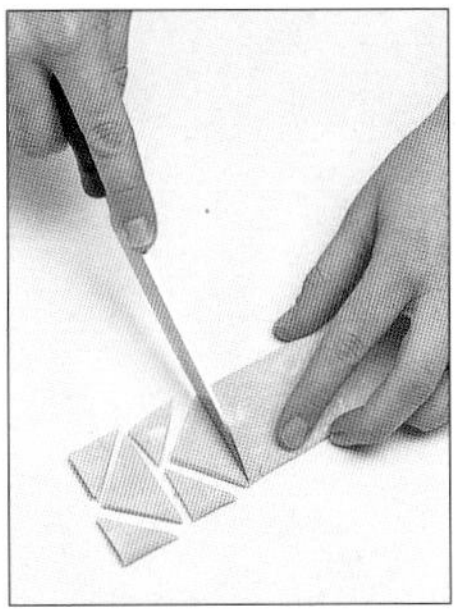

1 Dust one pasta sheet lightly with flour. Starting from one long edge, roll the sheet up into a cylinder. Lightly flatten the cylinder, then, with a sharp knife, slice off the corners at one end, making two diagonal cuts to form two sides of a triangle. Cut straight across to complete the triangle. Repeat all the way along the cylinder, then unfold the maltagliati.

2 Spread out the maltagliati on floured dish towels. Sprinkle the shapes with a little more flour and leave them to dry for at least 15 minutes before cooking.

Cook's Tip

Maltagliati means badly cut, so don't worry if the pasta is misshapen – it is meant to be. Quadrucci and maltagliati can also be cut from fresh lasagne rectangles, but this will take slightly longer.

Making Short Pasta Shapes

Most small pasta shapes are best left to the professionals, because they either take too long to make in any quantity or require specialist equipment. There are a couple of shapes that are an exception: garganelli and farfalle. Garganelli are traditionally made with a special tool called *il pettine*, but you can improvise with an old-fashioned butter paddle and a round pencil.

Making Garganelli

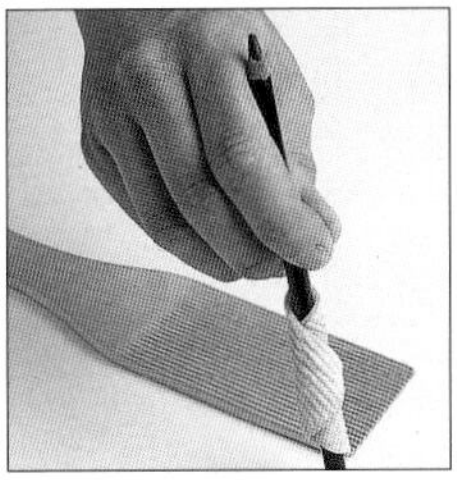

1 Cut the pasta sheets into 5cm/2in squares. Lay the butter paddle ridges horizontally on the work surface, with the ridges facing towards you. Angle the square so that it is diamond-shaped and place it over the ridges. Put a pencil diagonally across the corner of the square that is closest to you.

2 Roll the pasta square up around the pencil, pressing down hard on the ends of the pencil as you go. The ridges of the butter paddle will imprint themselves on the pasta.

3 Stand the pencil upright on the work surface and tap the end so that the tube of pasta slides off.

4 Spread the garganelli out in a single layer on floured dish towels, sprinkle them with more flour and leave them to dry for at least 15 minutes before cooking.

Making Farfalle

1 With a fluted pasta wheel, cut the pasta sheets into rectangles measuring 4 x 2.5cm/ 1 1/4 x 1in. Pinch the long sides of each rectangle between your index finger and thumb and squeeze hard to make a bow-tie shape. If the pasta will not hold the shape, moisten your fingers with water and squeeze again.

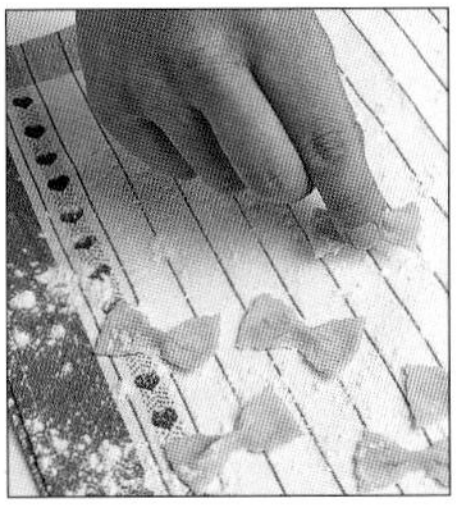

2 Spread the farfalle out in a single layer on floured dish towels, sprinkle them with a little more flour and leave to dry for at least 15 minutes before cooking.

Making Pasta Shapes Using a Machine

Rolling the Dough

A machine makes light work of rolling pasta dough. It makes thinner, smoother pasta than you can make by hand, and the thickness is always even. Some shapes, such as lasagne, are cut by hand, but for cutting noodles, a machine is invaluable.

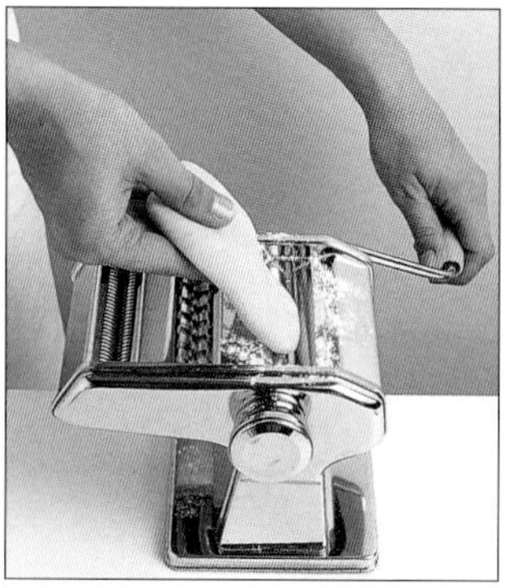

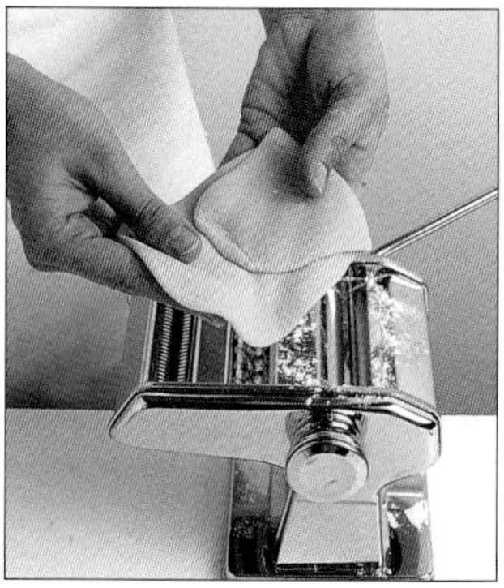

1 Clamp the machine securely to your work surface and insert the handle in the roller slot. Set the rollers at their widest setting and sprinkle them lightly with flour. Unwrap the ball of pasta and cut it into quarters. Work with one quarter at a time, wrapping the other three pieces of pasta dough in clear film.

2 Flatten the quarter of dough with lightly floured hands and make it into a rough rectangle, just a little narrower in width than the rollers of the machine. Feed this through the rollers of the machine.

3 Fold the dough into thirds, then feed it lengthways through the rollers. Repeat the folding and rolling five times.

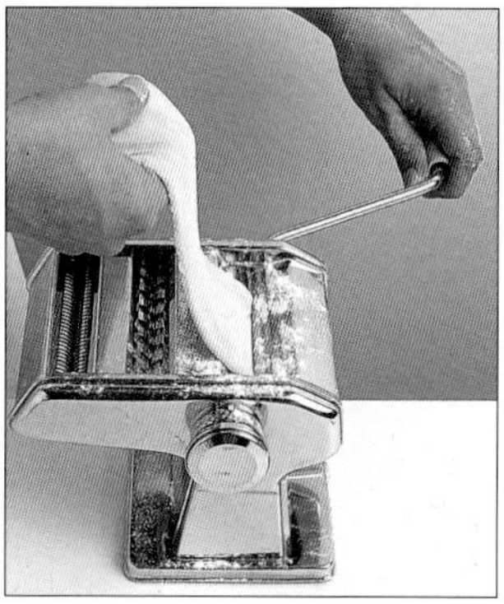

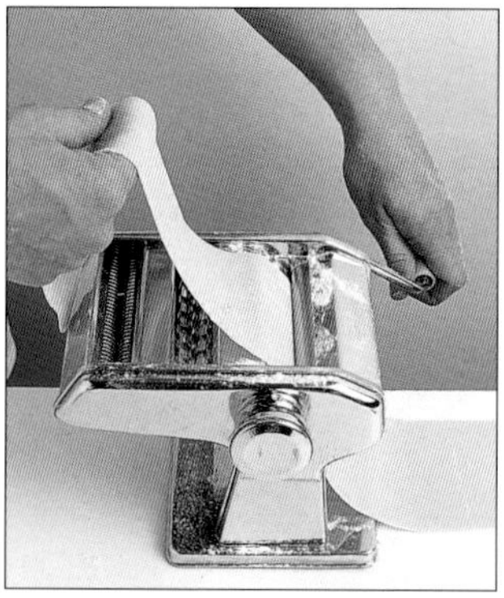

4 Turn the roller setting one notch. Sprinkle the pasta lightly with flour and feed it through the rollers again, only this time unfolded.

5 Turn the roller setting another notch and repeat the rolling, then continue in this way without folding the dough until you get to the last setting, turning the roller setting another notch after each rolling and sprinkling it lightly with flour if it becomes sticky. The dough will get longer and thinner with every rolling until it reaches 90cm–1 metre/35in–3feet in length. Once the dough has been rolled, it is ready for cutting into the required shape.

Cook's Tips

- *About halfway through the rolling process, you may find that the pasta strip becomes too unwieldy and difficult to handle because it is so long. In this case, cut the strip in half or into thirds and work with one piece at a time. Remember to return the notch on the roller to the setting where you left off when you start with the next piece of dough.*
- *You may find that the dough is thin enough on the penultimate setting, in which case you can stop there. This will definitely be the case if you are going to make tonnarelli or spaghetti alla chitarra.*
- *Keep sprinkling the pasta dough lightly with flour if it becomes sticky, and keep the rollers lightly floured to prevent the pasta sticking to the machine.*
- *Any trimmings and leftover pieces of pasta dough can be re-rolled and more shapes cut from them.*
- *Once they are dry, noodles and pasta shapes can be stored in a paper bag for 3–4 days, or frozen in plastic bags for up to 1 month.*

Cutting Lasagne and Cannelloni

1 Using a sharp knife, cut the rolled pasta strip into 15–18 x 7.5–10cm/5–6 x 3–4in rectangles, or whatever size fits your baking dish best.

2 Spread out the rectangles in a single layer on floured dish towels and sprinkle with flour.

Cook's Tip

•Leave the lasagne sheets to dry on the dish towels while rolling and cutting the remaining three pieces of dough.

•Stack each successive batch of lasagne sheets on top of the previous one, with a floured dish towel in between.

Cutting Tagliatelle and Fettuccine

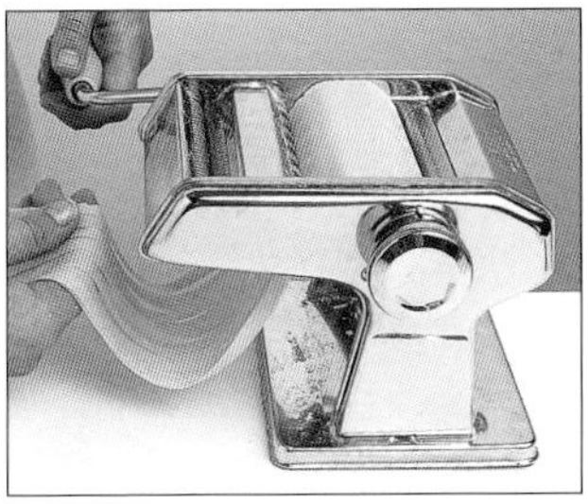

1 Insert the handle in the slot for the widest cutters and sprinkle these cutters lightly with flour. Cut the pasta strip to about 30cm/12in long if you haven't done so already, and sprinkle it lightly with flour. Feed the pasta through the widest cutters.

2 Continue turning the handle of the pasta machine slowly and steadily, guiding the strands with your other hand.

3 Toss the tagliatelle or fettuccine in flour and spread the noodles out on a floured dish towel. Leave to dry while rolling and cutting the remaining dough.

Cutting Tonnarelli and Spaghetti alla Chitarra

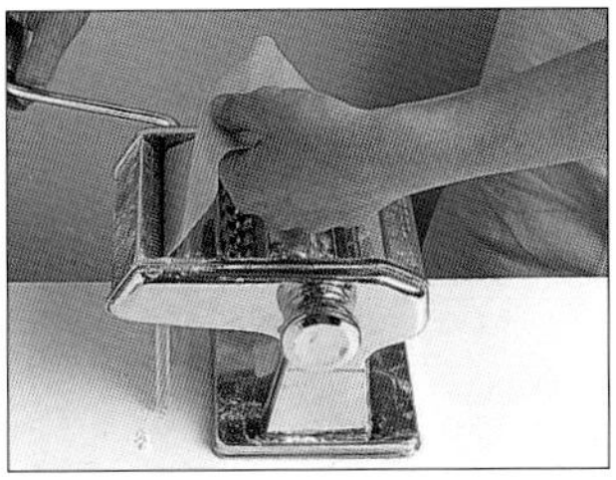

1 Stop rolling the pasta strip after the last but two or last but one setting, then insert the handle in the slot for the narrowest cutters and feed the pasta through the machine.

2 Proceed as for tagliatelle or fettuccine, turning the handle and guiding the long strands with your other hand. Toss the tonnarelli or spaghetti in flour and spread out on floured dish towels.

Cook's Tip

When making spaghetti alla chitarra, the thickness and width of the pasta should be equal so the noodles come out square. You may need to experiment with this shape a few times until you get it just the right thickness.

Variations

To make tagliarini or spaghettini, insert the pasta machine handle in the slot for the narrowest cutters and proceed as for tonnarelli and spaghetti alla chitarra.

Making Ravioli

1 Using a large sharp knife, cut the rolled pasta strip into two 45–50cm/ 18–20in lengths, if this has not been done already.

2 Using a teaspoon, put 10–12 little mounds of your chosen filling along one side of one of the pasta strips, spacing them evenly.

3 Using a pastry brush, carefully brush a little water on to the pasta strip around each mound of filling.

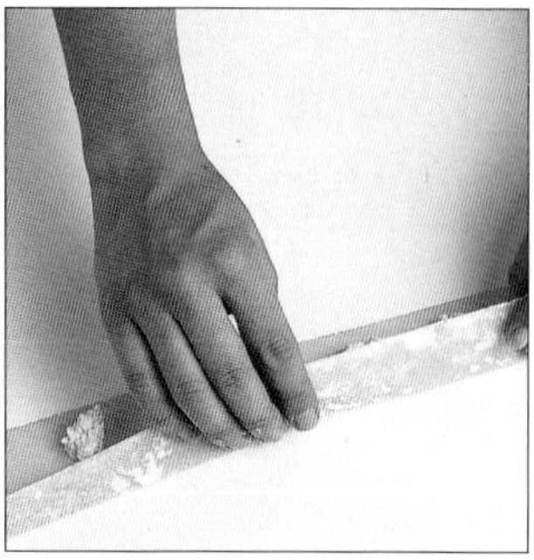

4 Fold the plain side of the pasta strip over the filling.

5 Starting from the folded edge, press down gently with your fingertips around each mound, pushing the air out at the unfolded edge. Sprinkle lightly with flour.

6 With a fluted pasta wheel, cut along each long side, then in between each mound to make small square shapes.

7 Put the ravioli on floured dish towels, sprinkle lightly with more flour and leave to dry while repeating the process with the remaining dough. For a 3-egg dough, you should get 80–96 ravioli, more if you re-roll the trimmings.

Cook's Tips

• *Ravioli made in this way are not perfectly square, but they look charmingly home-made. If you prefer a more precise finish, you should use a ravioli tray, which you can buy from a specialist kitchenware shop. The ravioli tray can be bought on its own or as an extra accessory to a pasta machine. Another alternative is to use a hand-held ravioli cutter or a round, plain or fluted biscuit cutter.*

• *Have ready 3 or 4 floured dish towels before you begin cutting the pasta shapes. Arrange the stuffed shapes on the towels, well-spaced and in one layer, because if you overlap them, they may stick together.*

• *Once they are dry, stuffed pasta shapes can be frozen for up to 1 month, layered between sheets of clear film in plastic bags.*

Fillings for Stuffed Pasta

These vary from one or two simple ingredients to special traditional recipes. The ingredients are mixed together and often bound with beaten egg, Seasoning is added to taste.

Simple ideas

• *spinach, Parmesan, ricotta and nutmeg*

• *crab, mascarpone, lemon, parsley and chillies*

• *taleggio cheese and fresh marjoram*

Regional specialities

• *minced pork and turkey with fresh herbs, ricotta and Parmesan*

• *fresh herbs, ricotta, Parmesan and garlic*

• *puréed cooked pumpkin, prosciutto, mozzarella and parsley*

Making Agnolotti

1 Using a sharp knife, cut the rolled strip of pasta dough by hand into two 45–50cm/18–20in lengths, if this has not been done already.

2 Using a teaspoon, put 8–10 little mounds of your chosen filling along one side of one of the pasta strips, spacing them evenly.

3 Using a pastry brush, carefully brush a little water on to the pasta strip around each mound of filling.

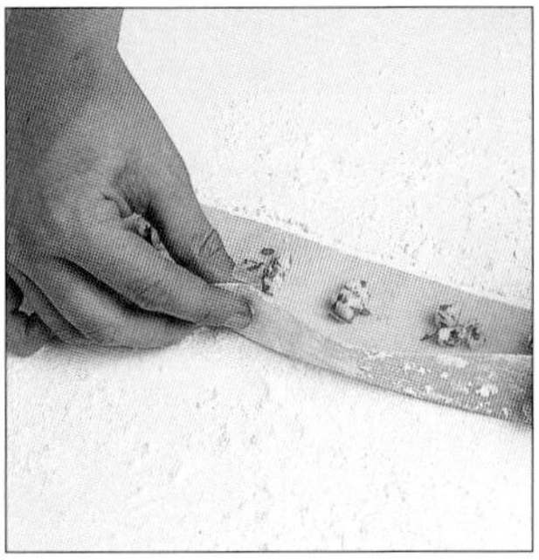

4 Fold the plain side of the pasta strip over the filling.

5 Starting from the folded edge, press down gently with your fingertips around each mound, pushing the air out at the unfolded edge. Sprinkle lightly with flour.

6 Using only half of a 5cm/2in fluted round ravioli or biscuit cutter, cut around each mound of filling to make a half-moon shape.

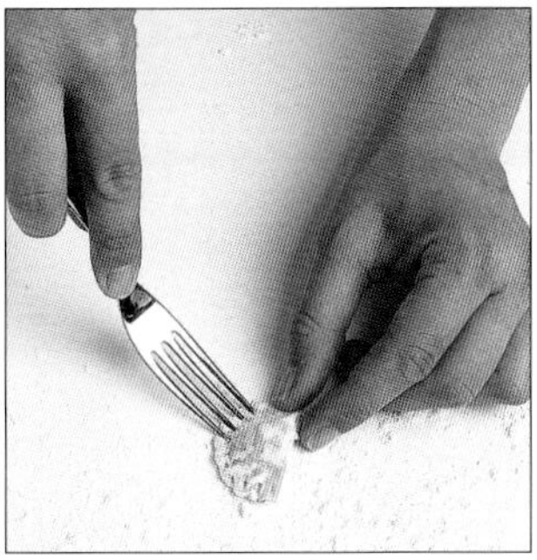

7 If you like, press the cut edges of the agnolotti with the tines of a fork to give a decorative effect.

8 Put the agnolotti on floured dish towels, sprinkle lightly with more flour and leave to dry while repeating the process with the remaining dough. For a 3-egg dough, you should get 64–80 agnolotti, more if you re-roll the trimmings.

Cook's Tips

- *When cutting out the agnolotti, make sure that the folded edge is the straight edge.*
- *Don't re-roll the trimmings after cutting each pasta strip, but wait until you have done them all. If there is no filling left for the rolled pasta trimmings, you can use them to make noodles or small shapes for soup.*

Making Tortellini / Tortelloni

1 Using a sharp knife, cut the rolled strip of pasta dough by hand into two 45–50cm/18–20in lengths, if this has not been done already.

2 To make tortellini: with a 5cm/2in fluted ravioli or biscuit cutter, cut out 8–10 discs from one of the pasta strips. For tortelloni use a 6cm/2½in cutter.

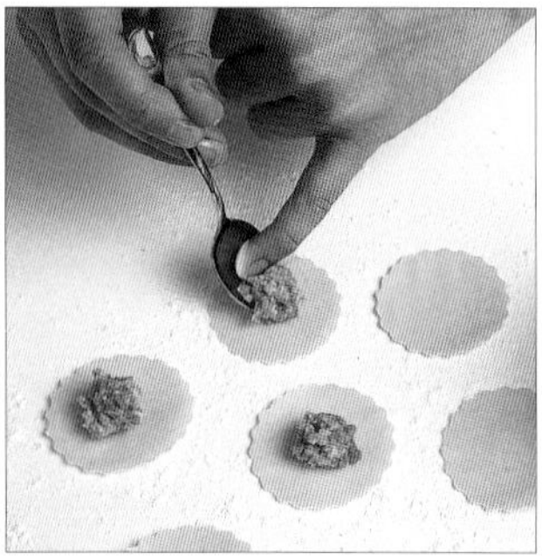

3 Using a teaspoon and a fingertip, put a little mound of your chosen filling in the centre of each disc.

4 Brush a little water around the edge of each disc.

5 Fold the disc in half over the filling so that the top and bottom edges do not quite meet. Press to seal.

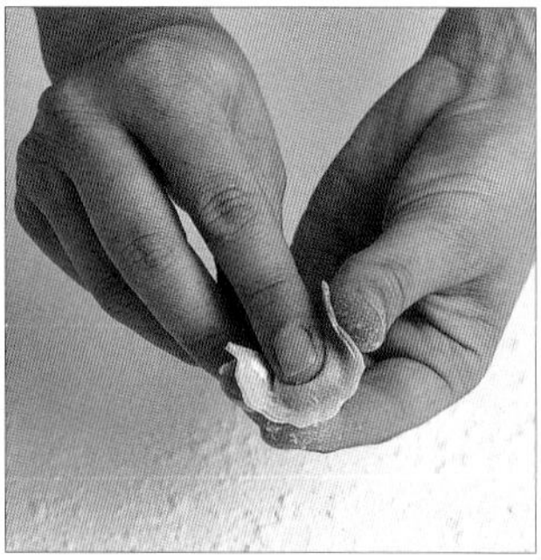

6 Wrap the half-moon shape around an index finger and pinch the ends together to seal.

7 Put the tortellini or tortelloni on floured dish towels, sprinkle with flour and leave to dry while repeating the process with the remaining dough. For a 3-egg dough, you should get 64–80 tortellini, more if you re-roll the trimmings.

Making Pansotti and Cappelletti / Cappellacci

Pansotti are made from 5cm/2in squares of pasta that are folded in half over the filling to make triangles. Moisten the edges of the triangles and press to seal in the filling.

Cappelletti and cappellacci are made in the same way as tortellini, using squares of pasta rather than discs. The edges are turned up so they look like little hats.

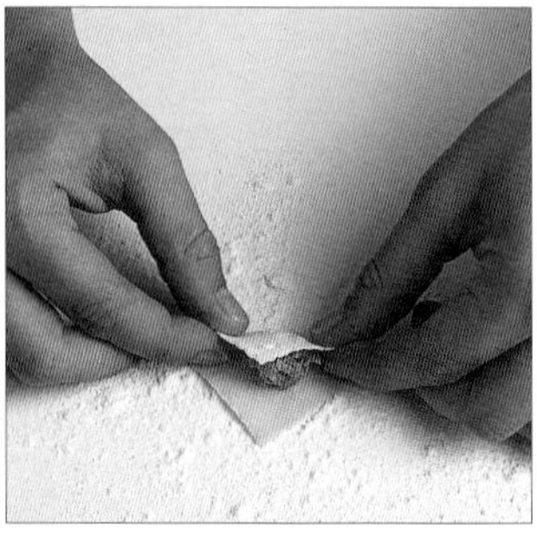

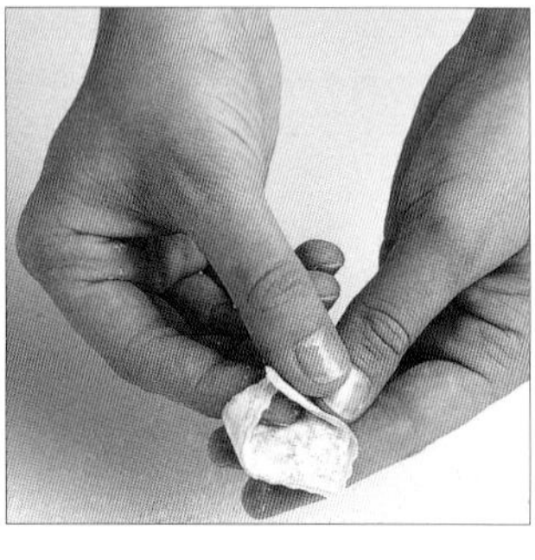

Making Flavoured and Coloured Pasta

There are many different ingredients you can use to change the flavour and colour of pasta, whether you are making the dough by hand or machine, although you will find it easier to get a more even colour with a machine. Some flavours are more trouble than they are worth, so it is best to restrict your choice to the tried and tested ones. The following flavourings are the most successful, and the amounts of ingredients given are for a 3-egg quantity of pasta all'uovo (pasta dough with eggs).

Black pepper

Chilli

Porcini

Tomato

Black pepper

Put 30ml/2 tbsp black peppercorns or mixed peppercorns in a mortar and crush them coarsely with a pestle. Add to the eggs in the well before you start to incorporate the flour.

Chilli

Add 5–10ml/1–2 tsp crushed dried red chillies to the eggs in the well before you start to incorporate the flour.

Porcini

Soak 15g/½oz porcini (dried wild mushrooms) in 175ml/6fl oz/¾ cup warm water. Drain the porcini and squeeze to remove as much water as possible. Dry the mushrooms thoroughly on kitchen paper, then chop them finely and add them to the eggs in the well before you start to incorporate the flour. The dough will be stickier than usual, so you will need to add more flour during kneading, rolling and cutting. If you like, you can add the porcini soaking water to the water for boiling the pasta. This will intensify the mushroom flavour of the pasta.

Tomato

Add 30ml/2 tbsp tomato purée to the eggs in the well before you start to incorporate the flour. The pasta dough will be stickier than usual, so you will need to add more flour during kneading, rolling and cutting.

Spinach

Wash 150g/5oz fresh spinach leaves and place them in a large saucepan with only the water that clings to the leaves. Add a pinch of salt, then cover the pan and cook over a medium heat for about 8 minutes or until the spinach is wilted and tender. Drain the spinach, leave for a few minutes until cool enough to handle, then squeeze it hard in your hands to remove as much water as possible. Dry the spinach thoroughly on several sheets of kitchen paper, then finely chop it using a large sharp knife or a food processor and add it to the eggs in the well before you start to incorporate the flour. The pasta dough will be much stickier than usual, so you will need to add a little extra flour during kneading and when rolling and cutting the dough.

Squid ink

Add two 4g sachets of squid ink to the eggs in the well before you start to incorporate the flour. The dough will be stickier than usual, so you will need to add more flour during kneading, rolling and cutting.

Herb

Wash and dry three small handfuls of fresh herbs. Basil, flat leaf parsley, sage and thyme are all good choices, either singly or together. Finely chop the herbs and add them to the eggs in the well before you start to incorporate the flour. The dough may be a little more sticky than usual, in which case you may need to add a little extra flour during kneading and when rolling and cutting it.

Saffron

Sift 3 or 4 sachets of saffron powder with the flour before starting to make the pasta dough.

Spinach

Squid ink

Herb

Saffron

Making Striped Pasta

You can use different colours to make striped dough that can be cut into rectangles for lasagne and cannelloni. It is quite fiddly, and the rolling out is best done with a pasta machine.

Plain or saffron yellow and spinach doughs look very good together, and another excellent combination is plain or saffron yellow dough contrasted with dough coloured with tomato or squid ink. To make pasta tricolore (three-coloured pasta), mix stripes of tomato dough, squid ink or spinach dough and plain dough. Some creative chefs make check and tartan patterns with coloured pasta, but this is very time-consuming for the home cook.

1 Roll out two different coloured pieces of dough on a pasta machine, keeping them separate and taking them up to and including the last setting but two.

2 With a fluted pasta wheel, cut one strip of each colour lengthways into three or four narrower strips. Select three strips of one colour and two of the other, setting the rest aside for the next batch of striped pasta.

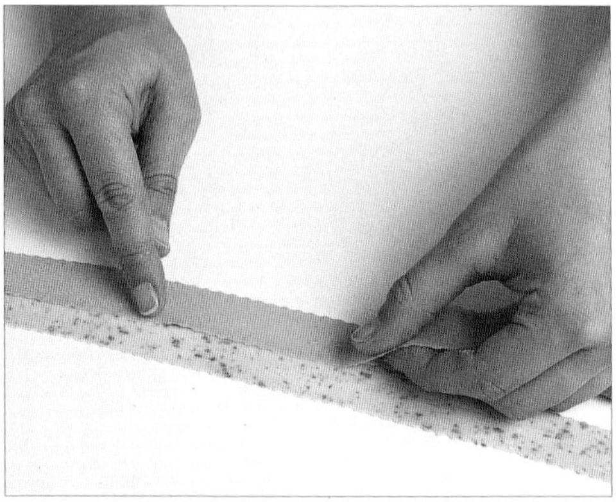

3 The aim is to join the pasta strips together, using water as glue. Brush one long edge of one pasta strip with a little water, then join a pasta of a different colour to it, placing it over the moistened edge and pressing it firmly to seal the join. Repeat this process, alternating the pasta colours until you have a length of pasta that resembles a scarf, with three stripes of one colour and two stripes of the other.

4 Sprinkle the pasta liberally with flour, lift it very carefully and put it through the pasta machine, which should be set to the last but one setting.

5 Cut the dough into rectangles or squares for cannelloni or lasagne and spread these out in a single layer on floured dish towels. Sprinkle them with flour and leave to dry for at least 15 minutes before cooking.

Cook's Tips

- *When cutting flavoured tagliatelle or tagliarini on a pasta machine, sprinkle the cutters liberally with flour before putting the dough through. The noodles tend to stick together as they come through the machine, so you may need to separate them gently with floured hands before putting them on dish towels and tossing them in more flour.*
- *When cooking flavoured pasta, start testing for doneness earlier than usual. The ingredients added for some flavours make the pasta more moist and soft than usual, and this means that it cooks a little more quickly.*
- *You can use striped pasta for making ravioli: keep the strips fairly narrow and make sure that they are well sealed, otherwise the ravioli may split open during cooking.*

Making Silhouette Pasta

Fresh herbs can be rolled between sheets of pasta to give a very pretty decorative effect. The pasta needs to be very thin, so it is best to roll it out on a pasta machine. Use only soft, leafy herbs such as flat leaf parsley, chervil, green or purple basil or sage. Silhouette pasta can be boiled and served with melted butter and grated Parmesan, or cooked in a clear soup (*in brodo*).

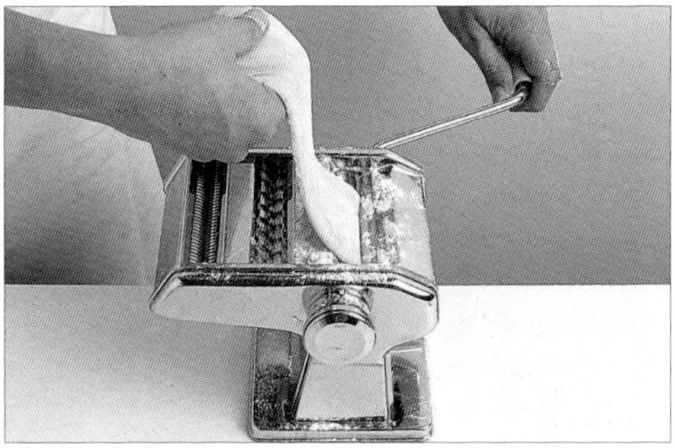

1 Roll out a piece of dough on a pasta machine, taking it up to and including the last setting. Moisten one side of the strip of dough lightly with water. A mister or spray gun is ideal for this.

Above: Fresh herbs, such as basil (top left), flat leaf parsley (left) and sage (right), can be rolled between sheets of dough to make pretty silhouette pasta.

2 Arrange individual fresh herb leaves on the moistened half of the dough, placing them at regular intervals. Fold the dry half of the dough over the herbs and press the edges firmly to seal.

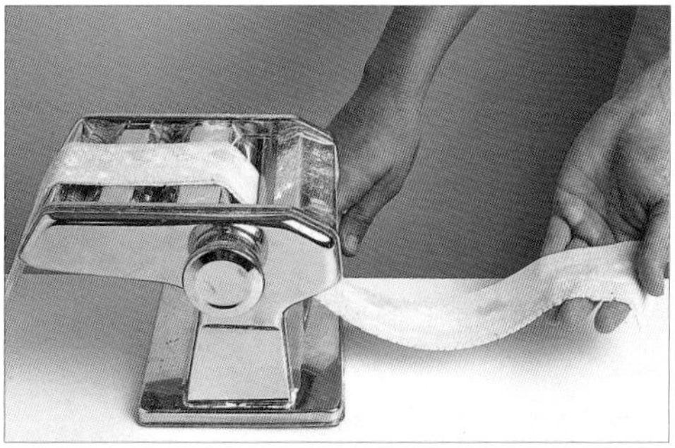

3 Sprinkle the pasta liberally with flour and put it through the machine, on the penultimate setting.

4 With a floured pasta wheel, cut around each herb leaf to make square ravioli shapes. Spread the shapes out in a single layer on floured dish towels. Sprinkle them with more flour and leave to dry for at least 15 minutes before cooking.

As an alternative to using a pasta wheel for cutting out rectangular shapes, use a small, fluted biscuit cutter and stamp out round shapes.

The Pasta Pantry

Certain ingredients crop up time and time again in sauces for pasta. Some can be kept in the pantry or storecupboard, while fresh ones must either be bought just before use, or kept in the fridge. Fresh herbs and leaves, spices, oils, vinegars and other less well-known ingredients are used to add flavour.

Canned and dried fish and shellfish are useful additions to your store cupboard, while fresh vegetables, such as aubergines, tomatoes and peppers, along with garlic and sun-dried vegetables, play an important part in many pasta dishes. Cheese and cream are used in sauces, in fillings and for baked pasta dishes.

Fresh Herbs and Leaves

These are used extensively for flavouring sauces for pasta, and for presentation and garnishing. Italian cooks keep pots of fresh herbs growing on the windowsill or in the garden, and think nothing of tossing in a handful of this or that herb to freshen up the flavour of their cooking. Herbs are added according to the individual cook's taste, and are seldom measured.

Basil

Basil

Basilico

The variety known as sweet basil is used in Italian cooking, and this is the one you are most likely to find in the shops. It is used all over Italy, but most of all in Liguria, where it grows prolifically and is used in large quantities for pesto. Basil has a special affinity with tomatoes, and is frequently used with them in sauces for pasta. It is best torn or shredded and added at the last moment. Fine chopping and long cooking spoil its pungent flavour.

Bay leaves

Bay

Alloro/lauro

Both fresh and dried bay leaves are used all over Italy for flavouring soups and broths and long-cooking sauces, especially those made with meat, poultry and game. The leaves are removed before serving.

Marjoram

Marjoram and Oregano

Maggiorana e Origano

These two herbs are closely related, but their flavours are quite different. Marjoram is sweet and delicate, while oregano, a wild variety of marjoram, is a pungent herb that should be used sparingly. They are both used in sauces for pasta, especially tomato-based ones, but marjoram is used more in Liguria and the north of Italy and oregano in the south, where it is perhaps best known for being sprinkled over pizza. Both marjoram and oregano are best chopped quite finely. They are sometimes used dried in the winter.

Oregano

Mint

Mint

Mentuccia

Mint is not usually associated with Italian cooking, but it is frequently used in Roman dishes, in the cooking of central Italy, and even as far south as Calabria. Mentuccia is a particular kind of wild mint with small leaves grown in Rome, and there is also another variety called nepitella. You may come across the flavour of fresh mint in pasta soups, and very occasionally in sauces for pasta.

Parsley

Prezzemolo

Italians use the flat leaf variety of parsley, which is sometimes sold here as continental or Italian parsley. It looks very similar to coriander, and has a stronger flavour than curly parsley. It is used frequently in sauces for pasta, in fairly large quantities, and is often roughly chopped and fried in olive oil with a *battuto* of onion and garlic at the beginning of sauce making. It is popular all over Italy, and is only ever used fresh.

Flat leaf parsley

Radicchio di Treviso

Radicchio di Verona

Radicchio

Radicchio

This ruby red and white salad leaf is a member of the chicory family. The most common variety, *radicchio di Verona*, is small and round with very tightly furled leaves, but there is another type called *radicchio di Treviso*, which is streaked creamy white and red with looser, long and tapering leaves. Both have a bitter flavour, which is much appreciated in small quantities in pasta sauces. Shredded leaves should be added at the last moment, to preserve their colour.

Rocket

Rocket

Rucola

Peppery hot *rucola* loses its pungency when cooked, so it is added to pasta sauces at the last minute, or strewn liberally over tl top of pasta dishes just before serving. Bunches of large-leaved *rucola* from the greengrocer are best; the small packets s(in supermarkets are very expensive and seem to lack flavour. Use *rucola* as soon a possible after purchase because the leave can quickly go limp and yellow, especially warm weather.

Rosemary

Rosemary

Rosmarino

This most fragrant and pungent herb is very popular all over Italy. Rosemary is used sparingly in meat and tomato sauces, either very finely chopped or on the sprig, which is then removed from the sauce before serving. Dried rosemary is sometimes used in the winter months.

Sage

Salvia

Along with parsley, basil and rosemary, sage is one of Italy's favourite herbs. It is frequently used by Roman cooks who sizzle fresh sage in butter to create a classic sauce to serve with ravioli. Fresh sage leaves are also used with meat, sausage, poultry and game sauces, either finely shredded or chopped or as whole leaves, which are removed before serving. Fresh sage is preferred to dried, but dried sage is occasionally used in the winter, in sauces that are cooked for a long time.

Thyme

Timo

This aromatic and distinctively flavoured herb is used both fresh and dried. It is a Mediterranean herb that goes well with tomato-based sauces and with meat and poultry, and it is also good mixed with rosemary and bay.

Thyme

Spices and Salt

Spicy, highly seasoned foods are not normally associated with Italian cooking, but the use of spices in cooking dates back to Roman – and even Etruscan – times, when spices were used freely, often to excess. Nowadays, spices tend to be used more sparingly and the range tends to be limited to a few favourites.

Dried chillies

Fresh chillies

Chilli flakes

Chilli
Peperoncino

Small red chillies are immensely popular in the south of Italy and Sardinia, and they are frequently used in sauces for pasta. Sometimes the sauce is a classic that depends on chillies for its essential flavour – the hot and spicy *Penne all'Arrabbiata* from Rome being perhaps the most famous. Most often, however, chillies are added more sparingly with the aim of livening up a sauce and intensifying its flavour rather than giving it a fiery flavour.

Fresh chillies tend to be fried with a *soffritto* of olive oil, onion, garlic and parsley at the beginning of sauce making, whereas dried chillies are popped into the sauce when it is bubbling. Both fresh and dried chillies are often added whole to sauces in order to impart a subtle flavour. They are later lifted out and either discarded or chopped or crumbled, then returned to the sauce. The seeds may be included or left out, depending on the degree of heat required (the seeds contain most of the heat). Crushed dried red chillies or chilli flakes (sold in little jars) are very handy when just a pinch or two of chilli is required in a recipe.

Cinnamon
Cannella

Ground cinnamon is used in stuffings for pasta, both with meat and cheese. It gives a fragrant aroma and subtle sweetness, and is always used sparingly.

Nutmeg
Noce moscata

Whole nutmeg is grated fresh when needed. It is used for flavouring *la beschiamella* (béchamel sauce) and is often used in combination with spinach and ricotta cheese. In Emilia-Romagna, it is traditionally used for flavouring meat sauces and stuffings for pasta.

Pepper
Pepe

Black peppercorns are ground fresh from a pepper mill as and when they are needed, both in cooking and at the table. Black pepper is used in just about every pasta sauce that is made, and it is also used to speckle and flavour home-made pasta. If coarsely crushed peppercorns are required, they are ground with a mortar and pestle.

Saffron
Zafferano

The most expensive spice in the world, saffron comes in two different forms. Threads of saffron, the actual dried stigmas of the crocus, are usually wrapped in cellophane and sold in sachets. They can be sprinkled into a sauce, but are more often soaked in warm water for 20–30 minutes, so that the water can be strained off and used for colouring and flavouring. Saffron powder is sold in sachets and can be sprinkled directly into sauces. It is less expensive than the threads and considered by many to be inferior, but it is more convenient to use. Saffron has a delicate but distinctive flavour, which is good with both cream and butter-based sauces as well as with fish and shellfish. The spice is also used to colour home-made pasta.

Saffron

Salt
Sale

Coarse sea salt and rock salt are ground in a salt mill and used both as a seasoning in cooking and at the table. It is essential that salt is added to the water when boiling pasta to give it flavour, but for this you can use refined cooking salt rather than the more expensive sea or rock salt. Just about every pasta sauce will have salt as a seasoning, except perhaps those containing salty anchovies or bottarga (air-dried mullet or tuna roe).

Peppercorns (left) and sea salt

Oils and Vinegars

Oil and vinegar are essential store-cupboard items for the Italian cook. Don't buy cheap brands; it will be false economy. Good olive oil and wine or balsamic vinegar will lift the flavour of a sauce or salad and enhance the other ingredients in it.

Olive oil
Olio d'oliva

Extra virgin olive oil is the best and most expensive of the olive oils. This is literally the oil that is secreted when the olives are crushed mechanically by cold presses.

No other processing nor any heat is involved in the making of extra virgin olive oil. It should have an acidity level of one per cent or less, but as this information is seldom on the label of the bottle, this is difficult to check.

Extra virgin is the oil to use for salads, since heating may spoil its natural olive flavour. It is also the one to use for sprinkling over warm food or for tossing with pasta in dishes, such as *Spaghetti Aglio e Olio*, that rely on olive oil for their predominant flavour.

Fruity, often peppery, Tuscan oil is reputed to be among the best of the extra virgin olive oils, although some cooks prefer oil from Umbria, or from Veneto or Liguria, which are more delicate. Oils from the South are stronger and more intensely flavoured, and these may be more to your taste. Brands vary enormously, so experiment to find what suits you best.

For cooking and heating, virgin olive oil is the one to use. This is less expensive than extra virgin because it has a higher acidity level (up to four per cent), but it is cold pressed and not refined in any way so it still has a good, full flavour. Many pasta sauces start with the frying of flavouring ingredients, such as onion, garlic, celery, parsley, chillies and carrot. If these are fried in an oil with a good flavour, the sauce will have a strong base (*soffritto*), the flavour of which will then permeate through the other ingredients during cooking.

Virgin olive oil (left), extra virgin olive oil (centre) and balsamic vinegar (right)

Vinegar
Aceto

Occasionally a splash of red or white wine vinegar may be added to a pasta sauce, but wine vinegar is more often used in salad dressings. Flavourwise, red and white vinegars are interchangeable, but the colour of the salad ingredients may dictate whether you use red or white.

Balsamic vinegar (aceto balsamico) from Modena in Emilia-Romagna is a different thing altogether. It is a dark, syrupy vinegar which is aged in wooden casks for many years. The best and most authentic *aceto balsamico* will have been aged in casks or barrels of different woods for 40–50 years. Labelled *tradizionale di Modena*, this vinegar is only used a drop at a time, usually at the moment of serving on fish or meat, salads and even fresh strawberries. For flavouring a pasta sauce or salad, use the much less expensive balsamic vinegar that has been aged between five and ten years. Its flavour does not compare with the genuine article, but it is musky and slightly sweet, and very good.

Flavourings

Some special ingredients are used in different regions of Italy, and you may need to buy them for a particular sauce.

Salted capers

Capers bottled in brine

Capers
Capperi

Capers are the fruit of a flowering shrub that grows in the Mediterranean. They are sold in various ways. The best are the large, salted capers sold in small jars in Italian delicatessens. Check before buying that the salt is white and has not discoloured at all. Yellow salt is a sign that the capers are past their best and may have a rancid taste. Before use, salted capers need to be soaked in several changes of water for 10–15 minutes, then drained, rinsed in fresh water and dried, but after this initial preparation they taste very fresh and good. They can be chopped and used to add piquancy to sauces – you will often find them in recipes from the south of Italy and Sicily and Sardinia.

It is also possible to buy tiny capers sold in small bottles of brine or vinegar. These have a strong flavour and should be rinsed well before use. They almost always taste sharp and vinegary, so use them sparingly.

Olives
Olive

Both black and green olives are used in making sauces and salads, although black olives are more highly favoured. The best type for pasta sauces are the small, shiny, very black *gaeta* olives from Liguria. Buy the plain ones for cooking, not those with additional flavourings, such as herbs, garlic, chillies and other spices, which are intended for antipasto. Olives are best added to a sauce towards the end of cooking. They need no cooking, only heating through, and if added too early they can impart a bitter flavour. When using olives in a pasta sauce or salad, pit them first, because the stones are awkward to manage when you are eating pasta.

Olives

Pancetta
Pancetta

This is cured belly of pork, the Italian equivalent of bacon, which has a spicy, sweet flavour and aroma. Unsmoked pancetta is sold in a roll at Italian delicatessens, and is called pancetta arrotolata or pancetta coppata. A machine is used to slice it very thinly to order and it can be eaten as it is for an antipasto, or cut into strips or diced for use in cooking. Pancetta affumicata is smoked and comes in rashers, which look like streaky bacon complete with rind. There is a version called pancetta stesa, which is long and flat. Smoked pancetta is cut into strips or dice and used as the base for ragù and many other pasta sauces, the most famous of which is carbonara. Some supermarkets sell packets of ready-diced pancetta. The quality and flavour are generally good, so these are well worth buying for convenience. If you are unable to get pancetta, streaky bacon can be used instead, and you can buy smoked or unsmoked, whichever flavour you prefer.

Smoked (left) and unsmoked pancetta

Pine nuts
Pinoli

Best known for their inclusion in pesto, these small, creamy white nuts have an unusual waxy texture and resinous flavour. They look and taste good sprinkled over pasta salads, and they add a welcome crunchy bite. To enhance their flavour, they are often toasted before use. Only buy the quantity of pine nuts you need because they do not keep well and quickly go rancid. They are sold ready-shelled in small packets, in supermarkets and delicatessens.

Pine nuts

Fish and Shellfish

Pasta sauces made with fish or shellfish are quick and delicious. Fresh seafood is often the main ingredient, but there are a few other fishy staples that are used over and over again.

Anchovies
Acciughe

The best anchovies are the salted ones that are packed in large cans. You see them on the counters of Italian delicatessens, where they are sold loose by the kilo or pound. They must be rinsed, skinned and filleted before use, but are plumper and more flavoursome than the fillets sold in jars and cans, so repay the effort. Anchovies are used in sauces for pasta all over Italy, but particularly in the hot South and in Sicily and Sardinia where strong and salty flavours are so popular. When chopped and heated gently with a little olive oil, they melt down to a creamy paste that is packed with flavour, so you only need to use a small quantity at a time. If you can't get salted anchovies, try to locate anchovy fillets that are bottled in olive oil. These taste better than the ones canned in vegetable oil.

Anchovies in brine (left) and salt

Bottarga
Bottarga

This is the salted and air-dried roe of mullet or tuna. The best is the mullet, bottarga di muggine. It is a great delicacy in Sardinia, Sicily and the Veneto, where they like it grated over pasta or very thinly sliced as an antipasto with lemon juice and olive oil. You can buy bottarga quite easily in Italian delicatessens, where it is kept in vacuum packs in the fridge. Mullet bottarga is delicate, moist and golden, like a pale, thin version of smoked cod's roe, and bears little resemblance to tuna bottarga, which

Tuna bottarga

Ready-grated bottarga

Mullet bottarga

comes in a thick, dark block. For grating over pasta you need only a small quantity and it can be kept in the fridge for a long time (check the use-by date). You can also buy ready-grated bottarga in small jars, but this product has a dry texture and the flavour does not compare with that of freshly grated bottarga.

Clams
Vongole

In Italy, small fresh clams are frequently used in pasta sauces on the coast and in Sicily and Sardinia, but they are not always easy to get in other parts of the country or further afield. Names vary from one region and one country to another, but the name is not important; it is the size that counts.

Fresh clams (left) and canned clams

Small *vongole* cook quickly and have a tender texture and sweet flavour, which make them ideal for pasta sauces. Don't be tempted to buy the large ones. Some fishmongers sell frozen small clams, which are a good substitute for fresh; otherwise you should buy the bottled shelled clams in natural juice that are sold at Italian delicatessens. Check labels carefully and don't buy the ones in vinegar or brine – these are intended for antipasto; their sharp flavour will spoil a pasta sauce. You can also buy bottled clams in their shells. These are packed in oil and, although intended primarily for antipasto, they also make an attractive garnish for a clam sauce.

Squid ink
Nero di seppia

If you want to colour home-made pasta black, you can buy handy little sachets of squid ink at fishmongers and Italian delicatessens. There is usually about 4g of ink in each sachet and the sachets are sold in pairs. Two sachets are enough to colour a 3-egg quantity of *pasta all'uovo.*

Tuna
Tonno

For pasta sauces, use only best-quality canned tuna in olive oil, not the kind packed in vegetable oil, water or brine. Some supermarkets sell it; otherwise you will have to go to an Italian delicatessen. The flesh of good-quality canned tuna is moist and meaty. The cost of a good can of tuna is generally less than that of fresh fish, so no matter how much you spend on it, pasta with a tuna sauce will still be an inexpensive meal.

Canned tuna

Vegetables

Tomatoes are not the only vegetable to be used in sauces for pasta. Many others play an important part, either as a main ingredient or in a more minor role. Dried vegetables such as porcini mushrooms, peppers and tomatoes are used almost as often as fresh; valued for the intense flavour they impart to pasta sauces and soups.

Dried chargrilled aubergines

Aubergines
Melanzane

Fresh aubergines are used as a main ingredient in many pasta sauces, especially in southern Italy, Sicily and Sardinia. Dried aubergines are not used as a substitute for fresh, but are added to fresh vegetables for their characteristic earthy flavour and meaty texture. Sold in cellophane packets, they are thin slices of aubergine that have been dried in the sun, and are a good storecupboard item in that you can use as few or as many as you like. They need to be rehydrated in boiling water with a splash of white wine vinegar for 2 minutes before use, then drained and dried. They can then be snipped into strips and either added immediately to a simmering pasta sauce or fried first in olive oil.

Garlic

Aglio

Crushed, sliced and chopped garlic is used in many pasta sauces, but especially in those from the south of Italy, and whole garlic cloves are sometimes fried in olive oil at the beginning of cooking, then removed to leave behind a subtly flavoured base for a sauce. One famous Roman pasta dish, *Spaghetti Aglio e Olio*, holds garlic in such high esteem that the sauce contains only two ingredients – garlic and olive oil – and in Rome they maintain it is the best cure for a hangover. The best Italian garlic is pink or purple tinged, with plump juicy cloves. In spring and early summer you can buy it fresh at some green-grocers, markets and Italian delicatessens.

Garlic

This is the newly picked garlic that is sweet, moist and mild. As it dries out it becomes more pungent, so you need to adjust quantities accordingly. Buy garlic little and often so it neither sprouts green shoots nor becomes papery and dry.

Porcini mushrooms

Funghi porcini

Dried porcini (*boletus edulis*) are invaluable for the intense, musky aroma and flavour they impart to pasta sauces and soups. Italians use them all year round, not as a substitute for fresh porcini, but as a valued ingredient in its own right. A few dried porcini added to ordinary fresh mushrooms, for example, will give them the flavour of wild mushrooms. Don't buy cheap porcini, but look for packets containing large pale-coloured pieces. Although they will seem expensive, a little goes a long way, and 15–25g/½–1oz is the most you will need in a recipe that serves 4–6 people. Before use, dried porcini must

Dried porcini mushrooms

be reconstituted in warm water for 15–20 minutes. Drain, rinse and squeeze dry, then slice or chop as required. Don't throw the soaking liquid away. Strain it to remove any grit and use it in soups and stocks, or add it to the water when cooking pasta to impart a mushroomy flavour – this is especially effective with fresh pasta.

Dried peppers

Peppers

Peperoni

Sun-dried red peppers are sold in cellophane packets. They resemble sun-dried tomatoes, but their flavour is more peppery and piquant. They are used in the same way as tomatoes, to add a firm meaty bite to sauces and soups, especially those made with vegetables. Before use they should be rinsed under the cold tap, then dried and cut into thin strips or chopped.

Roasted peppers can be bought loose or in jars, packed in olive oil or brine. Although you can easily roast fresh peppers yourself when you need them, it is handy to keep a jar of commercially roasted peppers in the fridge. Just one piece of roasted pepper, sliced or chopped, will add a wonderful smoky flavour to pasta sauces, salads and soups. The best ones come from Italian delicatessens, who chargrill the peppers themselves and sell them loose in extra virgin olive oil.

Bottled roasted peppers

Tomatoes

Pomodori

In summer, when fresh Italian plum tomatoes are ripe and full of flavour, it is wonderful to use these for sauce making, but at other times of the year you will get a far better flavour and colour by using preserved tomatoes.

There are plenty of excellent tomato products to choose from, most of which come from southern Italy, where the hot sun ripens the tomatoes on the vine to an incomparable flavour.

Canned peeled plum tomatoes (*pomodori pelati*) come whole and chopped. Don't buy cheap brands; instead, opt for the top-quality Italian brands,

Chopped canned plum tomatoes

Filetti di pomodoro (plum tomatoes in water and salt)

especially those that identify the tomatoes as San Marzano on the label. If you ask at your local Italian delicatessen, they will give you good advice. Plain chopped tomatoes are a good buy because they save you having to chop them yourself, but they are slightly more expensive. If they are labelled polpa di pomodoro, they are likely to be very finely chopped or even crushed. Flavourings, such as garlic and herbs, should be added fresh, so don't buy chopped canned tomatoes containing these.

Filetti di pomodoro are sold in jars at good Italian delicatessens and specialist food shops. These are plum tomatoes that have been halved or quartered and bottled *al naturale* in water and salt. They are about the nearest thing you can get to bottling tomatoes yourself at home, which Italians do in summer to preserve surplus tomatoes for winter use.

Crushed tomatoes come in many guises, and are a real boon for sauce making because they take all the hard work out of peeling, seeding and chopping. They are plum tomatoes that have been mechanically peeled and crushed, then sieved to remove the seeds. You can choose from passata, which is quite smooth, to polpa and sugocasa, which are quite chunky.

Bottles and jars of these products are good in that they allow you to see what you are buying. Cartons of very smooth passata take up less room and are lighter to carry; they are very popular with Italian cooks for making almost instant sauces.

Sun-dried tomatoes (*pomodori secchi*) are sold in two different forms – as dry pieces and in oil. Both types are piquant in flavour, but the dry pieces have a chewier texture than those in oil. Dried tomatoes are sold in cellophane packets and can be snipped directly into a long-cooking pasta sauce to intensify its tomato flavour, but generally they are best if softened in hot water for 2–3 hours before use. Sun-dried tomatoes in oil are sold in jars and can also be bought loose at some delicatessens. For the best flavour, buy the ones in olive oil. They are soft and juicy and can be used as they are, either sliced or chopped, in sauces and salads.

Sun-dried tomato paste is a thick mixture of sun-dried tomatoes and olive oil. It can be used on its own as a quick sauce for pasta or added by the spoonful to tomato sauces to colour and enrich them.

Although thick in texture, the flavour of sun-dried tomato paste is sweet and mild compared with tomato purée, and the colour is paler.

Sun-dried tomato paste (left) and tomato purée

Sun-dried tomatoes bottled in oil (top), and dry pieces

Tomato purée or concentrate (*concentrato di pomodoro*) is a very strong, thick paste made commercially from tomatoes, salt and citric acid. You can buy it in tubes, jars or cans, and its strength varies according to the manufacturer.

Clockwise from left, sugocasa, polpa and passata

Get to know the brand you like because some are quite bitter and sharp, and can overwhelm other flavours in a sauce. Only use tomato purée in small quantities or it may make a dish too acidic. A way to counteract acidity is to add a pinch or two or a lump of sugar.

Cheese and Cream

Italy's magnificent cheeses are famous all over the world, both as table cheeses and for their use in cooking. Many of them are used in sauces for pasta, in fillings for stuffed pasta and baked dishes.

Fontina

Fontina

A mountain cheese from the Val d'Aosta in the northwest of Italy, fontina is used in baked pasta dishes, such as lasagne. It has superb melting qualities and a wonderful nutty, slightly sweet flavour. Some large supermarkets sell it; otherwise you can get it at delicatessens and cheese shops.

Gorgonzola

This blue-veined cheese comes from Lombardy. Although it is a table cheese, it melts quickly and well, so it is good in sauces and stuffed pasta, and its sharp flavour tastes very good combined with cream and leafy greens, such as spinach,

Gorgonzola

sorrel and herbs. Gorgonzola piccante is the very strong version, while dolcelatte is milder and sweeter, almost buttery.

Mascarpone

This is a full-fat cream cheese with a smooth silky texture, often used in pasta

Mascarpone

sauces instead of cream. It melts without curdling and has a slightly tangy flavour. It is widely available in tubs in delicatessens and supermarkets.

Mozzarella

A soft white cheese, which is used in both salads and cooking, mozzarella melts quickly in hot sauces to serve with pasta, but must not be overcooked or it may become stringy. The whey should be drained off and discarded before the cheese is used. By

Mozzarella

tradition mozzarella should be made with buffalo's milk, but today it is often made with cow's or sheep's milk. Buy only the type that is swimming in whey in little bags – blocks of mozzarella are rubbery and tasteless. Mozzarella di bufala has the best texture and the most flavour, but it is more expensive than cow's or sheep's milk mozzarella and not so easy to find.

Parmesan

Grated Parmesan is most often used for sprinkling over pasta at the table, although it is also tossed with pasta after draining or added to sauces at the end of cooking. Genuine Parmigiano Reggiano has its name stamped on the rind and comes only from the area between Parma, Modena, Reggio-Emilia, Bologna and Mantua. It must be aged for a minimum of 2 years, which is one of the reasons why it is so costly. Grana Padano is a similar, less expensive, cheese, which is used in the same way as Parmigiano Reggiano. Both are excellent melting cheeses, but Reggiano has a milder,

Pecorino (left) and Parmigiano Reggiano

less salty flavour and its texture is more flaky. Never buy these cheeses ready grated. Buy them in the piece and grate them as and when you need them, or shave into curls with a vegetable peeler.

Pecorino

This salty, hard sheep's milk cheese is called Pecorino Romano if it comes from Lazio and Pecorino Sardo if it is Sardinian. It is used for grating in the same way as Parmesan, but because its flavour is sharper, it is used with the strong-tasting and spicy sauces associated with southern Italian and Sardinian cooking.

Ricotta salata (right) and ricotta

Dressing up Commercial Sauces

There are lots of bottled sauces for serving with pasta, ranging from chopped tomato sugocasa to classics, such as vongole, arrabbiata and carbonara, as well as unusual combinations of ingredients created by individual manufacturers. Generally speaking it is best to stick to the Italian brands that are sold in delicatessens and supermarkets, because these are the ones that Italians keep in their own store cupboards for times when they want to serve pasta at a moment's notice. You can use these sauces just as they are, but they will taste more home-made if you liven them up by adding something fresh.

Pesto

Both classic basil pesto and red pesto – made using sun-dried tomatoes – are available in jars, and are useful store cupboard standbys. Grate a little fresh Parmesan cheese over the pasta before tossing with the pesto, and add a spoonful or two of extra virgin olive oil for a more fruity flavour. For a richer pesto sauce, add a spoonful or two of mascarpone cheese or cream (*below left*). Just before serving, sprinkle the pasta with more freshly grated Parmesan or with toasted pine nuts or shredded basil leaves.

Sugocasa/Chopped tomatoes

Add a little sun-dried tomato paste and/or a splash of red or white wine when heating up sugocasa, and season well with salt and ground black pepper. If you like a creamy tomato sauce, add up to 150ml/$\frac{1}{4}$ pint/$\frac{2}{3}$ cup *panna da cucina*, double cream or crème fraîche. For a spicy kick, add a sprinkling of crushed dried red chillies. Finish the sauce off with a small handful of shredded fresh basil or rocket, or use 15–30ml/1–2 tbsp chopped fresh marjoram or oregano.

Arrabbiata

Strew a generous handful of finely shredded rocket leaves on top of the tossed pasta and sauce just before serving.

Carbonara

Stir a few spoonfuls of fresh cream into the sauce while it is heating up, then top with thin shavings of Parmesan cheese once the sauce and pasta have been tossed together.

Vongole

Add a splash of wine, some chopped fresh parsley and garlic. You can add all of these ingredients or just one or two of them. A few pitted and sliced black olives also look and taste good with a vongole sauce.

Ricotta

Fresh ricotta is a very soft white cheese, sold loose by the kilo/pound in Italian delicatessens. It has superb melting qualities and is used in fillings for stuffed and baked pasta dishes, and for tossing with fresh raw vegetables, such as tomatoes, spinach and rocket for uncooked sauces. Ricotta is low in fat and has a bland flavour, so it goes well with flavoursome ingredients, such as herbs and garlic. Fresh ricotta does not keep well, so check before buying and only buy it if it is snowy white in colour. If not, it is better to buy the ricotta sold in tubs – these are widely available at supermarkets. Ricotta salata is a hard, salted version of ricotta, cut from the block in Italian delicatessens. It too is very white and low in fat. Ricotta salata is used for grating or crumbling over soups and pasta, especially in the south of Italy. You will find it saltier than Parmesan, Grana Padano or Pecorino, so will need less.

Cream

Panna da cucina

For creamy pasta sauces, Italians use a type of cream called *panna da cucina* (cream for cooking). It is sold in little tubs, often joined together in pairs. Each tub contains 100ml/3$\frac{1}{2}$fl oz/scant $\frac{1}{2}$ cup, which is enough to make a pasta sauce to serve 4 people. Panna da cucina is a long-life product, so it is well worth buying to keep in the store cupboard for making impromptu sauces. It is widely available in Italian delicatessens.

Panna da cucina

Pasta Recipes

Pasta proves its enormous versatility in this section. There are complete recipes, plus many variations, and since there are very few hard-and-fast rules with sauces for pasta you can personalize them to your heart's content – and make even more. The recipes in the Broths and Soups chapter range from clear light liquids supporting delicate pieces of pasta to gutsy substantial soups that make meals in themselves. Tomato Sauces can be smooth and subtle, fiery or chunky, while Cream Sauces are deliciously rich and luxurious, and unbelievably quick to make. The Fish and Shellfish recipes have fabulous flavours, some of which are surprisingly spicy and strong. They make good first courses and after-work suppers, as do the recipes in Meat and Poultry, many of which you will recognize as traditional and regional favourites. In Vegetables and Vegetarian, some of the recipes are classic, but most are new. They're quick and easy, colourful and light, and they look and taste absolutely stunning. There's a choice of both family favourites and dinner party dishes in Baked Pasta, while in the Stuffed Pasta chapter you can have fun making your own dough. You'll be amazed how easy it is, and delighted with the results too. The chapter devoted to Fresh and Healthy recipes proves the point that pasta not only looks and tastes good, but it's nutritionally sound too, something that can also be said of delicious Pasta Salads. And finally, there is a section on Noodles, the Chinese equivalent of pasta, to prove just how versatile this food really is.

Broths and Soup

Soups made with pasta range from clear broths with just a surface scattering of *pastina* to filling and substantial *minestre* or *zuppe*, which include chunkier pieces of pasta and vegetables, fish or meat. Broth, called *brodo* in Italian, is generally served as a first course or *primo piatto*, especially for evening meals. It also makes a marvellous pick-me-up if you are tired, unwell or simply under the weather. The chunkier pasta soups are more likely to make a meal in themselves, especially when served with bread.

This chapter explores the full range of pasta soups. Some, like *Minestrone alla Genovese* and *Millecosedde*, are regional classics, others are less well known yet equally delicious, but all are gloriously adaptable: use a different shape or size of pasta if you prefer, and don't worry too much about exact quantities.

Cappelletti in Brodo

Little Stuffed Hats in Broth

THIS SOUP IS SERVED in northern Italy on Santo Stefano (St Stephen's Day – our Boxing Day) and on New Year's Day. It makes a welcome light change from all the special celebration food the day before. In Italy, the stock is traditionally made with the Christmas capon carcass.

INGREDIENTS

1.2 litres/2 pints/5 cups chicken stock
90–115g/3½–4oz/1 cup fresh or dried cappelletti
30ml/2 tbsp dry white wine (optional)
about 15ml/1 tbsp finely chopped fresh flat leaf (Italian) parsley (optional)
salt and ground black pepper
about 30ml/2 tbsp freshly grated Parmesan cheese, to serve
shredded flat leaf (Italian) parsley, to garnish

Serves 4

1 Pour the chicken stock into a large pan and bring to the boil. Add a little salt and pepper to taste, then drop in the pasta.

2 Stir well and bring back to the boil. Lower the heat to a simmer and cook according to the instructions on the packet, until the pasta is *al dente*. Stir frequently during cooking to ensure the pasta cooks evenly.

3 Swirl in the wine and parsley, if using, then taste for seasoning. Ladle into four warmed soup plates, then sprinkle with grated Parmesan and flat leaf parsley. Serve immediately.

COOK'S TIP

Cappelletti is just another name for tortellini, which come from Romagna. You can buy them or make your own.

Pastina in Brodo

Tiny Pasta in Broth

IN ITALY THIS SOUP is often served with bread for a light evening supper.

INGREDIENTS

1.2 litres/2 pints/5 cups beef stock
75g/3oz/¾ cup dried tiny soup pasta, e.g. funghetti
2 pieces bottled roasted red (bell) pepper, about 50g/2oz
salt and ground black pepper
coarsely shaved Parmesan cheese, to serve

Serves 4

COOK'S TIP

Stock (bouillon) cubes are not really suitable for a recipe like this in which the flavour of the broth is so important. If you don't have time to make your own stock, use two 300g/11oz cans of condensed beef consommé, adding water as instructed on the labels.

1 Bring the beef stock to the boil in a large pan. Add salt and pepper to taste, then drop in the dried soup pasta. Stir well and bring the stock back to the boil.

2 Lower the heat to a simmer and cook until the pasta is *al dente*: 7–8 minutes or according to the packet instructions. Stir frequently during cooking to prevent the pasta shapes from sticking together.

3 Drain the pieces of roasted pepper and dice them finely. Place them in the bottom of four warmed soup plates. Taste the soup for seasoning. Ladle into the soup plates and serve immediately, with shavings of Parmesan handed separately.

VARIATION

You can use other dried tiny soup pastas in place of the funghetti.

Minestrone alla Genovese

Genoese Minestrone

IN GENOA they often make minestrone like this, with pesto stirred in towards the end of cooking. It is packed full of vegetables and has a good strong flavour, making it an excellent vegetarian supper dish when served with bread. There is Parmesan cheese in the pesto, so there is no need to serve extra with the soup.

INGREDIENTS

1 onion
2 celery sticks
1 large carrot
45ml/3 tbsp olive oil
150g/5oz green beans, cut into 5cm/2in pieces
1 courgette (zucchini), thinly sliced
1 potato, cut into 1cm/½in cubes
¼ Savoy cabbage, shredded
1 small aubergine (eggplant), cut into 1cm/½in cubes
200g/7oz can cannellini beans, drained and rinsed
2 Italian plum tomatoes, chopped
1.2 litres/2 pints/5 cups vegetable stock
90g/3½oz dried vermicelli or spaghetti
salt and ground black pepper

For the pesto

about 20 fresh basil leaves
1 garlic clove
10ml/2 tsp pine nuts
15ml/1 tbsp freshly grated Parmesan cheese
15ml/1 tbsp freshly grated Pecorino cheese
30ml/2 tbsp olive oil

Serves 4–6

1 Chop the onion, celery and carrot finely, either in a food processor or by hand. Heat the oil in a large pan, add the chopped mixture and cook over a low heat, stirring frequently, for 5–7 minutes.

2 Mix in the green beans, courgette, potato and cabbage. Stir-fry over a medium heat for about 3 minutes. Add the aubergine, cannellini beans and tomatoes, and stir-fry for 2–3 minutes more. Pour in the stock with salt and pepper to taste. Bring to the boil. Stir well, cover and lower the heat. Simmer for about 40 minutes, stirring occasionally.

3 Meanwhile, process all the pesto ingredients in a food processor until the mixture forms a smooth sauce, adding 15–45ml/1–3 tbsp water through the feeder tube if necessary.

4 Break the pasta into small pieces and add it to the soup. Simmer, stirring frequently, for 5 minutes. Add the pesto sauce and stir it in well, then simmer for 2–3 minutes more, or until the pasta is *al dente*. Taste for seasoning. Serve hot, in warmed soup plates or bowls.

COOK'S TIP

If you don't want to go to the trouble of making your own pesto, use the bottled variety – the traditional green basil pesto rather than the red sun-dried tomato pesto. You will need about 45ml/3 tbsp.

Minestrone Ricco

Rich Minestrone

THIS IS A SPECIAL minestrone made with chicken. Served with crusty Italian bread, it makes a hearty meal.

INGREDIENTS

15ml/1 tbsp olive oil
2 chicken thighs
3 rindless streaky (fatty) bacon rashers (strips), chopped
1 onion, finely chopped
a few fresh basil leaves, shredded
a few fresh rosemary leaves, finely chopped
15ml/1 tbsp chopped fresh flat leaf (Italian) parsley
2 potatoes, cut into 1cm/½in cubes
1 large carrot, cut into 1cm/½in cubes
2 small courgettes (zucchini), cut into 1cm/½in cubes
1–2 celery sticks, cut into 1cm/½in cubes
1 litre/1¾ pints/4 cups chicken stock
200g/7oz/1¾ cups frozen peas
90g/3½oz/scant 1 cup dried tiny soup pasta
salt and ground black pepper
coarsely shaved Parmesan cheese, to serve
fresh basil leaves, to garnish

Serves 4–6

1 Heat the oil in a large frying pan, add the chicken thighs and fry for about 5 minutes on each side. Remove with a slotted spoon and set aside.

2 Lower the heat, add the bacon, onion and herbs to the pan and stir well. Cook gently, stirring constantly, for about 5 minutes. Add all the vegetables, except the frozen peas, and cook for 5–7 minutes more, stirring frequently.

3 Return the chicken thighs to the pan, add the stock and bring to the boil. Cover and cook over a low heat for 35–40 minutes, stirring the soup occasionally.

4 Remove the chicken thighs with a slotted spoon and place them on a board. Stir the peas and pasta into the soup and bring back to the boil. Simmer, stirring frequently until the pasta is *al dente*: 7–8 minutes or according to the instructions on the packet.

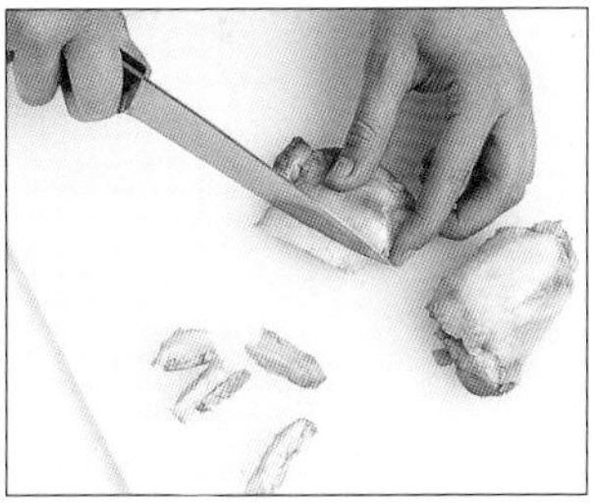

5 Meanwhile, remove and discard the chicken skin, then remove the meat from the bones and cut it into 1cm/½in pieces. Return the meat to the soup and heat through. Taste for seasoning. Serve hot in soup bowls; sprinkle over Parmesan shavings and garnish with one or two basil leaves.

COOK'S TIP

For extra flavour, add any Parmesan rind to the simmering soup.

Millecosedde

Pasta, Bean and Vegetable Soup

THIS IS A CALABRIAN speciality. The name comes from the Italian word *millecose*, meaning "a thousand things". Literally anything edible can go in this soup. In Calabria they include a bean called *cicerchia* that is peculiar to the region.

INGREDIENTS

75g/3oz/scant 1/2 cup brown lentils
15g/1/2oz dried mushrooms
60ml/4 tbsp olive oil
1 carrot, diced
1 celery stick, diced
1 onion, finely chopped
1 garlic clove, finely chopped
a little chopped fresh flat leaf (Italian) parsley
a good pinch of crushed red chillies (optional)
1.5 litres/2 1/2 pints/6 1/4 cups vegetable stock
150g/5oz/scant 1 cup each canned red kidney beans, cannellini beans and chickpeas, rinsed and drained
115g/4oz/1 cup dried small pasta shapes, e.g. rigatoni, penne or penne rigate
salt and ground black pepper
freshly grated Pecorino cheese, to serve
chopped flat leaf (Italian) parsley, to garnish

Serves 4–6

1 Put the lentils in a medium pan, add 475ml/16fl oz/2 cups water and bring to the boil over a high heat. Lower the heat to a gentle simmer and cook, stirring occasionally, for 15–20 minutes or until the lentils are just tender. Meanwhile, soak the dried mushrooms in 175ml/6fl oz/3/4 cup warm water for 15–20 minutes.

2 Place the lentils into a strainer to drain, then rinse under the cold tap. Drain the soaked mushrooms and reserve the soaking liquid. Finely chop the mushrooms and set aside.

3 Heat the oil in a large pan and add the carrot, celery, onion, garlic, parsley and chillies, if using. Cook over a low heat, stirring constantly, for 5–7 minutes.

4 Add the stock, then the mushrooms and their soaking liquid. Bring to the boil, then add the beans, chickpeas and lentils, with salt and pepper to taste. Cover, and simmer gently for 20 minutes.

5 Add the pasta and bring the soup back to the boil, stirring. Simmer, stirring frequently, until the pasta is *al dente*: 7–8 minutes or according to the instructions on the packet. Season, then serve hot in soup bowls, with grated Pecorino and chopped parsley.

COOK'S TIP

If you like, you can freeze the soup at the end of Step 4. To serve, thaw and bring to the boil, then add the pasta and simmer until it is just tender.

Zuppa di Vongole e Pastina

Clam and Pasta Soup

SUBTLY SWEET AND SPICY, this soup is substantial enough to be served on its own for lunch or supper. A crusty Italian loaf such as pugliese is the ideal accompaniment.

INGREDIENTS

30ml/2 tbsp olive oil
1 onion, finely chopped
leaves from 1 fresh or dried thyme sprig, chopped, plus extra to garnish
2 garlic cloves, crushed
5–6 fresh basil leaves, plus extra to garnish
1.5–2.5ml/¼–½ tsp crushed red chillies
1 litre/1¾ pints/4 cups fish stock
350ml/12fl oz/1½ cups passata (bottled strained tomatoes)
5ml/1 tsp sugar
90g/3½oz/scant 1 cup frozen peas
65g/2½oz/⅔ cup dried small pasta shapes, such as chifferini
225g/8oz frozen shelled clams or bottled clams in their shells
salt and ground black pepper

Serves 4–6

1 Heat the oil in a large pan, add the onion and cook gently for about 5 minutes until softened, but not coloured. Add the thyme, then stir in the garlic, basil leaves and chillies.

2 Add the stock, passata and sugar to the pan, with salt and pepper to taste. Bring to the boil, then lower the heat and simmer gently, stirring occasionally, for 15 minutes. Add the frozen peas and cook for a further 5 minutes.

3 Add the pasta to the stock and bring to the boil, stirring. Lower the heat and simmer, stirring frequently, until the pasta is only just *al dente*: about 5 minutes or according to the packet instructions.

4 Turn the heat down to low, add the frozen or bottled clams and heat through for 2–3 minutes. Taste for seasoning. Serve hot in warmed bowls, garnished with basil and thyme.

COOK'S TIP

Frozen shelled clams are available at good fishmongers and supermarkets; if you can't get them, use bottled or canned clams in natural juice (not vinegar). Italian delicatessens sell jars of clams in their shells. These both look and taste delicious and they are not too expensive. For a special occasion, stir some into the soup.

Minestrone di Orecchiette e Broccoli

Broccoli, Anchovy and Pasta Soup

This soup is from Puglia in the south of Italy, where anchovies and broccoli are often used together.

INGREDIENTS

30ml/2 tbsp olive oil
1 small onion, finely chopped
1 garlic clove, finely chopped
1/4–1/3 fresh red chilli, seeded and finely chopped
2 drained canned anchovies
200ml/7fl oz/scant 1 cup passata (bottled strained tomatoes)
45ml/3 tbsp dry white wine
1.2 litres/2 pints/5 cups vegetable stock
300g/11oz/2 cups broccoli florets
200g/7oz/1 3/4 cups dried orecchiette
salt and ground black pepper
freshly grated Pecorino cheese, to serve

Serves 4

1 Heat the oil in a large pan. Add the onion, garlic, chilli and anchovies and cook over a low heat, stirring all the time, for 5–6 minutes.

2 Add the passata and wine, with salt and pepper to taste. Bring to the boil, cover the pan, then cook over a low heat, stirring occasionally, for 12–15 minutes.

3 Pour in the stock. Bring to the boil, then add the broccoli and simmer for about 5 minutes. Add the pasta and bring back to the boil, stirring. Simmer, stirring frequently, until the pasta is *al dente*: 7–8 minutes or according to the instructions on the packet. Taste for seasoning. Serve hot, in warmed bowls. Hand around grated Pecorino separately.

Brodo di Quadrucci e Piselli

Pasta Squares and Peas in Broth

This thick soup is from Lazio, where it is traditionally made with fresh home-made pasta and peas. In this modern version, ready-made pasta is used with frozen peas, to save time.

INGREDIENTS

25g/1oz/2 tbsp butter
50g/2oz pancetta or rindless smoked streaky (fatty) bacon, roughly chopped
1 small onion, finely chopped
1 celery stick, finely chopped
400g/14oz/3 1/2 cups frozen peas
5ml/1 tsp tomato purée (paste)
5–10ml/1–2 tsp finely chopped fresh flat leaf (Italian) parsley
1 litre/1 3/4 pints/4 cups chicken stock
300g/11oz fresh lasagne sheets
about 50g/2oz prosciutto crudo (Parma ham), cut into cubes
salt and ground black pepper
freshly grated Parmesan cheese, to serve

Serves 4–6

1 Melt the butter in a large pan and add the pancetta or bacon, with the onion and celery. Cook over a low heat, stirring constantly, for 5 minutes.

2 Add the peas and cook, stirring, for 3–4 minutes. Stir in the tomato purée and parsley, then add the chicken stock, with salt and pepper to taste. Bring to the boil. Cover, lower the heat and simmer for 10 minutes. Meanwhile, cut the lasagne sheets into 2cm/3/4in squares.

3 Taste the stock for seasoning. Drop in the pasta, stir and bring to the boil. Simmer for 2–3 minutes or until the pasta is *al dente*, then stir in the prosciutto. Serve hot in warmed bowls, with grated Parmesan handed around separately.

Cook's Tip

Take care when adding salt, because of the saltiness of the pancetta and the prosciutto.

Zuppa di Fagioli con la Pasta

Bean and Pasta Soup

THIS HEARTY MAIN MEAL soup sometimes goes by the simpler name of *Pasta e Fagioli*, while some Italians refer to it as *Minestrone di Pasta e Fagioli*. Traditional country recipes use dried beans and a ham bone, and require the soup to be cooked for a long time.

INGREDIENTS

1 onion
1 carrot
1 celery stick
30ml/2 tbsp olive oil
115g/4oz pancetta or rindless smoked streaky (fatty) bacon, diced
1.75 litres/3 pints/7½ cups beef stock
1 cinnamon stick or a good pinch of ground cinnamon
90g/3½oz/scant 1 cup dried pasta shapes, e.g. conchiglie or corallini
400g/14oz can borlotti beans, rinsed and drained
1 thick slice cooked ham, about 225g/8oz, diced
salt and ground black pepper
coarsely shaved Parmesan cheese, to serve

Serves 4–6

1 Chop the vegetables. Heat the oil in a large pan, add the pancetta or bacon and cook, stirring, until lightly coloured. Add the chopped vegetable mixture to the pan and cook for about 10 minutes, stirring frequently, until lightly coloured. Pour in the stock, add the cinnamon with salt and pepper to taste, and bring to the boil. Cover and simmer gently for 15–20 minutes.

2 Add the pasta. Bring back to the boil, stirring all the time. Lower the heat and simmer, stirring frequently, for 5 minutes. Add the beans and diced ham and simmer until the pasta is *al dente*: 2–3 minutes or according to the instructions on the packet.

3 Taste the soup for seasoning. Serve hot in warmed bowls, sprinkled with shavings of Parmesan.

VARIATIONS

- *Use spaghetti or tagliatelle instead of the small pasta shapes, breaking it into small pieces over the pan.*
- *Use cannellini or white haricot (navy) beans instead of the borlotti. Alternatively, use dried beans that have been soaked, drained and boiled for 1 hour or until tender. Add them to the pan after the stock in Step 1.*
- *If you like, add 15ml/1 tbsp passata (bottled strained tomatoes) or tomato purée (paste), or 1 large ripe tomato, skinned and chopped, with the beans and diced ham.*

Minestrone di Pasta e Ceci

Pasta and Chickpea Soup

A SIMPLE, COUNTRY-STYLE soup. The shape of the pasta and the beans complement one another beautifully.

INGREDIENTS

1 onion
2 carrots
2 celery sticks
60ml/4 tbsp olive oil
400g/14oz can chickpeas, rinsed and drained
200g/7oz can cannellini beans, rinsed and drained
150ml/¼ pint/⅔ cup passata (bottled strained tomatoes)
120ml/4fl oz/½ cup water
1.5 litres/2½ pints/6¼ cups vegetable or chicken stock
2 fresh or dried rosemary sprigs
200g/7oz/scant 2 cups dried conchiglie
salt and ground black pepper
freshly grated Parmesan cheese, to serve

Serves 4–6

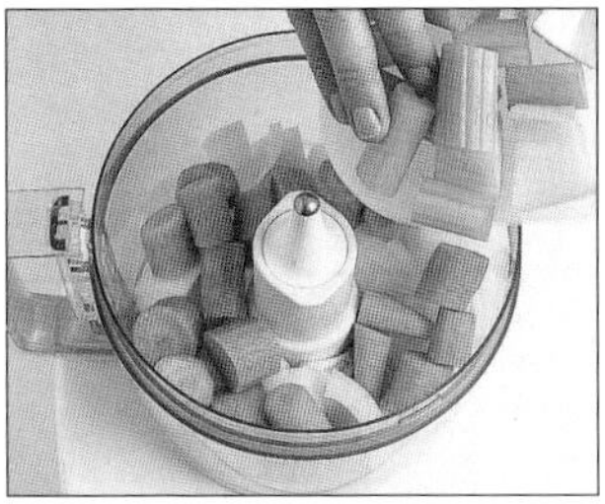

1 Chop the onion, carrots and celery finely, either in a food processor or by hand.

2 Heat the oil in a large pan, add the chopped vegetable mixture and cook over a low heat, stirring frequently, for 5–7 minutes.

3 Add the chickpeas and cannellini beans, stir well to mix, then cook for 5 minutes. Stir in the passata and water. Cook, stirring, for 2–3 minutes.

4 Add 475ml/16fl oz/2 cups of the stock, one of the rosemary sprigs and salt and pepper to taste. Bring to the boil, cover, then simmer gently, stirring occasionally, for 1 hour.

5 Pour in the remaining stock, add the pasta and bring to the boil, stirring. Lower the heat and simmer, stirring frequently, until the pasta is *al dente*: 7–8 minutes or according to the instructions on the packet. Taste for seasoning. Remove the rosemary and serve the soup hot, in warmed bowls, topped with grated Parmesan and a few rosemary leaves.

VARIATIONS

- *You can use other pasta shapes, but conchiglie are ideal because they scoop up the chickpeas and beans.*
- *If you like, crush 1–2 garlic cloves and fry them with the vegetables.*

Minestrone alla Pugliese

Puglia-style Minestrone

THIS IS A TASTY SOUP for a Monday supper, because it can be made with the leftover carcass of Sunday's roast chicken. The sprinkling of salty ricotta salata at the finish is typical of Puglian cooking.

INGREDIENTS

1 roast chicken carcass
1 onion, quartered lengthways
1 carrot, roughly chopped
1 celery stick, roughly chopped
a few black peppercorns
1 small handful mixed fresh herbs, such as parsley and thyme
1 chicken stock (bouillon) cube
50g/2oz/½ cup tubetti
salt and ground black pepper
50g/2oz ricotta salata, coarsely grated or crumbled and 30ml/2 tbsp fresh mint leaves, to serve

Serves 4

1 Break the chicken carcass into pieces and place these in a large pan. Add the onion, carrot, celery, peppercorns and herbs, then crumble in the stock cube and add a good pinch of salt. Cover the chicken generously with cold water (you will need about 1.5 litres/2½ pints/6¼ cups) and bring to the boil over a high heat.

2 Lower the heat, half cover the pan and simmer gently for about 1 hour. Remove the pan from the heat and leave to cool, then strain the liquid through a colander or sieve (strainer) into a clean large pan.

3 Remove any meat from the chicken bones, cut it into bitesize pieces and set aside. Discard the carcass and flavouring ingredients.

4 Bring the stock in the pan to the boil, add the pasta and simmer, stirring frequently, until only just *al dente*: 5–6 minutes or according to the instructions on the packet.

5 Add the pieces of chicken and heat through for a few minutes, by which time the pasta will be ready. Taste for seasoning. Serve hot in warmed bowls, sprinkled with the ricotta salata and mint leaves.

COOK'S TIPS

- *Use other small, hollow pasta shapes, such as chifferini or pennette, for this soup, if you like.*
- *Ricotta salata is a salted and dried version of ricotta cheese. It is firmer than the traditional soft white ricotta, and can be easily diced, crumbled and even grated. It is available from some delicatessens, good cheese shops and large supermarkets. If you can't locate it, use feta cheese instead.*

Zuppa di Lenticchie e Pastina

Lentil and Pasta Soup

THIS RUSTIC VEGETARIAN soup makes a warming winter meal and goes well with granary or crusty Italian bread.

INGREDIENTS

175g/6oz/¾ cup brown lentils
3 garlic cloves
1 litre/1¾ pints/4 cups water
45ml/3 tbsp olive oil
25g/1oz/2 tbsp butter
1 onion, finely chopped
2 celery sticks, finely chopped
30ml/2 tbsp sun-dried tomato purée (paste)
1.75 litres/3 pints/7½ cups vegetable stock
a few fresh marjoram leaves
a few fresh basil leaves
leaves from 1 fresh thyme sprig
50g/2oz/½ cup dried small pasta shapes, such as tubetti
salt and ground black pepper
tiny fresh herb leaves, to garnish

Serves 4–6

COOK'S TIP

Use green lentils instead of brown if you like, but the orange or red ones go mushy.

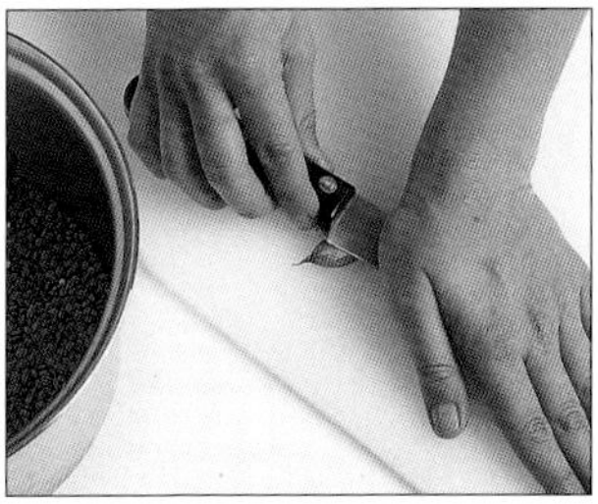

1 Put the lentils in a large pan. Smash 1 garlic clove (there's no need to peel it first) and add it to the lentils. Pour in the water and bring to the boil. Lower the heat to a gentle simmer and cook, stirring occasionally, for about 20 minutes or until the lentils are just tender. Place the lentils into a sieve (strainer), remove the garlic and set it aside. Rinse the lentils under the cold tap, then leave them to drain.

2 Heat 30ml/2 tbsp of the oil with half of the butter in a large pan. Add the onion and celery and cook over a low heat, stirring frequently, for 5–7 minutes until softened.

3 Crush the remaining garlic, then peel and mash the reserved garlic. Add to the vegetables with the remaining oil, the tomato purée and the lentils. Stir, then add the stock, the fresh herbs and salt and pepper to taste. Bring to the boil, stirring. Simmer for 30 minutes, stirring occasionally.

4 Add the pasta and bring the water back to the boil, stirring. Simmer, stirring frequently, until the pasta is *al dente*: 7–8 minutes or according to the packet instructions. Add the remaining butter and taste for seasoning. Serve hot in warmed bowls, sprinkled with the herb leaves.

Zuppa Casalinga

Farmhouse Soup

ROOT VEGETABLES FORM the base of this chunky, minestrone-style main meal soup. You can vary the vegetables according to what you have to hand.

INGREDIENTS

30ml/2 tbsp olive oil
1 onion, roughly chopped
3 carrots, cut into large chunks
175–200g/6–7oz turnips, cut into large chunks
about 175g/6oz swede (rutabaga), cut into large chunks
400g/14oz can chopped Italian tomatoes
15ml/1 tbsp tomato purée (paste)
5ml/1 tsp dried mixed herbs
5ml/1 tsp dried oregano
50g/2oz/½ cup dried bell peppers, washed and thinly sliced (optional)
1.5 litres/2½ pints/6¼ cups vegetable stock or water
50g/2oz/½ cup dried small macaroni
400g/14oz can red kidney beans, rinsed and drained
30ml/2 tbsp chopped fresh flat leaf (Italian) parsley
salt and ground black pepper
freshly grated Parmesan cheese, to serve

Serves 4

1 Heat the oil in a large pan, add the onion and cook over a low heat for about 5 minutes until softened. Add the fresh vegetables, canned tomatoes, tomato purée, dried herbs and dried peppers, if using. Stir in salt and pepper to taste. Pour in the stock or water and bring to the boil. Stir well, cover, lower the heat and simmer for 30 minutes, stirring occasionally.

COOK'S TIP

Packets of dried Italian peppers are sold in many supermarkets and in delicatessens. They are piquant and firm with a "meaty" bite to them, which makes them ideal for adding substance to vegetarian soups.

2 Add the pasta and bring to the boil, stirring. Lower the heat and simmer, uncovered, until the pasta is only just *al dente*: about 5 minutes or according to the instructions on the packet. Stir frequently.

3 Stir in the beans. Heat through for 2–3 minutes, then remove from the heat and stir in the parsley. Taste the soup for seasoning.

4 Serve hot in warmed soup bowls, with grated Parmesan handed separately.

Minestra con Pasta e Pomodori

Roasted Tomato and Pasta Soup

WHEN THE ONLY TOMATOES you can buy are not particularly flavoursome, make this soup. The oven-roasting compensates for any lack of flavour in the tomatoes, and the soup has a wonderful smoky taste.

INGREDIENTS

450g/1lb ripe Italian plum tomatoes, halved lengthways
1 large red (bell) pepper, quartered lengthways and seeded
1 large red onion, quartered lengthways
2 garlic cloves, unpeeled
15ml/1 tbsp olive oil
1.2 litres/2 pints/5 cups vegetable stock or water
good pinch of sugar
90g/3½oz/scant 1 cup dried small pasta shapes, such as tubetti or small macaroni
salt and ground black pepper
fresh basil leaves, to garnish

Serves 4

1 Preheat the oven to 190°C /375°F/ Gas 5. Spread out the tomatoes, red pepper, onion and garlic in a roasting pan and drizzle with the olive oil. Roast for 30–40 minutes until the vegetables are soft and charred, stirring and turning them halfway.

2 Transfer the vegetables into a food processor, add about 250ml/ 8fl oz/1 cup of the stock or water and process until puréed. Scrape into a sieve (strainer) placed over a large pan and press the purée through into the pan.

3 Add the remaining stock or water, the sugar and salt and pepper to taste. Bring to the boil, stirring.

4 Add the pasta and simmer, stirring frequently, until *al dente*: 7–8 minutes or according to the instructions on the packet. Taste for seasoning. Serve hot in warmed bowls, garnished with the fresh basil.

COOK'S TIPS

- *You can roast the vegetables in advance, allow them to cool, then leave them in a covered bowl in the refrigerator overnight before puréeing.*
- *The soup can be frozen without the pasta. Thaw and bring to the boil before adding the pasta.*

Pasta in Brodo con Piselli e Fegatini

Pasta Soup with Chicken Livers

A SOUP THAT CAN BE served as either a first or main course. The fried fegatini are so delicious that even if you do not normally like chicken livers you will find yourself loving them in this soup.

INGREDIENTS

115g/4oz/⅔ cup chicken livers, thawed if frozen
3 sprigs each fresh parsley, marjoram and sage
leaves from 1 fresh thyme sprig
5–6 fresh basil leaves
15ml/1 tbsp olive oil
knob of butter
4 garlic cloves, crushed
15–30ml/1–2 tbsp dry white wine
2 x 300g/11oz cans condensed chicken consommé
225g/8oz/2 cups frozen peas
50g/2oz/½ cup dried pasta shapes, such as farfalle
2–3 spring onions (scallions), sliced
salt and ground black pepper

Serves 4–6

1 Cut the chicken livers into small pieces with scissors. Chop the herbs. Heat the oil and butter in a frying pan, add the garlic and herbs, with salt and pepper to taste, and fry gently for a few minutes. Add the livers, increase the heat to high and stir-fry for a few minutes until they change colour and become dry. Pour the wine over the livers, cook until the wine evaporates, then remove the livers from the heat and taste for seasoning.

2 Empty both cans of condensed chicken consommé into a large pan and add water to the condensed soup as directed on the labels. Add an extra can of water, then stir in a little salt and pepper to taste and bring to the boil.

3 Add the frozen peas to the pan and simmer for about 5 minutes, then add the small pasta shapes and bring the soup back to the boil, stirring. Allow to simmer, stirring frequently, until the pasta is only just *al dente*: about 5 minutes or according to the instructions on the packet.

4 Add the fried chicken livers and spring onions and heat through for 2–3 minutes. Taste for seasoning. Serve hot, in warmed bowls.

Pallottoline e Pasta in Brodo

Meatball and Pasta Soup

EVEN THOUGH THIS SOUP comes from sunny Sicily, it is substantial enough for a hearty supper on a winter's day.

INGREDIENTS

2 x 300g/11oz cans condensed beef consommé
90g/3½oz/¾ cup dried very thin pasta, e.g. fidelini or spaghettini
fresh flat leaf (Italian) parsley, to garnish
freshly grated Parmesan cheese, to serve

For the meatballs

1 very thick slice of white bread, crusts removed
30ml/2 tbsp milk
225g/8oz/1 cup minced (ground) beef
1 garlic clove, crushed
30ml/2 tbsp freshly grated Parmesan cheese
30–45ml/2–3 tbsp fresh flat leaf (Italian) parsley leaves, coarsely chopped
1 egg
nutmeg
salt and ground black pepper

Serves 4

1 Make the meatballs. Break the bread into a small bowl, add the milk and set aside to soak. Meanwhile, put the minced beef, garlic, Parmesan, parsley and egg in another large bowl. Grate fresh nutmeg liberally over the top and add salt and pepper to taste.

2 Squeeze the bread with your hands to remove as much milk as possible, then add the bread to the meatball mixture and mix everything together well with your hands. Wash your hands, rinse them under the cold tap, then form the mixture into tiny balls about the size of small marbles.

3 Pour both cans of consommé into a large pan, add water as directed on the labels, then add an extra can of water. Stir in salt and pepper to taste and bring to the boil.

4 Drop in the meatballs, then break the pasta into small pieces and add it to the soup. Bring the soup to the boil, stirring gently. Simmer, stirring frequently, until the pasta is *al dente*: 7–8 minutes or according to the instructions on the packet. Taste for seasoning. Serve hot in warmed bowls, sprinkled with parsley and freshly grated Parmesan cheese.

Tomato Sauces

It was the Neapolitans who first discovered the delights of pasta and tomato sauce. Tomatoes originally came to Italy from the New World. They were yellow, which is why they were called golden apples (*pomodori*), and were originally used only as ornamental plants. They quickly took to the sunshine of southern Italy, however, and by the 18th century the red tomato was being enjoyed in salads. It wasn't long before they were partnered with pasta – and so began one of the most successful marriages in culinary history.

Tomato sauces, simple and uncooked or simmered for a longish while, are typically southern Italian. They go best with the dried, commercially produced pasta of the south, and taste divine with those other wonderful southern ingredients – basil, garlic and olive oil. Most recipes in this chapter give advice on the best type of pasta to serve with the sauce, while some go further and include pasta as part of the recipe.

Spaghetti is the pasta most often used with tomato sauces, but all the sauces work well with a wide range of pastas, so feel free to mix and match.

La Pommarola

Fresh Tomato Sauce

THIS IS THE FAMOUS Neapolitan sauce that is made in summer when tomatoes are very ripe and sweet. It is very simple, so that nothing detracts from the flavour of the tomatoes themselves. It is served here with spaghetti, which is the traditional choice of pasta.

INGREDIENTS

675g/1½lb ripe Italian plum tomatoes
60ml/4 tbsp olive oil
1 onion, finely chopped
350g/12oz fresh or dried spaghetti
1 small handful fresh basil leaves
salt and ground black pepper
coarsely shaved Parmesan cheese, to serve

Serves 4

1 With a sharp knife, cut a cross in the bottom (flower) end of each tomato. Bring a medium pan of water to the boil and remove from the heat. Plunge a few of the tomatoes into the water, leave for 30 seconds or so, then lift them out with a slotted spoon. Repeat with the remaining tomatoes, then peel off the skin and roughly chop the flesh.

2 Heat the oil in a large pan, add the onion and cook over a low heat, stirring frequently, for about 5 minutes until softened and lightly coloured. Add the tomatoes, with salt and pepper to taste, bring to a simmer, then turn the heat down to low and cover the pan. Cook, stirring occasionally, for 30–40 minutes until thick.

3 Meanwhile, cook the pasta according to the instructions on the packet. Shred the basil leaves finely.

4 Remove the sauce from the heat, stir in the basil and taste for seasoning. Drain the pasta, transfer it into a warmed bowl, pour the sauce over and toss. Serve immediately, with shaved Parmesan handed separately.

COOK'S TIPS

• *The Italian plum tomatoes called San Marzano are the best variety to use. When fully ripe, they have thin skins that peel off easily.*

• *In Italy, cooks often make this sauce in bulk in the summer months and freeze it for later use. Let it cool, then freeze in usable quantities in rigid containers. Thaw before reheating.*

VARIATIONS

Some Neapolitan cooks add a little crushed garlic with the onion and some use chopped fresh oregano or flat leaf parsley with the basil; it is a matter of personal taste.

Rigatoni con Sugo di Pomodoro Invernale

Rigatoni with Winter Tomato Sauce

IN WINTER, WHEN FRESH tomatoes are not at their best, this is the sauce the Italians make. Canned tomatoes combined with *soffritto* (the sautéed mixture of chopped onion, carrot, celery and garlic) and herbs give a better flavour than winter tomatoes.

INGREDIENTS

1 onion
1 carrot
1 celery stick
60ml/4 tbsp olive oil
1 garlic clove, thinly sliced
a few leaves each fresh basil, thyme and oregano or marjoram
2 x 400g/14oz cans chopped Italian plum tomatoes
15ml/1 tbsp sun-dried tomato purée (paste)
5ml/1 tsp sugar
about 90ml/6 tbsp dry red or white wine (optional)
350g/12oz/3 cups dried rigatoni
salt and ground black pepper
coarsely shaved Parmesan cheese, to serve

Serves 6–8

1 Chop the onion, carrot and celery stick finely, either in a food processor or by hand.

2 Heat the olive oil in a medium pan, add the garlic slices and stir over a very low heat for 1–2 minutes.

3 Add the chopped vegetables and the fresh herbs. Cook over a low heat, stirring frequently, for 5–7 minutes until the vegetables have softened and are lightly coloured.

4 Add the canned tomatoes, tomato purée and sugar, then stir in the wine, if using. Add salt and pepper to taste. Bring to the boil, stirring, then lower the heat to a gentle simmer. Cook, uncovered, for about 45 minutes, stirring occasionally.

5 Cook the pasta according to the instructions on the packet. Drain it and transfer it into a warmed bowl. Taste the sauce for seasoning, pour the sauce over the pasta and toss well. Serve immediately, with shavings of Parmesan handed separately. If you like, garnish with extra chopped herbs.

Spaghetti al Rancetto

Spaghetti with Tomatoes and Pancetta

This sauce comes from Spoleto in Umbria. It is a fresh, light sauce in which the tomatoes are cooked for a short time, so it should only be made in summer when tomatoes have a good flavour.

INGREDIENTS

350g/12oz ripe Italian plum tomatoes
150g/5oz pancetta or rindless streaky (fatty) bacon, diced
30ml/2 tbsp olive oil
1 onion, finely chopped
350g/12oz fresh or dried spaghetti
2–3 fresh marjoram sprigs, leaves stripped
salt and ground black pepper
freshly grated Pecorino cheese, to serve
shredded fresh basil, to garnish
Serves 4

1 With a sharp knife, cut a cross in the bottom (flower) end of each plum tomato. Bring a medium pan of water to the boil and remove from the heat. Plunge a few of the tomatoes into the water, leave for 30 seconds or so, then lift them out with a slotted spoon and set aside. Repeat with the remaining tomatoes, then peel off the skin and finely chop the flesh.

Cook's Tip

Do try to find pancetta – bacon can be substituted but the sauce will not taste precisely the same. You can buy ready diced pancetta in packets in supermarkets. Alternatively, you can buy it thinly sliced, sometimes cut from a roll (arrotolata), and dice it yourself.

2 Put the pancetta or bacon in a medium pan with the oil. Stir over a low heat until the fat runs. Add the onion and stir to mix. Cook gently for about 10 minutes, stirring.

3 Add the tomatoes, with salt and pepper to taste. Stir well and cook, uncovered, for about 10 minutes. Meanwhile, cook the pasta according to the instructions on the packet.

4 Remove the sauce from the heat, stir in the marjoram and taste for seasoning. Drain the pasta and transfer it into a warmed bowl. Pour the sauce over the pasta and toss well. Serve immediately, sprinkled with shredded basil. Hand around grated Pecorino.

Penne all'Arrabbiata

Penne with Tomato and Chilli Sauce

THIS IS ONE OF ROME'S most famous pasta dishes – penne tossed in a tomato sauce flavoured with chilli. Literally translated, *arrabbiata* means "enraged" or "furious" but in this context it should be translated as "fiery". Make the sauce as hot as you like by adding more chillies to taste.

INGREDIENTS

25g/1oz dried porcini mushrooms
90g/3½oz/7 tbsp butter
150g/5oz pancetta or rindless smoked streaky (fatty) bacon, diced
1–2 dried red chillies, to taste
2 garlic cloves, crushed
8 ripe Italian plum tomatoes, peeled and chopped
a few fresh basil leaves, torn, plus extra to garnish
350g/12oz/3 cups fresh or dried penne
50g/2oz/⅔ cup freshly grated Parmesan cheese
25g/1oz/⅓ cup freshly grated Pecorino cheese
salt
Serves 4

1 Soak the dried mushrooms in warm water to cover for 15–20 minutes. Drain, then squeeze dry with your hands. Finely chop the mushrooms.

2 Melt 50g/2oz/4 tbsp of the butter in a medium pan or frying pan. Add the pancetta or bacon and stir-fry over a medium heat until golden and slightly crispy. Remove the pancetta with a slotted spoon and set it aside.

3 Add the chopped mushrooms to the pan and cook in the same way. Remove and set aside with the pancetta or bacon. Crumble 1 chilli into the pan, add the garlic and cook, stirring, for a few minutes until the garlic turns golden.

4 Add the tomatoes and basil and season with salt. Cook gently, stirring occasionally, for 10–15 minutes. Meanwhile, cook the penne in a pan of salted boiling water, according to the instructions on the packet.

5 Add the pancetta or bacon and the mushrooms to the tomato sauce. Taste for seasoning, adding more chillies if you prefer a hotter flavour. If the sauce is too dry, stir in a little of the pasta water.

6 Drain the pasta and transfer it into a warmed bowl. Dice the remaining butter, add it to the pasta with the cheeses, then toss until well coated. Pour the sauce over the pasta, toss well and serve immediately, with a few basil leaves sprinkled on top.

Spaghetti alla Puttanesca

Spaghetti with Tomatoes, Anchovies, Olives and Capers

FROM CAMPANIA IN THE SOUTH, this classic sauce has a strong flavour. *Alla puttanesca* means "prostitute style".

INGREDIENTS

30ml/2 tbsp olive oil
1 small onion, finely chopped
1 garlic clove, finely chopped
4 drained canned anchovies
50g/2oz/½ cup pitted black olives, sliced
15ml/1 tbsp capers
400g/14oz can chopped Italian plum tomatoes
45ml/3 tbsp water
15ml/1 tbsp chopped fresh flat leaf (Italian) parsley
350g/12oz fresh or dried spaghetti
salt and ground black pepper

Serves 4

1 Heat the oil in a medium pan and add the onion, garlic and drained anchovies. Cook over a low heat, stirring constantly, for 5–7 minutes or until the anchovies break down to form a very soft pulp. Add the black olives and capers and stir-fry for a minute or so.

2 Add the tomatoes, water, half the parsley and salt and pepper to taste. Stir well and bring to the boil, then lower the heat and cover the pan. Simmer gently for 30 minutes, stirring occasionally. Meanwhile, cook the pasta according to the packet instructions.

3 Drain the pasta and transfer it into a warmed bowl. Taste the sauce for seasoning, pour it over the pasta and toss. Serve immediately, with the remaining parsley sprinkled on top.

COOK'S TIP

Use good-quality, shiny black olives – Gaeta olives from Liguria are very good.

Bucatini all'Amatriciana

Bucatini with Tomato and Chilli Sauce

AMATRICIANA IS A CLASSIC tomato sauce named after the town of Amatrice in the Sabine hills, Lazio. If you visit Rome, you will see it on many restaurant menus served with either bucatini or spaghetti.

INGREDIENTS

15ml/1 tbsp olive oil
1 small onion, finely sliced
115g/4oz smoked pancetta or rindless smoked streaky (fatty) bacon, diced
1 fresh red chilli, seeded and cut into thin strips
400g/14oz can chopped Italian plum tomatoes
30–45ml/2–3 tbsp dry white wine or water
350g/12oz dried bucatini
30–45ml/2–3 tbsp freshly grated Pecorino cheese, plus extra to serve (optional)
salt and ground black pepper

Serves 4

1 Heat the oil in a medium pan and cook the onion, pancetta and chilli over a low heat for 5–7 minutes, stirring. Add the tomatoes and wine or water, with salt and pepper to taste. Bring to the boil, stirring, then cover and simmer for 15–20 minutes, stirring occasionally. If the sauce is too dry, stir in a little of the pasta water.

2 Meanwhile, cook the pasta in a pan of salted boiling water according to the packet instructions.

3 Drain the pasta and transfer it into a warmed bowl. Taste the sauce for seasoning, pour it over the pasta and add the grated Pecorino. Toss well. Serve immediately, with more grated Pecorino served separately.

COOK'S TIP

Always take care when dealing with chillies. They contain a substance called capsaicin, which will irritate delicate skin, so it's a good idea to wear rubber gloves.

Fusilli con Salsa di Pomodori all'Aceto Balsamico

Fusilli with Tomato and Balsamic Vinegar Sauce

THIS IS A MODERN CAL-ITAL recipe (Californian/Italian). The intense, sweet-sour flavour of balsamic vinegar gives a pleasant kick to a sauce made with canned tomatoes.

INGREDIENTS

2 x 400g/14oz cans chopped Italian plum tomatoes
2 pieces of drained sun-dried tomato in olive oil, thinly sliced
2 garlic cloves, crushed
45ml/3 tbsp olive oil
5ml/1 tsp sugar
350g/12oz/3 cups fresh or dried fusilli
45ml/3 tbsp balsamic vinegar
salt and ground black pepper
coarsely shaved Pecorino cheese and rocket (arugula) salad, to serve

Serves 6–8

1 Put the canned and sun-dried tomatoes in a medium pan with the garlic, olive oil and sugar. Add salt and pepper to taste. Bring to the boil, stirring. Lower the heat and simmer for about 30 minutes until reduced.

2 Meanwhile, cook the pasta in salted boiling water according to the instructions on the packet.

3 Add the balsamic vinegar to the sauce and stir to mix evenly. Cook for 1–2 minutes, then remove from the heat and taste for seasoning.

4 Drain the pasta and turn it into a warmed bowl. Pour the sauce over the pasta and toss well. Serve immediately, with rocket salad and the shaved Pecorino handed separately.

Linguine con Pesto di Pomodori Secchi

Linguine with Sun-dried Tomato Pesto

TOMATO PESTO WAS ONCE a rarity, but is becoming increasingly popular. To make it, sun-dried tomatoes are used instead of basil. The result is absolutely delicious.

INGREDIENTS

25g/1oz/⅓ cup pine nuts
25g/1oz/⅓ cup freshly grated Parmesan cheese
50g/2oz/½ cup sun-dried tomatoes in olive oil
1 garlic clove, roughly chopped
60ml/4 tbsp olive oil
350g/12oz fresh or dried linguine
ground black pepper
coarsely shaved Parmesan cheese, to serve
basil leaves, to garnish

Serves 4

1 Put the pine nuts in a small non-stick frying pan and toss over a low to medium heat for 1–2 minutes or until the nuts are lightly toasted and golden.

2 Place the nuts into a food processor. Add the Parmesan, sun-dried tomatoes and garlic, with pepper to taste. Process until finely chopped.

3 With the machine running, gradually add the olive oil through the feeder tube until it has all been incorporated evenly. Process until the ingredients have formed a smooth-looking paste.

4 Cook the pasta according to the packet instructions. Drain well, reserving a little of the cooking water. Transfer the pasta into a warmed bowl, add the pesto and a few spoonfuls of the water and toss well. Serve immediately garnished with basil leaves. Hand round Parmesan shavings separately.

COOK'S TIP

You can make this pesto up to 2 days in advance and keep it in a bowl in the refrigerator until ready to use. Pour a thin film of olive oil over the pesto in the bowl, then cover the bowl tightly with clear film (plastic wrap) to prevent the pesto from tainting other foods in the refrigerator.

Cappelletti con Pomodoro e Panna

Cappelletti with Tomatoes and Cream

TOMATOES, CREAM AND FRESH BASIL are a winning combination. In this very quick and easy recipe, the sauce coats little pasta hats filled with soft cheeses to make a substantial supper dish for vegetarians. If you prefer a lighter dish, you can use the sauce to coat plain, unstuffed pasta. Small shapes such as penne, farfalle or conchiglie are best.

INGREDIENTS

400ml/14fl oz/1⅔ cups passata (bottled strained tomatoes)
90ml/6 tbsp dry white wine
150ml/¼ pint/⅔ cup double (heavy) cream
225g/8oz/2½ cups fresh cappelletti
1 small handful of fresh basil leaves
60ml/4 tbsp freshly grated Parmesan cheese
salt and ground black pepper
Serves 4–6

1 Pour the passata and wine into a medium pan and stir to mix. Bring to the boil over a medium heat, then add the cream and stir until evenly mixed and bubbling. Turn the heat down to low and leave to simmer.

2 Cook the pasta until *al dente*: 5–7 minutes or according to the instructions on the packet. Meanwhile, finely shred most of the basil leaves and set aside with the whole leaves.

3 Drain the pasta well, return it to the pan and toss it with the grated Parmesan. Taste the sauce for seasoning, pour it over the pasta and toss well. Serve immediately, sprinkled with the shredded basil and whole basil leaves.

COOK'S TIPS

- *Cappelletti with a variey of fillings are available at supermarkets and Italian delicatessens.*
- *Other stuffed pasta shapes, such as tortelloni, ravioli, or the more unusual sacchettini (little purses), can be used with this sauce.*
- *The tomato sauce can be made up to a day ahead, then chilled until ready to use. Reheat gently in a heavy pan while the pasta is cooking.*

La Crudaiola

Raw Tomato Sauce

THIS IS A WONDERFULLY simple uncooked tomato sauce that goes well with many different kinds of pasta, both long strands and short shapes. It is always made in summer when plum tomatoes have ripened on the vine in the sun and have their fullest flavour.

INGREDIENTS

500g/1¼lb ripe Italian plum tomatoes
1 large handful fresh basil leaves
75ml/5 tbsp extra virgin olive oil
115g/4oz ricotta salata cheese, diced
1 garlic clove, crushed
salt and ground black pepper
coarsely shaved Pecorino cheese, to serve
Serves 4

1 Roughly chop the plum tomatoes, removing the cores and as many of the seeds as you can. Tear the basil leaves into shreds with your fingers.

2 Put all the ingredients (except the cheese) in a bowl, adding salt and pepper to taste, and stir well. Cover and leave at room temperature for 1–2 hours to let the flavours mingle.

3 Taste the sauce to check the seasoning before tossing it with hot, freshly cooked pasta of your choice. Serve immediately with shavings of Pecorino handed separately.

COOK'S TIPS

- *Ricotta salata is a salted and dried version of ricotta cheese. It is firmer than the traditional soft white ricotta, and can be easily diced, crumbled and even grated. It is available from some delicatessens. If you can't locate it, use feta cheese instead.*
- *Long pasta goes well with this sauce, especially bucatini or spaghetti, or you could serve it with short shapes, such as fusilli or orecchiette.*

Sugo Finto

Meaty Tomato Sauce

THE WORD FINTO means "mock" or "pretend", and this Roman sauce takes its name from the days when meat was scarce and expensive, so cooks would put a little meat fat in a tomato sauce to make it taste of meat. Sometimes meat stock was used for the same purpose.

INGREDIENTS

1 small onion
1 small carrot
2 celery sticks
2 garlic cloves
1 small handful fresh flat leaf (Italian) parsley
50g/2oz ham or bacon fat, finely chopped
60–90ml/4–6 tbsp dry white wine, or more to taste
500g/1 ¼lb ripe Italian plum tomatoes, chopped
salt and ground black pepper

Serves 4

1 Chop the onion, carrot and celery finely in a food processor. Add the garlic cloves and parsley and process until finely chopped. Alternatively, chop everything by hand.

2 Put the chopped vegetable mixture in a medium shallow pan with the ham fat and cook, stirring, over a low heat for about 5 minutes. Add the wine, with salt and pepper to taste and simmer for 5 minutes, then stir in the tomatoes. Simmer for 40 minutes, stirring occasionally and adding a little hot water if the sauce seems too dry.

3 Have ready a large sieve (strainer) placed over a large bowl. Carefully pour in the sauce and press it through the sieve with the back of a metal spoon, leaving behind the tomato skins and any tough pieces of vegetable that won't go through.

4 Return the sauce to the clean pan and heat it through, adding a little more wine or hot water if it is too thick. Taste the sauce for seasoning, then toss with hot, freshly cooked pasta of your choice.

COOK'S TIPS

- *Capelli d'angelo, preferably made without egg, is the traditional pasta to serve with* sugo finto, *but you can use tagliolini or tagliarini if you prefer.*
- *If you like, you can add about 7g/¼oz dried porcini mushrooms, soaked, drained and squeezed dry, when first cooking the other vegetables.*

Farfalle al Sugo di Piselli

Farfalle with Tomatoes and Peas

THIS PRETTY SAUCE should be served with plain white pasta so that the red, green and white make it tricolore, the three colours of the Italian flag. Here farfalle (bow-tie shaped pasta) are used, but other pasta shapes will work just as well.

INGREDIENTS

15ml/1 tbsp olive oil
5–6 rindless streaky (fatty) bacon rashers, cut into strips
400g/14oz can chopped Italian plum tomatoes
60ml/4 tbsp water
350g/12oz/3 cups dried farfalle
225g/8oz/2 cups frozen peas
50g/2oz/4 tbsp mascarpone
a few fresh basil leaves, shredded
salt and ground black pepper
freshly grated Parmesan cheese, to serve
basil leaves, to garnish

Serves 4

1 Heat the olive oil in a medium pan and add the bacon. Cook over a low heat, stirring frequently, for about 5–7 minutes.

2 Add the tomatoes and water, with salt and pepper to taste. Bring to the boil. Lower the heat, cover and simmer gently for about 15 minutes, stirring from time to time.

3 Meanwhile, cook the pasta in salted boiling water according to the instructions on the packet.

4 Add the peas to the tomato sauce, stir well to mix and bring to the boil. Cover the pan and cook for 5–8 minutes until the peas are cooked and the sauce is quite thick. Taste the sauce for seasoning.

5 Turn off the heat under the pan and add the mascarpone and shredded basil. Mix well, cover the pan and leave to stand for 1–2 minutes. Drain the pasta and transfer it into a warmed bowl. Pour the sauce over the pasta and toss well. Serve immediately, garnished with basil, and hand round some grated Parmesan separately.

S
P

Cream Sauces

The northern Italians love cream sauce with pasta. Its unctuous texture goes well with *pasta all'uovo*, pasta made with egg. The pasta in the north is often fresh rather than dried, and cream sauces complement it perfectly. The cream used in Italy is different from our fresh cream. Called *panna da cucina* (cream for cooking), it has a thin, almost runny, consistency and a slight tang. You can buy it fresh in Italy, but beyond its borders you are more likely to see long-life *panna da cucina* in delicatessens and specialist stores.

Oddly enough, the most famous cream sauce of all does not come from northern Italy, but from Rome. *Fettuccine all'Alfredo* – a simple dish of fresh fettuccine tossed in nothing more than cream, butter and grated Parmesan – is one of the best pasta dishes of all time, and very hard to beat. You will find the recipe in this chapter, plus many other simple sauces based on cream to rival Alfredo's creation. From classic favourites, such as *Spaghetti alla Carbonara* and *Vermicelli al Limone* to recipes using seasonal vegetables, such as asparagus and wild mushrooms, or more unusual ingredients, such as radicchio, there is plenty of choice.

Pasta with a cream sauce is always special and makes a good dinner party first course, but keep portions small, because flavours are rich.

Spaghetti alla Carbonara

Spaghetti with Eggs, Bacon and Cream

AN ALL-TIME FAVOURITE that needs no introducing. This version has plenty of pancetta or bacon and is not too creamy, but you can vary the amounts as you please.

INGREDIENTS

30ml/2 tbsp olive oil
1 small onion, finely chopped
8 pancetta or rindless smoked streaky (fatty) bacon rashers (strips), cut into 1cm/½in strips
350g/12oz fresh or dried spaghetti
4 eggs
60ml/4 tbsp crème fraîche
60ml/4 tbsp freshly grated Parmesan cheese, plus extra to serve
salt and ground black pepper

Serves 4

1 Heat the oil in a large pan, add the finely chopped onion and cook over a low heat, stirring frequently, for about 5 minutes until softened.

2 Add the strips of pancetta or bacon to the onion in the pan and cook for about 10 minutes, stirring almost all the time. Meanwhile, cook the pasta in a pan of salted boiling water according to the instructions on the packet until *al dente*.

3 Put the eggs, crème fraîche and grated Parmesan in a bowl. Grind in plenty of pepper, then beat everything together well.

4 Drain the pasta, transfer it into the pan with the pancetta or bacon and toss well to mix. Turn the heat off under the pan. Immediately add the egg mixture and toss vigorously so that it cooks lightly and coats the pasta.

5 Quickly taste for seasoning, then divide among four warmed bowls and sprinkle with black pepper. Serve immediately, with extra grated Parmesan handed separately.

Fusilli di Bosco

Fusilli with Wild Mushrooms

A VERY RICH DISH WITH AN earthy flavour and lots of garlic, this makes an ideal main course for vegetarians, especially if it is followed by a crisp green salad.

INGREDIENTS

1/2 x 275g/10oz jar wild mushrooms in olive oil
25g/1oz/2 tbsp butter
225g/8oz/2 cups fresh wild mushrooms, sliced if large
5ml/1 tsp finely chopped fresh thyme
5ml/1 tsp finely chopped fresh marjoram or oregano, plus extra herbs to serve
4 garlic cloves, crushed
350g/12oz/3 cups fresh or dried fusilli
200ml/7fl oz/scant 1 cup panna da cucina *or double (heavy) cream*
salt and ground black pepper

Serves 4

1 Drain about 15ml/1 tbsp of the oil from the mushrooms into a medium pan. Slice or chop the bottled wild mushrooms into bitesize pieces, if they are large.

2 Add the butter to the oil in the pan and place over a low heat until sizzling. Add the bottled and the fresh mushrooms, the chopped herbs and the garlic, with salt and pepper to taste. Simmer over a medium heat, stirring frequently, for about 10 minutes or until the fresh mushrooms are soft and tender. Meanwhile, cook the pasta in salted boiling water according to the instructions on the packet.

3 As soon as the mushrooms are cooked, increase the heat to high and toss the mixture with a wooden spoon to drive off any excess liquid. Pour in the cream and bring to the boil, stirring, then taste and add more salt and pepper if needed.

4 Drain the pasta and transfer it into a warmed bowl. Pour the sauce over the pasta and toss well. Serve immediately, sprinkled with extra fresh herb leaves.

Farfalle Verdi e Rosa

Pink and Green Farfalle

IN THIS MODERN RECIPE, pink prawns and green courgettes combine prettily with cream and pasta bows to make a substantial main course. Serve with crusty Italian rolls or chunks of warm ciabatta bread.

INGREDIENTS

50g/2oz/¼ cup butter
2–3 spring onions (scallions), very thinly sliced on the diagonal
350g/12oz courgettes (zucchini), thinly sliced on the diagonal
60ml/4 tbsp dry white wine
300g/11oz/2¾ cups dried farfalle
75ml/5 tbsp crème fraîche
225g/8oz/1⅓ cups peeled cooked prawns (shrimp), thawed and thoroughly dried if frozen
15ml/1 tbsp finely chopped fresh marjoram or flat leaf (Italian) parsley, or a mixture
salt and ground black pepper
Serves 4

1 Melt the butter in a large pan, add the spring onions and cook over a low heat, stirring frequently, for about 5 minutes until softened. Add the courgettes, with salt and pepper to taste, and stir-fry for 5 minutes. Pour over the wine and let it bubble, then cover and simmer for 10 minutes.

VARIATION

Use penne instead of the farfalle, and asparagus instead of courgettes (zucchini).

2 Cook the pasta in a pan of salted boiling water according to the instructions on the packet. Meanwhile, add the crème fraîche to the courgette mixture and simmer for 10 minutes until well reduced.

3 Add the prawns to the courgette mixture, heat through gently and taste for seasoning. Drain the pasta and transfer it into a warmed bowl. Add the sauce and chopped herbs and toss well. Serve immediately.

Penne ai Gamberetti con Pernod

Penne with Prawns and Pernod

THIS IS A MODERN RECIPE, typical of those found on menus in the most innovative Italian restaurants. The Pernod and dill go well together, but you could use white wine and basil.

INGREDIENTS

200ml/7fl oz/scant 1 cup panna da cucina *or double (heavy) cream*
250ml/8fl oz/1 cup fish stock
350g/12oz/3 cups dried penne
30–45ml/2–3 tbsp Pernod
225g/8oz/1⅓ cups peeled cooked prawns (shrimp), thawed and dried if frozen
30ml/2 tbsp chopped fresh dill, plus extra to garnish
salt and ground black pepper
Serves 4

1 Put the cream and the fish stock in a medium pan and bring to the boil. Lower the heat and simmer, stirring occasionally, for 10–15 minutes until reduced by about half. Meanwhile, cook the dried pasta in a pan of salted boiling water according to the instructions on the packet.

2 Add the Pernod and prawns to the cream sauce, with salt and pepper to taste, if necessary. Heat the prawns through very gently. Drain the pasta and transfer it into a warmed bowl. Pour the sauce over the pasta, add the dill and toss well. Serve immediately, sprinkled with chopped dill.

Pipe Rigate ai Piselli e Prosciutto

Pipe Rigate with Peas and Ham

PRETTILY FLECKED WITH PINK and green, this is a lovely dish for a spring or summer supper party.

INGREDIENTS

25g/1oz/2 tbsp butter
15ml/1 tbsp olive oil
150g/5oz/1 1/4 cups frozen peas, thawed
1 garlic clove, crushed
150ml/1/4 pint/2/3 cup chicken stock, dry white wine or water
30ml/2 tbsp chopped fresh flat leaf (Italian) parsley
175ml/6fl oz/3/4 cup panna da cucina or double (heavy) cream
115g/4oz prosciutto crudo (Parma ham), shredded
350g/12oz/3 cups dried pipe rigate
salt and ground black pepper
chopped fresh herbs, to garnish

Serves 4

1 Melt half the butter with the olive oil in a medium pan until foaming. Add the thawed frozen peas and the crushed garlic to the pan, followed by the chicken stock, wine or water.

2 Sprinkle in the chopped parsley and add salt and pepper to taste. Cook over a medium heat, stirring frequently, for 5–8 minutes or until most of the liquid has been absorbed.

3 Add about half the cream, increase the heat to high and let the cream bubble, stirring constantly, until it thickens and coats the peas. Remove from the heat, stir in the prosciutto and taste for seasoning.

4 Cook the pasta according to the instructions on the packet. Transfer into a colander and drain well.

5 Immediately melt the remaining butter with the cream in the pan in which the pasta was cooked. Add the pasta and toss over a medium heat until it is evenly coated. Pour in the sauce, toss lightly to mix with the pasta and heat through. Serve immediately, sprinkled with fresh herbs.

COOK'S TIPS

- *Prosciutto is quite expensive, but it tastes very good in this dish. To cut the cost you could use ordinary cooked ham or pancetta.*
- *If you can't get pipe rigate, use conchiglie or orecchiette instead, all of which trap the peas.*

Fettuccine all'Alfredo

Alfredo's Fettuccine

THIS SIMPLE RECIPE WAS invented by a Roman restaurateur called Alfredo, who became famous for serving it with a gold fork and spoon.

INGREDIENTS

50g/2oz/¼ cup butter
200ml/7fl oz/scant 1 cup panna da cucina *or double (heavy) cream*
50g/2oz/⅔ cup freshly grated Parmesan cheese, plus extra to serve
350g/12oz fresh fettuccine
salt and ground black pepper

Serves 4

1 Melt the butter in a large pan. Add the cream and bring it to the boil. Simmer for 5 minutes, stirring, then add the Parmesan, with salt and black pepper to taste, and turn off the heat under the pan.

2 Bring a large pan of salted water to the boil. Drop in the pasta all at once and quickly bring back to the boil, stirring occasionally. Cook until *al dente*: 2–3 minutes, or according to the instructions on the packet. Drain well.

3 Turn on the heat under the pan of cream to low, add the pasta all at once and toss until it is coated in the sauce. Taste for seasoning. Serve immediately, with extra grated Parmesan handed around separately.

COOK'S TIPS

- *With so few ingredients, it is particularly important to use only the best-quality ones for this dish to be a success. Use good unsalted butter and top-quality Parmesan cheese. The best is Parmigiano-Reggiano – available from Italian delicatessens – which has its name stamped on the rind. Grate it only just before using.*
- *Fresh fettuccine is traditional, so either make it yourself or buy it from an Italian delicatessen. If you cannot get fettuccine, you can use tagliatelle instead.*

Linguine al Prosciutto e Mascarpone

Linguine with Ham and Mascarpone

MASCARPONE masquerades as cream in this recipe. Its thick, unctuous consistency makes it perfect for sauces. Have the water boiling, ready for the pasta, before you start making the sauce, because everything cooks so quickly.

INGREDIENTS

25g/1oz/2 tbsp butter
150g/5oz/¾ cup mascarpone
90g/3½oz cooked ham, cut into thin strips
30ml/2 tbsp milk
45ml/3 tbsp freshly grated Parmesan cheese, plus extra to serve
500g/1¼lb fresh linguine
salt and ground black pepper

Serves 6

1 Melt the butter in a medium pan, add the mascarpone, ham and milk and stir well over a low heat until the mascarpone has melted. Add 15ml/1 tbsp of the grated Parmesan and plenty of pepper and stir well.

2 Cook the pasta in a large pan of salted boiling water for 2–3 minutes until *al dente*.

3 Drain the cooked pasta well and transfer it into a warmed bowl. Pour the sauce over the pasta, add the remaining Parmesan and toss well.

4 Taste for seasoning and serve the pasta immediately, with more ground black pepper and extra grated Parmesan handed separately.

Farfalle alla Crema di Gorgonzola

Farfalle with Gorgonzola Cream

SWEET AND SIMPLE, this sauce has a nutty tang from the blue cheese. It is also good with long pasta, such as spaghetti or trenette.

INGREDIENTS

350g/12oz/3 cups dried farfalle
175g/6oz Gorgonzola cheese, any rind removed, diced
150ml/¼ pint/⅔ cup panna da cucina or double (heavy) cream
pinch of sugar
10ml/2 tsp finely chopped fresh sage, plus fresh sage leaves (some whole, some shredded) to garnish
salt and ground black pepper

Serves 4

1 Cook the pasta until *al dente*: 8–10 minutes or according to the instructions on the packet.

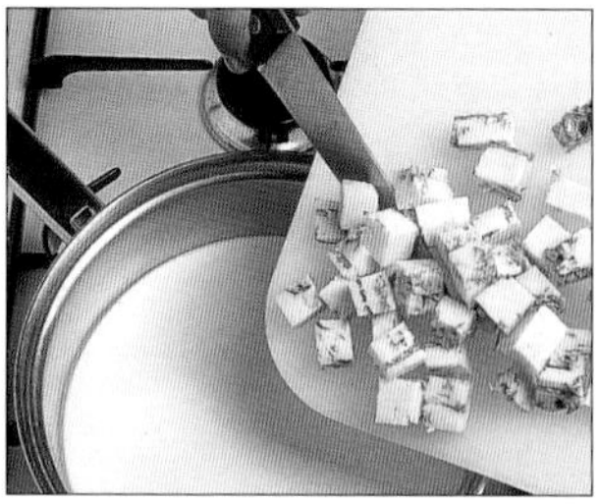

2 Meanwhile, put the Gorgonzola and cream in a medium pan. Add the sugar and plenty of ground black pepper and heat gently, stirring frequently, until the cheese has melted. Remove the pan from the heat.

3 Drain the cooked pasta well and return it to the pan in which it was cooked. Pour the sauce into the pan with the pasta.

4 Add the chopped sage to the pasta and toss over a medium heat until the pasta is evenly coated.

5 Taste for seasoning, adding salt if necessary, then divide among four warmed bowls. Garnish each portion with sage and serve immediately.

Vermicelli al Limone

Vermicelli with Lemon

FRESH AND TANGY, THIS MAKES an excellent first course for a dinner party. It doesn't rely on fresh seasonal ingredients, so it is good at any time of year. It is also a recipe to remember when you're pushed for time, because the sauce can easily be made in the time it takes to cook the pasta.

INGREDIENTS

350g/12oz dried vermicelli
juice of 2 large lemons
50g/2oz/¼ cup butter
200ml/7fl oz/scant 1 cup panna da cucina *or double (heavy) cream*
115g/4oz/1⅓ cups freshly grated Parmesan cheese
salt and ground black pepper

Serves 4

1 Cook the pasta in salted boiling water according to the instructions on the packet.

2 Meanwhile, pour the lemon juice into a medium pan. Add the butter and cream, then salt and pepper to taste.

3 Bring to the boil, then lower the heat and simmer for about 5 minutes, stirring occasionally, until the cream reduces slightly.

4 Drain the pasta and return it to the pan. Add the grated Parmesan, then taste the sauce for seasoning and pour it over the pasta. Toss quickly over a medium heat until the pasta is evenly coated with the sauce, then divide among four warmed bowls and serve immediately.

COOK'S TIP

Lemons vary in the amount of juice they yield. On average, a large fresh lemon will yield 60–90ml/4–6 tbsp. The lemony flavour of this dish is quite sharp – you can use less juice if you prefer.

VARIATIONS

- *Use spaghettini or spaghetti, or even small pasta shapes, such as fusilli, farfalle or orecchiette.*
- *For an even tangier taste, add a little grated lemon rind to the sauce when you add the butter and the cream to the pan in Step 2.*

Spaghetti allo Zafferano

Spaghetti with Saffron

A QUICK AND EASY DISH THAT makes a delicious midweek supper. The ingredients are all staples that you are likely to have in the refrigerator, so this recipe is perfect for impromptu meals.

INGREDIENTS

350g/12oz dried spaghetti
a few saffron strands
30ml/2 tbsp water
150g/5oz cooked ham, cut into thin strips
200ml/7fl oz/scant 1 cup panna da cucina *or double (heavy) cream*
50g/2oz/⅔ cup freshly grated Parmesan cheese, plus extra to serve
2 egg yolks
salt and ground black pepper

Serves 4

1 Cook the pasta in a pan of salted boiling water according to the instructions on the packet.

2 Meanwhile, put the saffron strands in a pan, add the water and bring to the boil immediately. Remove the pan from the heat and leave to stand for a while.

3 Add the strips of ham to the pan containing the saffron. Stir in the cream and Parmesan, with a little salt and pepper to taste. Heat gently, stirring all the time. When the cream starts to bubble around the edges, remove the sauce from the heat and add the egg yolks. Beat well to mix, then taste for seasoning.

4 Drain the pasta and transfer it into a warmed bowl. Immediately pour the sauce over the pasta and toss well. Serve immediately, with extra grated Parmesan handed separately.

COOK'S TIPS

- *Individual sachets of saffron powder, enough for four servings, are sold at Italian delicatessens and some supermarkets, and one sachet can be used for this sauce instead of the saffron strands. Simply sprinkle in the powder in Step 3, when adding salt and pepper.*
- *Use a heavy pan for heating the cream so that it does not catch on the bottom. Make sure you beat the sauce immediately once the eggs are added.*

Garganelli agli Asparagi e Panna

Garganelli with Asparagus and Cream

A LOVELY RECIPE FOR LATE spring when bunches of fresh young asparagus are on sale in shops and markets everywhere.

INGREDIENTS

1 bunch fresh young asparagus, 250–300g/9–11oz
350g/12oz/3 cups dried garganelli
25g/1oz/2 tbsp butter
200ml/7fl oz/scant 1 cup panna da cucina or double (heavy) cream
30ml/2 tbsp dry white wine
90–115g/3½–4oz/1–1⅓ cups freshly grated Parmesan cheese
30ml/2 tbsp chopped fresh mixed herbs, such as basil, flat leaf (Italian) parsley, chervil, marjoram and oregano
salt and ground black pepper

Serves 4

1 Trim off and throw away the woody ends of the asparagus – after trimming, you should have about 200g/7oz asparagus spears. Cut the spears diagonally into pieces that are roughly the same length and shape as the garganelli.

2 Blanch the asparagus spears in salted boiling water for 2 minutes, the tips for 1 minute. Immediately after blanching drain the asparagus spears and tips, rinse in cold water and set aside.

3 Cook the pasta according to the instructions on the packet. Meanwhile, put the butter and cream in a medium pan, add salt and pepper to taste and bring to the boil. Simmer for a few minutes until the cream reduces and thickens, then add the asparagus, wine and about half the grated Parmesan. Taste for seasoning and keep on a low heat.

4 Drain the pasta when cooked and transfer it into a warmed bowl. Pour the sauce over the pasta, sprinkle with the fresh herbs and toss well. Serve immediately, topped with the remaining grated Parmesan.

COOK'S TIPS

- *When buying asparagus look for thin stalks, which will be sweet and tender. Don't buy asparagus with thick or woody stalks, which will be tough.*
- *Garganelli all'uovo (with egg) are just perfect for this dish. You can buy packets of this pasta in Italian delicatessens.*
- *Penne (quills) or penne rigate (ridged quills) are an alternative pasta for this recipe. They are similar in shape and size to garganelli.*

Tagliatelle al Radicchio con Panna

Tagliatelle with Radicchio and Cream

THIS IS A MODERN RECIPE that is very quick and easy to make. It is deliciously rich, kand makes a good dinner party first course.

INGREDIENTS

225g/8oz dried tagliatelle
75–90g/3–3½oz pancetta or rindless streaky (fatty) bacon, diced
25g/1oz/2 tbsp butter
1 onion, finely chopped
1 garlic clove, crushed
1 head of radicchio, about 115–175g/4–6oz, finely shredded
150ml/¼ pint/⅔ cup panna da cucina or double (heavy) cream
50g/2oz/⅔ cup freshly grated Parmesan cheese
salt and ground black pepper

Serves 4

1 Cook the pasta according to the instructions on the packet.

2 Meanwhile, put the pancetta or bacon in a medium pan and heat gently until the fat runs. Increase the heat slightly and stir-fry the pancetta or bacon for 5 minutes.

3 Add the butter, onion and garlic to the pan and stir-fry for 5 minutes more. Add the radicchio and toss for 1–2 minutes until wilted.

4 Pour in the cream and add the grated Parmesan, with salt and pepper to taste. Stir for 1–2 minutes until the cream is bubbling and the ingredients are evenly mixed. Taste the sauce for seasoning.

5 Drain the pasta and transfer it into a warmed bowl. Pour the sauce over the pasta and toss well. Serve immediately.

COOK'S TIP

In Italy, cooks use a type of radicchio called radicchio di Treviso. It is very striking to look at, having long leaves that are dramatically striped in dark red and white. Radicchio di Treviso is available in some supermarkets and specialist greengrocers, but if you cannot get it you can use the round radicchio instead, which is very easy to obtain.

Fish and Shellfish

It is not surprising that seafood sauces are often served with pasta along the Italian coastline, and on the islands of Sicily and Sardinia, but they're very popular inland, too. Clams, mussels, tuna, prawns, anchovies, salmon, scallops and squid are the most common fish and shellfish used, but cooks in coastal areas also create unique pasta dishes using the local catch. These are hard to replicate elsewhere.

Sometimes seafood is cooked with tomatoes, sometimes with a cream-based sauce, so the look and taste of seafood pasta can vary considerably from one dish to another. Intense flavours are found in Sicilian recipes, such as *Spaghetti alla Siracusana* and *Spaghetti alla Bottarga*, while the popular modern classic *Penne, Panna e Salmone* is mild and creamy. *Spaghetti alla Caprese*, which comes from the island of Capri, is fresh and light.

Spaghetti is the traditional pasta to serve with seafood sauces, since so many of them are based on olive oil and tomatoes. It remains the all-time favourite, but other shapes work equally well. When partnered with seafood, pasta proves its versatility.

Vermicelli alla Napoletana

Vermicelli with Clam Sauce

THIS RECIPE TAKES ITS name from the city of Naples, where both fresh tomato sauce and seafood are traditionally served with vermicelli. Here the two are combined to make a very tasty dish.

INGREDIENTS

1kg/2¼lb fresh clams
250ml/8fl oz/1 cup dry white wine
2 garlic cloves, bruised
1 large handful fresh flat leaf (Italian) parsley
30ml/2 tbsp olive oil
1 small onion, finely chopped
8 ripe Italian plum tomatoes, peeled, seeded and finely chopped
½–1 fresh red chilli, seeded and finely chopped
350g/12oz dried vermicelli
salt and ground black pepper
Serves 4

1 Scrub the clams thoroughly under cold running water and discard any that are open or that do not close when sharply tapped against the work surface.

2 Pour the wine into a large pan, add the garlic cloves and half the parsley, then the clams. Cover tightly with the lid and bring to the boil over a high heat. Cook for about 5 minutes, shaking the pan frequently, until the clams have opened.

3 Place the clams in a large colander set over a bowl and let the liquid drain through. Leave the clams until cool enough to handle, then remove about two-thirds of them from their shells, tipping the clam liquor into the bowl of cooking liquid. Discard any clams that have failed to open. Set both shelled and unshelled clams aside, keeping the unshelled clams warm in a bowl covered with a lid.

4 Heat the oil in a pan, add the onion and cook gently, stirring frequently, for about 5 minutes until softened and lightly coloured. Add the tomatoes, then strain in the clam cooking liquid. Add the chilli and salt and pepper to taste.

5 Bring to the boil, half cover the pan and simmer gently for 15–20 minutes. Meanwhile, cook the pasta according to the packet instructions. Chop the remaining parsley finely.

6 Add the shelled clams to the tomato sauce, stir well and heat through very gently for 2–3 minutes.

7 Drain the cooked pasta well and transfer it into a warmed bowl. Taste the sauce for seasoning, then pour the sauce over the pasta and toss everything together well. Garnish with the reserved clams, sprinkle the parsley over the pasta and serve immediately.

Conchiglie di Mare

Seafood Conchiglie

THIS IS A VERY SPECIAL MODERN dish, a warm salad of scallops, pasta and fresh rocket flavoured with roasted pepper, chilli and balsamic vinegar. It makes an impressive dinner party starter, or a main course for a light lunch.

INGREDIENTS

8 large fresh scallops
300g/11oz/2¾ cups dried conchiglie
15ml/1 tbsp olive oil
15g/½oz/1 tbsp butter
120ml/4fl oz/½ cup dry white wine
90g/3½oz rocket (arugula) leaves, stalks trimmed
salt and ground black pepper

For the vinaigrette
60ml/4 tbsp extra virgin olive oil
15ml/1 tbsp balsamic vinegar
1 piece bottled roasted (bell) pepper, drained and finely chopped
1–2 fresh red chillies, seeded and chopped
1 garlic clove, crushed
5–10ml/1–2 tsp clear honey, to taste
Serves 4

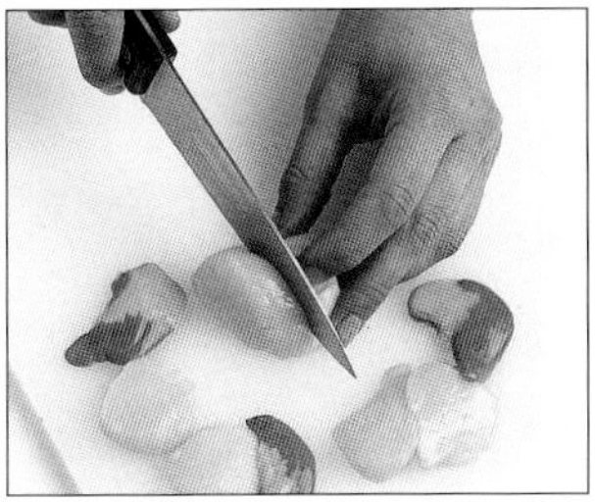

1 Cut each scallop into 2–3 pieces. If the corals are attached, pull them off and cut each piece in half. Season the scallops and corals with salt and pepper.

2 To make the vinaigrette, put the oil, vinegar, chopped pepper and chillies in a jug with the garlic and honey and whisk well.

3 Cook the pasta according to the instructions on the packet.

4 Meanwhile, heat the oil and butter in a non-stick frying pan until sizzling. Add half the scallops and toss over a high heat for 2 minutes. Remove with a slotted spoon and keep warm. Cook the remaining scallops in the same way.

5 Add the wine to the liquid remaining in the pan and stir over a high heat until the mixture has reduced to a few tablespoons. Remove from the heat and keep warm.

6 Drain the pasta and transfer it into a warmed bowl. Add the rocket, scallops, the reduced cooking juices and the vinaigrette and toss well to combine. Serve immediately.

COOK'S TIPS

- *Use only fresh scallops for this dish – they are available all year round in most fishmongers and from fish counters in supermarkets. Frozen scallops tend to be watery and tasteless, and often prove to be rubbery when cooked.*
- *For a more formal presentation, arrange the rocket leaves in a circle on each of four individual serving plates. Toss the pasta, scallops, reduced cooking juices and vinaigrette together and spoon into the centre of the rocket leaves.*

Spaghetti alla Siracusana

Spaghetti with Anchovies and Olives

THE STRONG FLAVOURS of this dish are typical of Sicilian cuisine.

INGREDIENTS

45ml/3 tbsp olive oil
1 large red (bell) pepper, seeded and chopped
1 small aubergine (eggplant), finely chopped
1 onion, finely chopped
8 ripe Italian plum tomatoes, peeled, seeded and finely chopped
2 garlic cloves, finely chopped
120ml/4fl oz/½ cup dry red or white wine
120ml/4fl oz/½ cup water
1 handful fresh herbs, such as basil, flat leaf (Italian) parsley and rosemary
300g/11oz dried spaghetti
50g/2oz canned anchovies, roughly chopped, plus extra whole anchovies to garnish
12 pitted black olives
15–30ml/1–2 tbsp capers, to taste
salt and ground black pepper

Serves 4

1 Heat the oil in a pan and add all the finely chopped vegetables and garlic. Cook gently, stirring frequently, for 10–15 minutes until the vegetables are soft. Pour in the wine and water, add the fresh herbs and pepper to taste and bring to the boil. Lower the heat and simmer, stirring occasionally, for 10–15 minutes. Meanwhile, cook the pasta in a large pan of salted boiling water according to the instructions on the packet.

2 Add the chopped anchovies, olives and capers to the sauce, heat through for a few minutes and taste for seasoning. Drain the pasta and transfer it into a warmed bowl. Pour the sauce over the pasta, toss well and serve immediately.

COOK'S TIP

If the anchovies are omitted, this makes a good sauce for vegetarians.

Spaghetti alla Caprese

Spaghetti with Tuna, Anchovies, Olives and Mozzarella

THIS RECIPE FROM CAPRI is fresh, light and full of flavour, so serve it as soon as it is cooked to enjoy it at its best.

INGREDIENTS

300g/11oz dried spaghetti
30ml/2 tbsp olive oil
6 ripe Italian plum tomatoes, chopped
5ml/1 tsp sugar
50g/2oz jar anchovies in olive oil, drained
about 60ml/4 tbsp dry white wine
200g/7oz can tuna in olive oil, drained
50g/2oz/½ cup pitted black olives, quartered lengthways
125g/4½oz packet mozzarella cheese, drained and diced
salt and ground black pepper
fresh basil leaves, to finish

Serves 4

1 Cook the pasta according to the instructions on the packet. Meanwhile, heat the oil in a medium pan. Add the tomatoes, sugar and pepper to taste, and toss over a medium heat for a few minutes until the tomatoes soften and the juices run. Snip a few anchovies at a time into the pan of tomatoes with kitchen scissors.

2 Add the wine, tuna and olives and stir once or twice until they are just evenly mixed into the sauce. Add the mozzarella and heat through without stirring. Taste and add salt if necessary. Drain the pasta and transfer it into a warmed bowl. Pour the sauce over, toss gently and sprinkle with basil leaves. Serve immediately.

Orecchiette con Acciughe e Broccoli

Orecchiette with Anchovies and Broccoli

WITH ITS ROBUST FLAVOURS, this pasta dish is typical of southern Italian and Sicilian cooking. Anchovies, pine nuts, garlic and Pecorino cheese are all very popular ingredients. Serve with crusty Italian bread for a light lunch or supper.

INGREDIENTS

300g/11oz/2 cups broccoli florets
40g/1½oz/½ cup pine nuts
350g/12oz/3 cups dried orecchiette
60ml/4 tbsp olive oil
1 small red onion, thinly sliced
50g/2oz jar anchovies in olive oil
1 garlic clove, crushed
50g/2oz/⅔ cup freshly grated Pecorino cheese
salt and ground black pepper

Serves 4

COOK'S TIP

Orecchiette (little ears) from Puglia are a special type of pasta with a chewy texture. You can get them in Italian delicatessens, or use conchiglie instead.

1 Break the broccoli florets into small sprigs and cut off the stalks. If the stalks are large, chop or slice them. Cook the broccoli florets and stalks in a pan of boiling salted water for 2 minutes, then drain and refresh under cold running water. Leave to drain on kitchen paper.

2 Put the pine nuts in a dry non-stick frying pan and toss over a low to medium heat for 1–2 minutes or until the nuts are lightly toasted and golden. Remove and set aside.

3 Cook the pasta according to the instructions on the packet.

4 Meanwhile, heat the oil in a frying pan, add the red onion and fry gently, stirring frequently, for about 5 minutes until softened. Add the anchovies with their oil, then add the garlic and fry over a medium heat, stirring frequently, for 1–2 minutes until the anchovies form a paste. Add the broccoli and plenty of pepper and toss over the heat for a minute or two until the broccoli is hot. Taste for seasoning.

5 Drain the pasta and transfer it into a warmed bowl. Add the broccoli mixture and grated Pecorino and toss well. Sprinkle the pine nuts over the top and serve immediately.

Trenette ai Frutti di Mare

Trenette with Shellfish

COLOURFUL AND DELICIOUS, this typical Genoese dish is ideal for a dinner party. The sauce is quite runny, so serve it with crusty bread and spoons as well as forks.

INGREDIENTS

45ml/3 tbsp olive oil
1 small onion, finely chopped
1 garlic clove, crushed
½ fresh red chilli, seeded and chopped
200g/7oz can chopped Italian plum tomatoes
30ml/2 tbsp chopped fresh flat leaf (Italian) parsley
400g/14oz fresh clams
400g/14oz fresh mussels
60ml/4 tbsp dry white wine
400g/14oz/3½ cups dried trenette
a few fresh basil leaves
90g/3½oz/⅔ cup peeled cooked prawns (shrimp), thawed and dried if frozen
salt and ground black pepper
chopped fresh herbs, to garnish

Serves 4

1 Heat 30ml/2 tbsp of the oil in a medium pan. Add the onion, garlic and chilli and cook over a medium heat for 1–2 minutes, stirring constantly. Stir in the tomatoes, half the parsley and pepper to taste. Bring to the boil, lower the heat, cover and simmer for about 15 minutes.

2 Meanwhile, scrub the clams and mussels under cold running water. Discard any that are open or that do not close when sharply tapped against the work surface.

3 In a large pan, heat the remaining oil. Add the clams and mussels, with the rest of the parsley and toss over a high heat for a few seconds. Pour in the wine, then cover tightly. Cook for about 5 minutes, shaking the pan frequently, until the clams and mussels have opened.

4 Remove the pan from the heat and transfer the clams and mussels to a bowl with a slotted spoon, discarding any shellfish that have failed to open.

5 Strain the cooking liquid into a measuring jug (cup) and set aside. Reserve eight clams and four mussels in their shells for the garnish, then remove the rest from their shells.

6 Cook the pasta according to the instructions on the packet. Meanwhile, add 120ml/4fl oz/½ cup of the reserved seafood liquid to the tomato sauce. Bring the sauce to the boil over a high heat, stirring. Lower the heat, tear in the basil leaves and add the prawns with the shelled clams and mussels. Stir well, then taste for seasoning.

7 Drain the pasta and transfer it into a warmed bowl. Add the seafood sauce and toss well to combine. Serve in individual bowls, sprinkle with herbs and garnish each portion with two reserved clams and one mussel in their shells.

Spaghetti alle Vongole

Spaghetti with Clam Sauce

THIS IS ONE OF ITALY'S most famous pasta dishes, sometimes translated as "white clam sauce" to distinguish it from clams in tomato sauce. It is how they serve clams with pasta in Venice.

INGREDIENTS

1kg/2¼lb fresh clams
60ml/4 tbsp olive oil
45ml/3 tbsp chopped fresh flat leaf (Italian) parsley
120ml/4fl oz/½ cup dry white wine
350g/12oz dried spaghetti
2 garlic cloves
salt and ground black pepper
Serves 4

1 Scrub the clams under cold running water, discarding any that are open or that do not close when sharply tapped against the work surface.

2 Heat half the oil in a large pan, add the clams and 15ml/1 tbsp of the parsley and cook over a high heat for a few seconds. Pour in the wine, then cover tightly. Cook for about 5 minutes, shaking the pan frequently, until the clams have opened. Meanwhile, cook the pasta in salted boiling water according to the instructions on the packet.

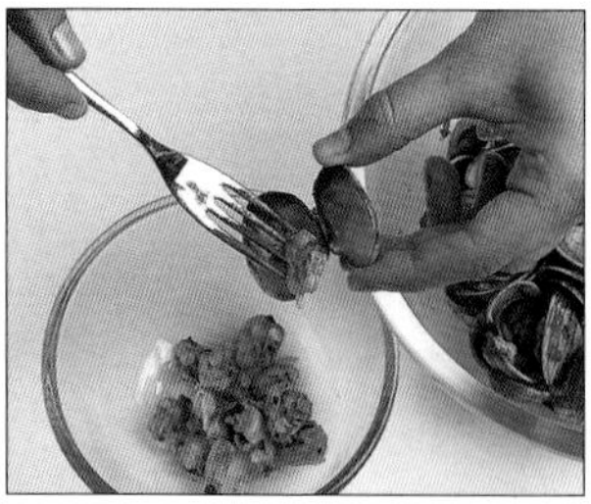

3 Using a slotted spoon, transfer the clams to a bowl, discarding any that have failed to open. Strain the liquid and set it aside. Put eight clams in their shells to one side for the garnish, then remove the rest from their shells.

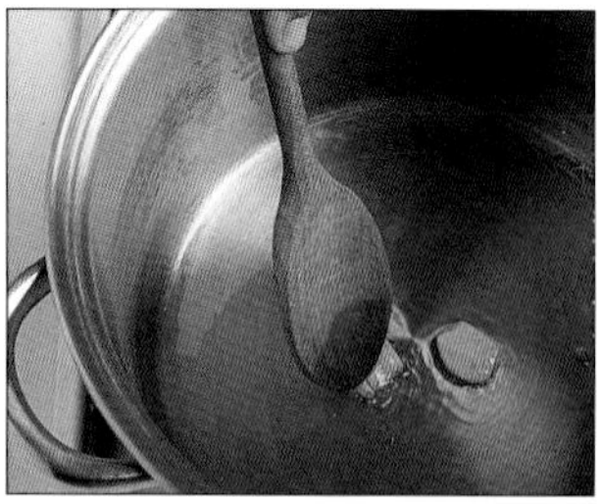

4 Heat the remaining oil in the clean pan. Fry the whole garlic cloves over a medium heat until golden, crushing them with the back of a spoon. Remove the garlic with a slotted spoon and discard.

5 Add the shelled clams to the oil remaining in the pan, gradually add some of the strained liquid from the clams, then add plenty of pepper. Cook for 1–2 minutes, gradually adding more liquid as the sauce reduces. Add the remaining parsley and cook for 1–2 minutes.

6 Drain the pasta, add it to the pan and toss well. Serve in individual dishes, scooping the shelled clams from the bottom of the pan and placing some of them on top of each serving. Garnish with the reserved clams in their shells and serve immediately.

Penne ai Gamberi e Carciofi

Penne with Prawns and Artichokes

THIS IS A GOOD DISH TO MAKE in early summer, when greeny-purple baby artichokes appear on market stalls.

INGREDIENTS

juice of 1/2 lemon
4 baby globe artichokes
90ml/6 tbsp olive oil
2 garlic cloves, crushed
30ml/2 tbsp chopped fresh mint
30ml/2 tbsp chopped fresh flat leaf (Italian) parsley
350g/12oz/3 cups dried penne
8–12 peeled cooked king or tiger prawns (jumbo shrimp), each cut into 2–3 pieces
25g/1oz/2 tbsp butter
salt and ground black pepper

Serves 4

1 Have ready a bowl of cold water to which you have added the lemon juice. To prepare the artichokes, cut off the artichoke stalks, if any, and cut across the tops of the leaves. Peel off and discard any tough or discoloured outer leaves.

2 Cut the artichokes lengthways into quarters and remove any hairy chokes from their centres. Finally, cut the pieces of artichoke lengthways into 5mm/1/4in slices and put these in the bowl of acidulated water.

3 Drain the slices of artichoke and pat them dry. Heat the olive oil in a non-stick frying pan and add the artichokes, the crushed garlic and half the mint and parsley to the pan.

4 Season with plenty of salt and pepper. Cook over a low heat, stirring frequently, for about 10 minutes or until the artichokes feel tender when pierced with a sharp knife.

5 Meanwhile, cook the pasta in a large pan of salted boiling water according to the instructions on the packet.

6 Add the prawns to the artichokes, stir well to mix, then heat through gently for 1–2 minutes.

7 Drain the pasta and transfer it into a warmed bowl. Add the butter and toss until it has melted. Spoon the artichoke mixture over the pasta and toss to combine. Serve immediately, sprinkled with the remaining herbs.

Pesce con Fregola

Fish with Fregola

THIS SARDINIAN SPECIALITY is a cross between a soup and a stew. Serve it with crusty Italian country bread to mop up the juices.

INGREDIENTS

75ml/5 tbsp olive oil
4 garlic cloves, finely chopped
½ small fresh red chilli, seeded and finely chopped
1 large handful fresh flat leaf (Italian) parsley, roughly chopped
1 red snapper, about 450g/1lb, cleaned, with head and tail removed
1 red or grey mullet (red snapper or pompano), about 500g/ 1¼lb, cleaned, with head and tail removed
350–450g/12oz–1lb thick cod fillet
400g/14oz can chopped Italian plum tomatoes
175g/6oz/1½ cups dried fregola
salt and ground black pepper

Serves 4–6

1 Heat 30ml/2 tbsp of the olive oil in a large flameproof casserole. Add the chopped garlic and chilli, with about half the chopped fresh parsley. Fry over a medium heat, stirring occasionally, for about 5 minutes.

2 Cut all of the fish into large chunks – including the skin and the bones in the case of the snapper and mullet – and add the pieces to the casserole as you cut them. Sprinkle the pieces with a further 30ml/2 tbsp of the olive oil and fry for a few minutes more.

3 Add the tomatoes, then fill the empty can with water and pour this into the pan. Bring to the boil. Stir in salt and pepper to taste, lower the heat and cook for 10 minutes, stirring occasionally.

4 Add the fregola and simmer for 5 minutes, then add 250ml/8fl oz/1 cup water and the remaining oil. Simmer for 15 minutes until the fregola is *al dente*.

5 If the sauce becomes too thick, add more water, then taste for seasoning. Serve hot, in warmed bowls, sprinkled with the remaining parsley.

COOK'S TIPS

- *You can make the basic fish sauce several hours in advance or even the day before, bringing it to the boil and adding ther fregola just before serving.*
- *Fregola is a tiny pasta shape from Sardinia. If you can't get it, use a tiny soup pasta* (pastina), *such as corallini or semi de melone.*

Farfalle al Sugo di Tonno

Farfalle with Tuna

A QUICK AND SIMPLE DISH that makes a good weekday supper if you have canned tomatoes and tuna in the storecupboard.

INGREDIENTS

30ml/2 tbsp olive oil
1 small onion, finely chopped
1 garlic clove, finely chopped
400g/14oz can chopped Italian plum tomatoes
45ml/3 tbsp dry white wine
8–10 pitted black olives, cut into rings
10ml/2 tsp chopped fresh oregano or 5ml/1 tsp dried oregano, plus extra fresh oregano to garnish
400g/14oz/3½ cups dried farfalle
175g/6oz can tuna in olive oil
salt and ground black pepper

Serves 4

1 Heat the olive oil in a medium pan, add the onion and garlic and fry gently for 2–3 minutes until the onion is soft and golden.

2 Add the plum tomatoes and bring to the boil, then add the white wine and simmer for a minute or so. Stir in the olives and oregano, with salt and pepper to taste, then cover and cook for 20–25 minutes, stirring from time to time.

3 Meanwhile, cook the pasta in a large pan of salted boiling water according to the instructions on the packet.

4 Drain the canned tuna and flake it with a fork. Add the tuna to the sauce with about 60ml/4 tbsp of the water used for cooking the pasta. Taste and adjust the seasoning.

5 Drain the cooked pasta well and transfer it into a warmed large serving bowl. Pour the tuna sauce over the top and toss to mix. Serve immediately, garnished with sprigs of oregano.

Paglia e Fieno con Salsa di Gamberi e Vodka

Paglia e Fieno with Prawns and Vodka

THE COMBINATION OF PRAWNS, vodka and pasta may seem unusual, but it has become something of a modern classic in Italy. Here it is stylishly presented with two-coloured pasta, but the sauce goes as well with short shapes such as penne and rigatoni.

INGREDIENTS

30ml/2 tbsp olive oil
1/4 large onion, finely chopped
1 garlic clove, crushed
15ml/1 tbsp sun-dried tomato purée (paste)
200ml/7fl oz/scant 1 cup panna da cucina or double (heavy) cream
350g/12oz fresh or dried paglia e fieno
12 raw tiger prawns (shrimp), peeled and chopped
30ml/2 tbsp vodka
salt and ground black pepper
Serves 4

1 Heat the oil in a medium pan, add the onion and garlic and cook gently, stirring frequently, for about 5 minutes until softened.

2 Add the tomato purée and stir for 1–2 minutes, then add the cream and bring to the boil, stirring. Season with salt and pepper to taste and let the sauce bubble until it starts to thicken slightly. Remove from the heat.

3 Cook the pasta according to the instructions on the packet. When it is almost ready, add the prawns and vodka to the sauce; toss quickly over a medium heat for 2–3 minutes until the prawns turn pink.

4 Drain the pasta and transfer it into a warmed bowl. Pour the sauce over and toss well. Divide among warmed bowls and serve immediately.

COOK'S TIP

This sauce is best served as soon as it is ready, otherwise the prawns (shrimp) will overcook and become tough. Make sure that the pasta has only a minute or two of cooking time left before adding the prawns to the sauce.

Penne, Panna e Salmone

Penne with Cream and Smoked Salmon

THIS MODERN WAY OF serving pasta is popular all over Italy. The three essential ingredients combine together beautifully, and the dish is very quick and easy to make.

INGREDIENTS

350g/12oz/3 cups dried penne
115g/4oz thinly sliced smoked salmon
2–3 fresh thyme sprigs
25g/1oz/2 tbsp butter
150ml/1/4 pint/2/3 cup extra-thick single (light) cream
salt and ground black pepper
Serves 4

1 Cook the pasta in a pan of salted boiling water according to the instructions on the packet.

2 Meanwhile, using kitchen scissors, cut the smoked salmon into thin strips, about 5mm/1/4in wide. Strip the leaves from the thyme sprigs.

3 Melt the butter in a large pan. Stir in the cream with about a quarter of the salmon and thyme leaves, then season with pepper. Heat gently for 3–4 minutes, stirring all the time. Do not allow to boil. Taste the sauce for seasoning.

4 Drain the pasta and toss it in the cream and salmon sauce. Divide among four warmed bowls and top with the remaining salmon and thyme leaves. Serve immediately.

VARIATION

Although penne is traditional with this sauce, it also goes very well with fresh ravioli stuffed with spinach and ricotta.

Spaghetti alla Bottarga

Spaghetti with Bottarga

ALTHOUGH THIS MAY SEEM an unusual recipe, with bottarga (salted and air-dried mullet or tuna roe) as the principal ingredient, it is very well known in Sardinia – and also in Sicily and parts of southern Italy. It is simplicity itself to make and tastes very, very good.

INGREDIENTS

350g/12oz fresh or dried spaghetti
about 60ml/4 tbsp olive oil
2–3 garlic cloves, peeled
ground black pepper
60–90ml/4–6 tbsp grated bottarga, to taste
Serves 4

1 Cook the pasta according to the instructions on the packet.

2 Meanwhile, heat half the olive oil in a large pan. Add the garlic and cook gently, stirring, for a few minutes. Remove the pan from the heat, scoop out the garlic with a slotted spoon and discard.

3 Drain the pasta very well. Return the pan of garlic-flavoured oil to the heat and add the pasta. Toss well, season with pepper and moisten with the remaining oil, or more to taste. Divide the pasta among four warmed bowls, sprinkle the grated bottarga over the top and serve immediately.

COOK'S TIP

You can buy bottarga in Italian delicatessens. Small jars of ready-grated bottarga are convenient, but the best flavour comes from vacuum-packed slices of mullet bottarga. This is very easy to grate on a box grater. Keep any leftover bottarga tightly wrapped in the refrigerator, so that it does not taint other foods.

Spaghetti alla Carrettiera

Spaghetti with Tuna, Mushrooms and Bacon

THE TERM ALLA CARRETTIERA means "cart-driver's style". The Romans lay claim to this recipe, but so do the Neapolitans and Sicilians, so there are many different versions of it.

INGREDIENTS

15g/½oz dried porcini mushrooms
175ml/6fl oz/¾ cup warm water
30ml/2 tbsp olive oil
1 garlic clove
75g/3oz pancetta or rindless streaky (fatty) bacon, cut into 5mm/¼in strips
225g/8oz/3 cups button (white) mushrooms, chopped
400g/14oz fresh or dried spaghetti
200g/7oz can tuna in olive oil, drained
salt and ground black pepper
freshly grated Parmesan cheese, to serve

Serves 4

1 Put the porcini in a small bowl. Pour over the warm water and leave to soak for 15–20 minutes.

2 Heat the oil in a large pan, add the garlic clove and cook gently for about 2 minutes, crushing it with a wooden spoon to release the flavour. Remove the garlic and discard. Add the pancetta or bacon to the oil remaining in the pan and cook for 3–4 minutes, stirring occasionally.

3 Meanwhile, drain the dried mushrooms, reserving the soaking liquid, and chop them finely.

4 Add both types of mushroom to the pan and cook, stirring, for 1–2 minutes, then add 90ml/6 tbsp of the reserved liquid from soaking the dried mushrooms, with salt and pepper to taste. Simmer for 10 minutes, stirring occasionally. Meanwhile, cook the pasta according to the instructions on the packet, adding the remaining soaking liquid from the mushrooms to the pasta cooking water.

5 Add the drained canned tuna to the mushroom sauce and fold it in gently. Taste for seasoning.

6 Drain the cooked pasta well and transfer it into a warmed serving bowl. Pour the sauce over the top, toss well and sprinkle liberally with some freshly grated Parmesan. Serve immediately, with more Parmesan handed around separately.

Capelli d'Angelo all'Aragosta

Capelli d'Angelo with Lobster

THIS IS A SOPHISTICATED, stylish dish for a special occasion. Some cooks make the sauce with champagne rather than sparkling white wine, especially when they are planning to serve champagne with the meal.

INGREDIENTS

meat from the body, tail and claws of 1 cooked lobster
juice of 1/2 lemon
40g/1 1/2oz/3 tbsp butter
4 fresh tarragon sprigs, leaves stripped and chopped
60ml/4 tbsp double (heavy) cream
90ml/6 tbsp sparkling dry white wine
60ml/4 tbsp fish stock
300g/11oz fresh capelli d'angelo
salt and ground black pepper
about 10ml/2 tsp lumpfish roe, to garnish (optional)

Serves 4

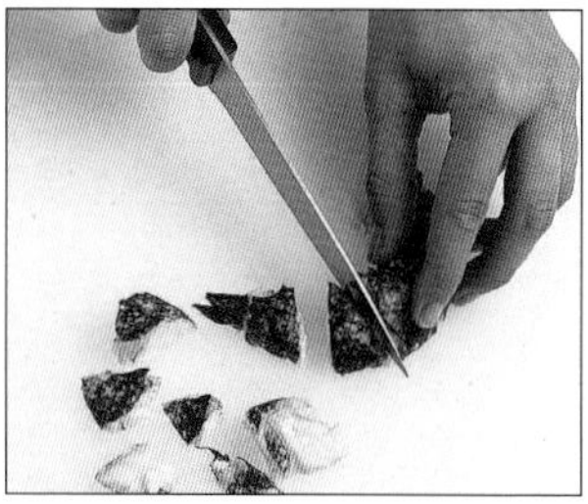

1 Cut the lobster meat into small pieces and put it in a bowl. Sprinkle with the lemon juice. Melt the butter in a frying pan, add the lobster meat and tarragon and stir over the heat for a few seconds. Add the cream and stir for a few seconds more, then pour in the wine and stock, with salt and pepper to taste. Simmer gently for 2 minutes, then remove from the heat and cover.

2 Cook the pasta according to the instructions on the packet. Drain well, reserving a few spoonfuls of the cooking water.

3 Place the pan of lobster sauce over a medium to high heat, add the pasta and toss for just long enough to combine and heat through; moisten with a little of the reserved water from the pasta. Serve immediately in warmed bowls, sprinkled with lumpfish roe if you like.

COOK'S TIP

To remove the meat from a lobster, place the lobster on a board with its underbelly facing uppermost. With a large sharp knife, cut the lobster in half lengthways. Spoon out the green liver and any pink roe (coral) and reserve these, then remove and discard the gravel sac (stomach). Pull the white tail meat out from either side of the shell and discard the black intestinal vein. Crack the claws with a nutcracker just below the pincers and remove the meat from the base. Pull away the small pincer, taking the white membrane with it, then remove the meat from this part of the shell. Pull the meat from the large pincer shell.

Linguine al Granchio

Linguine with Crab

THIS RECIPE COMES FROM Rome. It makes a very rich and tasty first course on its own, or can be served for a lunch or supper with crusty Italian bread. Some cooks like a finer sauce, and work the crabmeat through a sieve after pounding. If you fancy following their example, be warned – it's hard work.

INGREDIENTS

about 250g/9oz shelled crabmeat
45ml/3 tbsp olive oil
1 small handful fresh flat leaf (Italian) parsley, roughly chopped, plus extra to garnish
1 garlic clove, crushed
350g/12oz ripe Italian plum tomatoes, skinned and chopped
60–90ml/4–6 tbsp dry white wine
350g/12oz fresh or dried linguine
salt and ground black pepper
Serves 4

1 Put the crabmeat in a mortar and pound to a rough pulp with a pestle. If you do not have a mortar and pestle, use a sturdy bowl and the end of a rolling pin. Set aside.

2 Heat 30ml/2 tbsp of the oil in a large pan. Add the parsley and garlic, with salt and pepper to taste, and fry for a few minutes until the garlic begins to brown.

3 Add the tomatoes, pounded crabmeat and wine, cover the pan and simmer gently for 15 minutes, stirring occasionally.

4 Meanwhile, cook the pasta according to the instructions on the packet, draining it the moment it is *al dente*, and reserving a little of the cooking water.

5 Return the pasta to the clean pan, add the remaining oil and toss quickly over a medium heat until the oil coats the strands.

6 Add the tomato and crab mixture to the pasta and toss again, adding a little of the reserved cooking water if you think it necessary. Adjust the seasoning to taste. Serve hot, in warmed bowls, sprinkled with parsley.

COOK'S TIP

The best way to obtain crabmeat is to ask a fishmonger to remove it from the shell for you, or buy dressed crab from the supermarket. For this recipe you will need one large crab, and you should use both the white and dark meat.

Tagliatelle con Capesante

Tagliatelle with Scallops

SCALLOPS AND BRANDY MAKE this a relatively expensive dish, but it is so delicious that you will find it well worth the cost. Serve it for a dinner party first course.

INGREDIENTS

200g/7oz scallops, sliced
30ml/2 tbsp plain (all-purpose) flour
40g/1 1/2oz/3 tbsp butter
2 spring onions (scallions), cut into thin rings
1/2–1 small fresh red chilli, seeded and very finely chopped
30ml/2 tbsp finely chopped fresh flat leaf (Italian) parsley
60ml/4 tbsp brandy
105ml/7 tbsp fish stock
275g/10oz fresh spinach-flavoured tagliatelle
salt and ground black pepper
Serves 4

1 Toss the scallops in the flour, then shake off the excess. Bring a pan of salted water to the boil, ready for cooking the pasta.

2 Meanwhile, melt the butter in a frying pan. Add the spring onions, finely chopped chilli and half the parsley and fry, stirring frequently, for 1–2 minutes over a medium heat. Add the scallops and toss over the heat for 1–2 minutes.

3 Pour the brandy over the scallops, then set it alight with a match. As soon as the flames have died down, stir in the fish stock and salt and pepper to taste. Mix well. Simmer for 2–3 minutes, then cover the pan and remove it from the heat.

4 Add the pasta to the boiling water and cook it according to the instructions on the packet. Drain, add to the sauce and toss over a medium heat until mixed. Serve at once, in warmed bowls sprinkled with the remaining parsley.

COOK'S TIP

Buy fresh scallops, with their corals if possible. Fresh scallops always have a better texture and flavour than frozen scallops, which tend to be watery.

Spaghetti con Seppie e Piselli

Spaghetti with Squid and Peas

IN TUSCANY, SQUID IS often cooked with peas in a tomato sauce. This is a variation on this popular theme.

INGREDIENTS

450g/1lb prepared squid
30ml/2 tbsp olive oil
1 small onion, finely chopped
400g/14oz can chopped Italian plum tomatoes
1 garlic clove, finely chopped
15ml/1 tbsp red wine vinegar
5ml/1 tsp sugar
10ml/2 tsp finely chopped fresh rosemary
115g/4oz/1 cup frozen peas
350g/12oz fresh or dried spaghetti
15ml/1 tbsp chopped fresh flat leaf (Italian) parsley
salt and ground black pepper
Serves 4

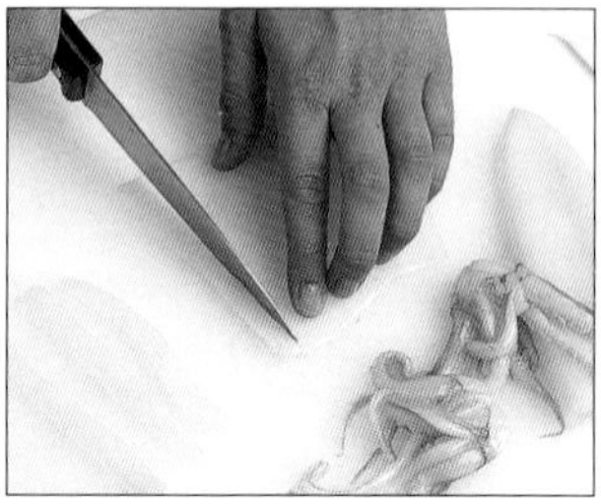

1 Cut the prepared squid into strips about 5mm/1/4in wide. Finely chop any tentacles.

2 Heat the oil in a frying pan, add the finely chopped onion and cook gently, stirring, for about 5 minutes until softened. Add the squid, tomatoes, garlic, red wine vinegar and sugar.

3 Add the rosemary, with salt and pepper to taste. Bring to the boil, stirring, then cover and simmer gently for 20 minutes. Uncover the pan, add the peas and cook for 10 minutes. Meanwhile, cook the pasta according to the instructions on the packet, then drain and transfer it into a warmed bowl. Pour the sauce over, add the parsley, then toss well and serve.

Spaghetti con Salmone e Gamberi

Spaghetti with Salmon and Prawns

THIS IS A LOVELY FRESH-TASTING pasta dish, perfect for an *al fresco* meal in summer. Serve it for lunch with warm ciabatta and a dry white wine.

INGREDIENTS

300g/11oz salmon fillet
200ml/7fl oz/scant 1 cup dry white wine
a few fresh basil sprigs, plus extra basil leaves, to garnish
6 ripe Italian plum tomatoes, peeled and finely chopped
150ml/¼ pint/⅔ cup double (heavy) cream
350g/12oz/3 cups fresh or dried spaghetti
115g/4oz/⅔ cup peeled cooked prawns (shrimp), thawed and thoroughly dried if frozen
salt and ground black pepper

Serves 4

1 Put the salmon skin side up in a wide shallow pan. Pour the wine over, then add the basil sprigs to the pan and sprinkle the fish with salt and pepper. Bring the wine to the boil, cover the pan and simmer gently for no more than 5 minutes. Using a fish slice or metal spatula, lift the fish out of the pan and set aside to cool a little.

2 Add the cream and tomatoes to the liquid remaining in the pan and bring to the boil. Stir well, then lower the heat and simmer, uncovered, for 10–15 minutes. Meanwhile, cook the pasta according to the instructions on the packet.

3 Flake the fish into large chunks, discarding the skin and any bones. Add the fish to the sauce with the prawns, shaking the pan until the fish and shellfish are well coated. Taste the sauce for seasoning.

4 Drain the pasta and transfer it into a warmed bowl. Pour the sauce over the pasta and toss to combine. Serve immediately, garnished with fresh basil leaves.

COOK'S TIP

Check the salmon fillet carefully for small bones when you are flaking the flesh. Although the salmon is already filleted, you will always find a few stray "pin" bones. Pick them out carefully using tweezers or your fingertips.

Tagliolini con Vongole e Cozze

Tagliolini with Clams and Mussels

SERVED ON WHITE CHINA, this makes a stunning looking dish for a dinner party first course. The sauce can be prepared a few hours ahead of time, then the pasta cooked and the dish assembled at the last minute.

INGREDIENTS

450g/1lb fresh mussels
450g/1lb fresh clams
60ml/4 tbsp olive oil
1 small onion, finely chopped
2 garlic cloves, finely chopped
1 large handful fresh flat leaf (Italian) parsley, plus extra parsley to garnish
175ml/6fl oz/¾ cup dry white wine
250ml/8fl oz/1 cup fish stock
1 small fresh red chilli, seeded and chopped
350g/12oz squid ink tagliolini or tagliatelle
salt and ground black pepper

Serves 4

1 Scrub the mussels and clams under cold running water and discard any that are open or damaged, or that do not close when sharply tapped against the work surface.

2 Heat half the oil in a large pan, add the onion and cook gently for about 5 minutes until softened. Sprinkle in the garlic, then add about half the parsley sprigs, with salt and pepper to taste. Add the mussels and clams and pour in the wine. Cover with the lid and bring to the boil over a high heat. Cook for about 5 minutes, shaking the pan frequently, until the shellfish have opened.

3 Place the mussels and clams in a fine sieve (strainer) set over a bowl and let the liquid drain through. Discard the aromatics in the sieve, together with any mussels or clams that failed to open. Return the liquid to the clean pan and add the fish stock. Chop the remaining parsley and add it to the liquid with the chopped chilli. Bring to the boil, then lower the heat and simmer, stirring, for a few minutes until slightly reduced. Turn off the heat.

4 Remove and discard the top shells from about half the mussels and clams. Put all the mussels and clams in the pan of liquid and seasonings, then cover the pan tightly and set aside.

5 Cook the pasta according to the instructions on the packet.

6 Drain well, then return to the clean pan; toss with the remaining olive oil. Put the pan of shellfish over a high heat and toss to quickly heat the shellfish through and combine with the liquid and seasonings.

7 Divide the pasta among four warmed plates, spoon the shellfish mixture over and around, then serve immediately, sprinkled with parsley.

Meat and Poultry

When we think of a meat sauce to serve with pasta, our minds automatically turn to Bolognese sauce, or *ragù alla Bolognese*, as it is correctly called in Italian. Thanks to Italian emigrés, Bolognese sauce has become one of the most famous pasta sauces outside Italy, especially in Great Britain and the United States. Beef, pork and pancetta simmered with wine and tomatoes until rich, intensely meaty and satisfying, is very hard to beat. Unfortunately, this superb sauce is almost always served with spaghetti outside Italy, which is incorrect. It should be teamed with tagliatelle.

Many meat sauces hail from the north of Italy, especially from the region of Emilia-Romagna, where both fresh meat and the famous hams, salami and sausages are enjoyed in abundance. The actual quantity of meat in the sauce is never very large, however, and the size of the pieces must be small or the sauce will simply slide off the pasta. The egg-enriched pasta of the northern regions is good with meat sauces because it holds the sauce well, but it is by no means the only possibility. Long, thin types of pasta, such as spaghetti and vermicelli, find favour precisely because they do not hold a great deal of sauce with each forkful, a point worth considering when a sauce is very rich.

Tagliatelle alla Bolognese

Tagliatelle with Meat Sauce

THIS RECIPE IS AN authentic meat sauce – ragù – from the city of Bologna in Emilia-Romagna. It is very rich, and is always served with tagliatelle, never with spaghetti.

INGREDIENTS

450g/1lb fresh or dried tagliatelle
salt and ground black pepper
freshly grated Parmesan cheese, to serve

For the Bolognese meat sauce

1 onion
2 carrots
2 celery sticks
2 garlic cloves
25g/1oz/2 tbsp butter
15ml/1 tbsp olive oil
130g/4½oz pancetta or rindless streaky (fatty) bacon, diced
250g/9oz lean minced (ground) beef
250g/9oz lean minced (ground) pork
120ml/4fl oz/½ cup dry white wine
2 x 400g/14oz cans crushed Italian plum tomatoes
475–750ml/16fl oz–1¼ pints/2–3 cups beef stock
100ml/3½fl oz/scant ½ cup panna da cucina or double (heavy) cream

Serves 6–8

1 Make the meat sauce. Chop all the fresh vegetables finely. Heat the butter and oil in a frying pan until sizzling. Add the vegetables and the pancetta or bacon and cook over a medium heat, stirring frequently, for 10 minutes or until the vegetables have softened.

2 Add the minced beef and pork, lower the heat and cook gently for 10 minutes, stirring frequently and breaking up any lumps in the meat with a wooden spoon. Stir in salt and pepper to taste, then add the wine and stir again. Simmer for about 5 minutes, or until reduced.

3 Add the canned tomatoes and 250ml/8fl oz/1 cup of the beef stock and bring to the boil. Stir the sauce well, then lower the heat. Half cover the pan with a lid and leave to simmer very gently for 2 hours. Stir occasionally during this time and add more stock as it becomes absorbed.

4 Pour the cream into the sauce, stir well to mix, then simmer, without a lid, for another 30 minutes, stirring frequently. Meanwhile, cook the pasta according to the packet instructions. Taste the sauce to check the seasoning. Drain the cooked pasta and transfer it into a warmed bowl. Pour the sauce over and toss well. Serve immediately, sprinkled with grated Parmesan.

VARIATION

Some cooks add a few chopped chicken livers when frying the meat at the beginning of Step 2. This gives the sauce a stronger, almost gamey, flavour.

Spaghetti con Polpettine

Spaghetti with Meatballs

Meatballs simmered in a sweet and spicy tomato sauce are truly delicious with spaghetti. Children love them and you can easily leave out the chillies.

INGREDIENTS

350g/12oz minced (ground) beef
1 egg
60ml/4 tbsp roughly chopped fresh flat leaf (Italian) parsley
2.5ml/½ tsp crushed dried red chillies
1 thick slice white bread, crusts removed
30ml/2 tbsp milk
about 30ml/2 tbsp olive oil
300ml/½ pint/1¼ cups passata (bottled strained tomatoes)
400ml/14fl oz/1¾ cups vegetable stock
5ml/1 tsp sugar
350–450g/12oz–1lb fresh or dried spaghetti
salt and ground black pepper
freshly grated Parmesan cheese, to serve

Serves 6–8

1 Put the minced beef in a large bowl. Add the egg, and half the parsley and half the crushed chillies. Season with plenty of salt and pepper.

2 Tear the bread into small pieces and place in a small bowl. Moisten with the milk. Leave to soak for a few minutes, then squeeze out the excess milk and crumble the bread over the meat mixture. Mix everything together with a wooden spoon, then use your hands to squeeze and knead the mixture so that it becomes smooth and quite sticky.

3 Wash your hands, rinse them under the cold tap, then pick up small pieces of the mixture and roll them between your palms to make about 40–60 small balls. Place the meatballs on a tray and chill in the fridge for about 30 minutes.

4 Heat the oil in a large non-stick frying pan. Cook the meatballs in batches until browned on all sides. Pour the passata and stock into a large pan. Heat gently, then add the remaining chillies and the sugar, with salt and pepper to taste. Add the meatballs to the passata mixture, then bring to the boil. Lower the heat and cover. Simmer for 20 minutes.

5 Cook the pasta according to the packet instructions. When it is *al dente*, drain and transfer it into a warmed large bowl. Pour the sauce over the pasta and toss gently. Sprinkle with the remaining parsley and serve with grated Parmesan handed separately.

Ragù d'Agnello e Peperoni

Lamb and Sweet Pepper Sauce

THIS SIMPLE SAUCE is a speciality of the Abruzzo-Molise region, east of Rome, where it is traditionally served with *maccheroni alla chitarra* – square-shaped long macaroni.

INGREDIENTS

60ml/4 tbsp olive oil
250g/9oz boneless lamb neck fillet, diced quite small
2 garlic cloves, finely chopped
2 bay leaves, torn
250ml/8fl oz/1 cup dry white wine
4 ripe Italian plum tomatoes, peeled and chopped
2 large red (bell) peppers, seeded and diced
salt and ground black pepper

Serves 4–6

1 Heat half the olive oil in a frying, add the small pieces of lamb and sprinkle with a little salt and pepper. Cook the meat over a medium to high heat for about 10 minutes, stirring often, until it is browned on all sides.

2 Sprinkle in the garlic and add the bay leaves, then pour in the wine and let it bubble until reduced.

3 Add the remaining oil, the tomatoes and the peppers; stir to mix with the lamb. Season again. Cover with the lid and simmer over a low heat for 45–55 minutes or until the lamb is very tender. Stir occasionally during cooking and moisten with water if the sauce becomes too dry. Remove the bay leaves from the sauce before serving it with pasta.

COOK'S TIPS

- *The peppers don't have to be red. Use yellow, orange or green if you prefer; either one colour or a mixture.*
- *If you need to add water to the sauce towards the end of cooking, take it from the pan used for cooking the pasta.*
- *You can make your own fresh* maccheroni alla chitarra *or buy the dried pasta from an Italian delicatessen. Alternatively, this sauce is just as good with ordinary long or short macaroni. You will need 350–425g/12–15oz.*

Fusilli con Salsicce

Fusilli with Sausage

SPICY HOT SAUSAGE and tomato sauce combine with spirals of pasta to make this really tasty dish from southern Italy. Pecorino cheese, with its strong and salty flavour, is the perfect accompaniment. Serve with a full-bodied red wine and crusty country bread.

INGREDIENTS

400g/14oz spicy pork sausages
30ml/2 tbsp olive oil
1 small onion, finely chopped
2 garlic cloves, crushed
1 large yellow (bell) pepper, seeded and cut into strips
5ml/1 tsp paprika
5ml/1 tsp dried mixed herbs
5–10ml/1–2 tsp chilli sauce
400g/14oz can Italian plum tomatoes
250–300ml/8–10fl oz/1–1¼ cups vegetable stock
300g/11oz/2¾ cups fresh or dried fusilli
salt and ground black pepper
freshly grated Pecorino cheese, to serve
Serves 4

1 Grill (broil) the sausages for about 10–12 minutes until they are browned on all sides, then drain them on kitchen paper.

2 Heat the oil in a frying pan, add the onion and garlic and cook over a low heat, stirring frequently, for 5–7 minutes until soft. Add the yellow pepper, paprika, herbs and chilli sauce to taste. Cook gently for 5–7 minutes, stirring occasionally.

3 Add in the canned tomatoes, breaking them up with a wooden spoon, then add salt and pepper to taste and stir well. Cook over a medium heat for 10–12 minutes, adding the vegetable stock gradually as the sauce reduces.

4 While the tomato sauce is cooking, cut the grilled sausages diagonally into 1cm/½in pieces.

5 Add the sausage pieces to the sauce, reduce the heat to low and cook for 10 minutes. Meanwhile, cook the pasta according to the instructions on the packet.

6 Taste the sauce for seasoning. Drain the pasta and add it to the pan of sauce. Toss well, then divide among four warmed bowls. Sprinkle each serving with a little grated Pecorino and serve immediately, with more Pecorino handed separately.

Malloreddus

Sardinian Sausage and Pasta

IN SARDINIA THEY CALL this dish simply "malloreddus", which is the local name for the type of pasta traditionally used to make it.

INGREDIENTS

30ml/2 tbsp olive oil
6 garlic cloves
200g/7oz Italian pure pork sausage, diced small
2 small handfuls fresh basil leaves
400g/14oz can chopped Italian plum tomatoes
a good pinch of saffron threads
15ml/1 tbsp sugar
350g/12oz/3 cups dried malloreddus *(gnocchi sardi)*
75g/3oz/1 cup freshly grated Pecorino Sardo cheese
salt and ground black pepper

Serves 4–6

1 Heat the oil in a frying pan. Add the garlic, sausage and half the basil leaves. Fry, stirring frequently, until the sausage is browned all over. Remove and discard the garlic. Add the tomatoes. Fill the empty can with water, pour it into the pan, then stir in the saffron, sugar, 5ml/1 tsp salt and pepper to taste. Bring to the boil, lower the heat and simmer for about 20–30 minutes, stirring occasionally.

2 Meanwhile, cook the pasta in a pan of salted boiling water according to the packet instructions.

3 Drain the pasta and transfer it into a warmed bowl. Taste the sauce for seasoning, pour it over the pasta and toss well. Add about one-third of the grated Pecorino and the remaining basil and toss well to mix again. Serve immediately, with the remaining pecorino sprinkled on top.

COOK'S TIP

In Sardinia, a special type of sausage is used for malloreddus. *It is flavoured with aniseed and black pepper and is called* sartizzu sardo. *A good alternative to* sartizzu sardo *would be the piquant* salsiccia piccante. *If, however, you prefer a slightly milder flavour, try* luganega, *which is much more widely available. Some butchers make their own Italian-style sausage on the premises, in which case you can always ask the butcher if he will season it for you with aniseed and black pepper if you want to try and create the authentic taste for yourself.*

Rigatoni alla Bresàola e Peperoni

Rigatoni with Bresàola and Peppers

BRESÀOLA – CURED RAW BEEF – is usually served thinly sliced as an antipasto. Here its strong, almost gamey, flavour is used to good effect.

INGREDIENTS

30ml/2 tbsp olive oil
1 small onion, finely chopped
150g/5oz bresàola*, cut into thin strips*
4 (bell) peppers, red and orange or yellow, diced
120ml/4fl oz/½ cup dry white wine
400g/14oz can chopped plum tomatoes
450g/1lb/4 cups dried rigatoni
50g/2oz/⅔ cup shaved Parmesan cheese
1 small handful fresh basil leaves
salt and ground black pepper

Serves 6

1 Heat the oil in a medium pan, add the onion and *bresàola*. Cover the pan and cook over a low heat for 5–8 minutes until the onion has softened. Add the peppers, wine, 5ml/1 tsp salt and plenty of pepper. Stir well, then simmer for 10–15 minutes.

2 Add the canned tomatoes to the pan and increase the heat to high. Bring to the boil, stirring, then lower the heat and replace the lid again. Simmer gently, stirring occasionally, for 20 minutes or until the peppers are very soft and quite creamy. Meanwhile, cook the pasta in a pan of salted boiling water according to the instructions on the packet.

3 Drain the cooked pasta and transfer it into a warmed bowl. Taste the sauce for seasoning, then pour over the pasta and add half the Parmesan. Toss well and serve immediately, with the basil leaves and the remaining Parmesan sprinkled on top.

Bucatini alla Posillipo

Bucatini with Sausage and Pancetta

This is a very rich and satisfying main course dish. Grated Parmesan cheese makes an excellent accompaniment, so you can hand some round in a separate bowl if you wish.

INGREDIENTS

115g/4oz pork sausage meat (bulk sausage)
400g/14oz can Italian plum tomatoes
15ml/1 tbsp olive oil
1 garlic clove, crushed
115g/4oz pancetta or rindless streaky (fatty) bacon, roughly chopped
30ml/2 tbsp chopped fresh flat leaf (Italian) parsley
400g/14oz dried bucatini
60–75ml/4–5 tbsp panna da cucina *or double (heavy) cream*
2 egg yolks
salt and ground black pepper

Serves 4

1 Remove any skin from the sausage-meat and break the meat up roughly with a knife. Purée the tomatoes in a food processor or blender.

2 Heat the oil in a frying pan, add the garlic and fry over a low heat for 1–2 minutes. Remove the garlic from the pan with a slotted spoon and discard it.

3 Add the pork sausage meat and pancetta or bacon and cook over a medium heat for 3–4 minutes. Stir constantly with a wooden spoon to break up the sausage meat – it will become brown and look crumbly.

4 Add the puréed tomatoes to the pan with half the parsley and salt and pepper to taste. Stir well and bring to the boil, scraping up any sediment from the sausage meat that has stuck to the bottom of the pan.

5 Lower the heat, cover and simmer for 30 minutes, stirring from time to time. Taste the sausage meat sauce for seasoning.

6 Meanwhile, cook the pasta according to the instructions on the packet. Put the cream and egg yolks in a warmed large bowl and mix with a fork. As soon as the pasta is *al dente*, drain it well and add it to the bowl of cream mixture. Toss until the pasta is coated, then pour the sausage meat sauce over the pasta and toss again. Serve immediately, sprinkled with the remaining parsley.

COOK'S TIPS

- *To save time puréeing the tomatoes, use passata (bottled strained tomatoes).*
- *For authenticity, buy* salsiccia a metro, *a pure pork sausage sold by the metre at Italian delicatessens.*
- *Bucatini is a long hollow pasta that looks like hard drinking straws; spaghetti works equally well.*

Rigatoni con Ragù di Maiale

Rigatoni with Pork

THIS IS AN EXCELLENT meat sauce using minced pork rather than the more usual minced beef. Here it is served with rigatoni, a short tubular pasta shape, but you could serve it with tagliatelle or spaghetti to make a pork version of Bolognese.

INGREDIENTS

1 small onion
½ carrot
½ celery stick
2 garlic cloves
25g/1oz/2 tbsp butter
30ml/2 tbsp olive oil
150g/5oz minced (ground) pork
60ml/4 tbsp dry white wine
400g/14oz can chopped Italian plum tomatoes
a few fresh basil leaves, plus extra basil leaves, to garnish
400g/14oz/3½ cups dried rigatoni
salt and ground black pepper
freshly shaved Parmesan cheese, to serve

Serves 4

1 Chop all the fresh vegetables finely, either in a food processor or by hand. Heat the butter and oil in a large frying pan until just sizzling, add the chopped vegetables and cook over a medium heat, stirring frequently, for 3–4 minutes.

2 Add the minced pork and cook gently for 2–3 minutes, breaking up any lumps in the meat with a wooden spoon.

3 Lower the heat and fry for a further 2–3 minutes, stirring frequently, then stir in the wine. Mix in the tomatoes, whole basil leaves, salt to taste and plenty of pepper. Bring to the boil, then lower the heat, cover and simmer for 40 minutes, stirring from time to time.

4 Cook the pasta according to the instructions on the packet. Just before draining it, add a ladleful or two of the cooking water to the sauce. Stir well, then taste the sauce for seasoning.

5 Drain the pasta, add it to the pan of sauce and toss well. Serve immediately, sprinkled with the basil and shaved Parmesan.

VARIATION

To give the sauce a more intense flavour, soak 15g/½oz dried porcini mushrooms in 175ml/ 6fl oz/¾ cup warm water for 15–20 minutes, then drain, chop and add with the meat.

Eliche con Salsiccie e Radicchio

Eliche with Sausage and Radicchio

SAUSAGE AND RADICCHIO may seem odd companions, but the combined flavour of these hearty ingredients is really delicious.

INGREDIENTS

30ml/2 tbsp olive oil
1 onion, finely chopped
200g/7oz Italian pure pork sausage
175ml/6fl oz/¾ cup passata (bottled strained tomatoes)
90ml/6 tbsp dry white wine
300g/11oz/2¾ cups dried eliche
50g/2oz radicchio leaves
salt and ground black pepper

Serves 4

1 Heat the olive oil in a large, deep frying pan. Add the finely chopped onion and cook over a low heat, stirring frequently, for about 5 minutes until softened.

2 Cut the end off the sausage skin and squeeze the sausage meat into the pan. With a wooden spoon, stir the sausage meat to mix it with the oil and onion and break it up.

3 Continue to fry the mixture, increasing the heat if necessary, until the sausage meat is brown all over and looks crumbly. Stir in the passata, then sprinkle in the wine, with salt and pepper to taste. Simmer over a low heat, stirring occasionally, for 10–12 minutes.

4 Meanwhile, cook the pasta according to the instructions on the packet. Just before draining the pasta, add a ladleful or two of the cooking water to the sausage sauce and stir it in well. Taste the sauce to check the seasoning.

5 Finely shred the radicchio leaves. Drain the cooked pasta and transfer it into the pan of sausage sauce. Add the shredded radicchio and toss well to combine everything together. Serve immediately.

COOK'S TIPS

- *The best sausage to use is the one you buy from the Italian delicatessen called* salsiccia puro suino. *It is made from 100 per cent pure pork plus flavourings and seasonings.*
- *If you can get it, use the long, tapering* radicchio di Treviso *for this dish; otherwise the tightly furled, round radicchio can be used.*

Spaghetti Bolognese

Spaghetti with Minced Beef Sauce

Spaghetti Bolognese is not an authentic Italian dish. It was "invented" by Italian emigrés in America in the sixties in response to popular demand for a spaghetti dish with meat sauce. This is a rich, spicy version.

INGREDIENTS

30ml/2 tbsp olive oil
1 onion, finely chopped
1 garlic clove, crushed
5ml/1 tsp dried mixed herbs
1.25ml/¼ tsp cayenne pepper
350–450g/12oz–1lb minced (ground) beef
400g/14oz can chopped Italian plum tomatoes
45ml/3 tbsp tomato ketchup
15ml/1 tbsp sun-dried tomato purée (paste)
5ml/1 tsp Worcestershire sauce
5ml/1 tsp dried oregano
450ml/¾ pint/1¾ cups beef or vegetable stock
45ml/3 tbsp red wine
400–450g/14oz–1lb dried spaghetti
salt and ground black pepper
freshly grated Parmesan cheese, to serve

Serves 4–6

1 Heat the oil in a medium pan, add the onion and garlic and cook over a low heat, stirring frequently, for about 5 minutes until softened. Stir in the mixed herbs and cayenne and cook for 2–3 minutes more. Add the minced beef and cook gently for about 5 minutes, stirring frequently and breaking up any lumps in the meat with a wooden spoon.

2 Stir in the canned tomatoes, ketchup, sun-dried tomato purée, Worcestershire sauce, oregano and plenty of black pepper. Pour in the stock and red wine and bring to the boil, stirring. Cover the pan, lower the heat and leave the sauce to simmer for 30 minutes, stirring occasionally.

3 Cook the pasta according to the instructions on the packet. Drain well and divide among warmed bowls. Taste the sauce and add a little salt if necessary, then spoon it on top of the pasta and sprinkle with a little grated Parmesan. Serve immediately, with grated Parmesan handed separately.

Tortellini con Prosciutto

Tortellini with Ham

THIS IS A VERY EASY RECIPE that can be made quickly from storecupboard ingredients. It is therefore ideal for an after-work supper.

INGREDIENTS

250g/9oz packet tortellini alla carne *(meat-filled tortellini)*
30ml/2 tbsp olive oil
1/4 large onion, finely chopped
115g/4oz cooked ham, diced
150ml/1/4 pint/2/3 cup strained crushed Italian plum tomatoes
100ml/3 1/2fl oz/scant 1/2 cup panna da cucina or double (heavy) cream
about 90g/3 1/2oz/generous 1 cup freshly grated Parmesan cheese
salt and ground black pepper
Serves 4

1 Cook the pasta according to the instructions on the packet.

2 Meanwhile, heat the oil in a large frying pan, add the onion and cook over a low heat, stirring frequently, for about 5 minutes until softened. Add the ham and cook, stirring occasionally, until it darkens.

3 Add the strained crushed tomatoes. Fill the empty carton with water and pour it into the pan. Stir well, then add salt and pepper to taste. Bring to the boil, lower the heat and simmer the sauce for a few minutes, stirring occasionally, until it has reduced slightly. Stir in the cream. Drain the pasta well and add it to the sauce.

4 Add a handful of grated Parmesan to the pan. Stir, toss well and taste for seasoning. Serve in warmed bowls, topped with the remaining Parmesan.

COOK'S TIP

Cartons of strained crushed tomatoes are handy for making quick sauces.

Ragù al Vino Rosso

Bolognese Sauce with Red Wine

THIS IS A VERSATILE meat sauce. You can toss it with freshly cooked pasta – the quantity here is enough for 450g/1lb tagliatelle, spaghetti penne or fusilli – or layer it in a lasagne.

INGREDIENTS

1 onion
1 small carrot
1 celery stick
2 garlic cloves
45ml/3 tbsp olive oil
400g/14oz minced (ground) beef
120ml/4fl oz/1/2 cup red wine
200ml/7fl oz/scant 1 cup passata (bottled strained tomatoes)
15ml/1 tbsp tomato purée (paste)
5ml/1 tsp dried oregano
15ml/1 tbsp chopped fresh flat leaf (Italian) parsley
about 350ml/12fl oz/1 1/2 cups beef stock
8 baby Italian tomatoes (optional)
salt and ground black pepper
Serves 4–6

1 Chop all the vegetables finely, either in a food processor or by hand. Heat the oil in a large pan, add the chopped vegetable mixture and cook over a low heat, stirring frequently, for about 5–7 minutes.

2 Add the minced beef and cook for 5 minutes, stirring frequently and breaking up any lumps in the meat with a wooden spoon. Stir in the wine and mix well.

3 Cook for 1–2 minutes, then add the passata, tomato purée, herbs and 60ml/4 tbsp of the stock. Season with salt and pepper to taste. Stir well and bring to the boil.

4 Cover the pan, and cook over a gentle heat for 30 minutes, stirring from time to time and adding more stock as necessary. Add the tomatoes, if using, and simmer for 5–10 minutes more. Taste for seasoning and toss with hot, freshly cooked pasta, or use in baked pasta dishes.

Fettuccine al Prosciutto e Piselli

Fettuccine with Ham and Peas

THIS SIMPLE DISH MAKES a very good first course for six people, or a main course for three to four. The ingredients are all easily available from the supermarket, so the recipe makes an ideal impromptu supper.

INGREDIENTS

50g/2oz/¼ cup butter
1 small onion, finely chopped
200g/7oz/1¾ cups fresh or frozen peas
100ml/3½fl oz/scant ½ cup chicken stock
2.5ml/½ tsp sugar
175ml/6fl oz/¾ cup dry white wine
350g/12oz fresh fettuccine
75g/3oz piece cooked ham, cut into bitesize chunks
115g/4oz/1⅓ cups freshly grated Parmesan cheese
salt and ground black pepper

Serves 3–6

1 Melt the butter in a frying pan, add the onion and cook over a low heat for about 5 minutes until softened but not coloured. Add the peas, stock and sugar, with salt and pepper to taste.

2 Bring to the boil, then lower the heat and simmer for 3–5 minutes or until the peas are tender. Add the wine, increase the heat and boil until the wine has reduced.

3 Cook the pasta according to the instructions on the packet. When it is almost ready, add the ham to the sauce, with about a third of the grated Parmesan. Heat through, stirring, then taste for seasoning.

4 Drain the pasta and transfer it into a warmed large bowl. Pour the sauce over the pasta and toss well. Serve immediately, sprinkled with the remaining grated Parmesan.

Pappardelle con Sugo di Coniglio

Pappardelle with Rabbit Sauce

THIS RICH-TASTING DISH comes from the north of Italy, where rabbit sauces for pasta are very popular.

INGREDIENTS

15g/½oz dried porcini mushrooms
175ml/6fl oz/¾ cup warm water
1 small onion
½ carrot
½ celery stick
2 bay leaves
25g/1oz/2 tbsp butter
15ml/1 tbsp olive oil
40g/1½oz pancetta or rindless streaky (fatty) bacon, chopped
15ml/1 tbsp roughly chopped fresh flat leaf (Italian) parsley, plus extra to garnish
250g/9oz boneless rabbit meat
90ml/6 tbsp dry white wine
200g/7oz can chopped Italian plum tomatoes or 200ml/7fl oz/scant 1 cup passata (bottled strained tomatoes)
300g/11oz fresh or dried pappardelle
salt and ground black pepper

Serves 4

1 Put the dried mushrooms in a bowl, pour over the warm water and leave to soak for 15–20 minutes. Finely chop the vegetables, either in a food processor or by hand. Make a tear in each bay leaf, so that they will release their flavour when added to the sauce.

2 Heat the butter and oil in a frying pan until just sizzling. Add the chopped vegetables, pancetta or bacon and the parsley and cook for about 5 minutes.

3 Add the pieces of rabbit and fry on both sides for 3–4 minutes. Pour the wine over and let it reduce for a few minutes, then add the tomatoes or passata. Drain the mushrooms and pour the soaking liquid into the pan. Chop the mushrooms and add them to the mixture, with the bay leaves and salt and pepper to taste. Stir well, cover and simmer for 35–40 minutes until the rabbit is tender, stirring occasionally.

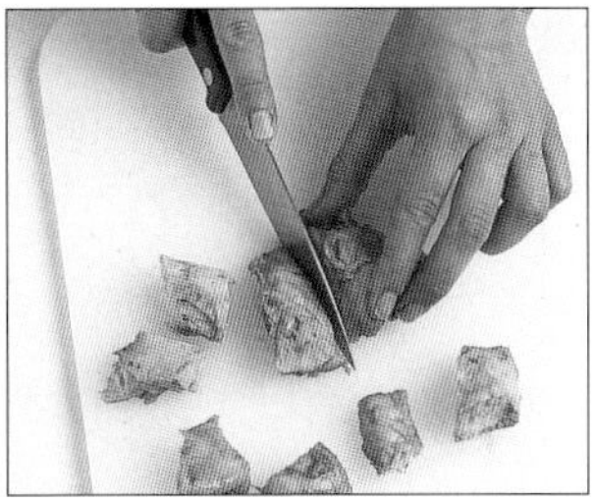

4 Remove the pan from the heat and lift out the pieces of rabbit with a slotted spoon. Cut them into bitesize chunks and stir them into the sauce. Remove and discard the bay leaves. Taste the sauce and add more salt and pepper, if needed. Cook the pasta according to the instructions on the packet. Meanwhile, reheat the sauce. Drain the pasta and toss with the sauce in a warmed bowl. Serve immediately, sprinkled with parsley.

Farfalle con Pollo e Pomodorini

Farfalle with Chicken and Cherry Tomatoes

QUICK TO PREPARE and easy to cook, this colourful dish is full of flavour. Serve it for a midweek supper, with a green salad to follow.

INGREDIENTS

350g/12oz skinless chicken breast fillets, cut into bitesize pieces
60ml/4 tbsp Italian dry vermouth
10ml/2 tsp chopped fresh rosemary, plus 4 fresh rosemary sprigs, to garnish
15ml/1 tbsp olive oil
1 onion, finely chopped
90g/3½oz piece Italian salami, diced
275g/10oz/2½ cups dried farfalle
15ml/1 tbsp balsamic vinegar
400g/14oz can Italian cherry tomatoes
good pinch of crushed dried red chillies
salt and ground black pepper

Serves 4

1 Put the pieces of chicken in a large bowl, pour in the dry vermouth and sprinkle with half the chopped rosemary and salt and pepper to taste. Stir well and set aside.

2 Heat the oil in a frying pan, add the onion and salami and fry over a medium heat for about 5 minutes, stirring frequently.

3 Cook the pasta according to the instructions on the packet.

4 Add the chicken and vermouth to the onion and salami, increase the heat to high and fry for 3 minutes or until the chicken is white on all sides. Sprinkle the vinegar over the chicken.

5 Add the cherry tomatoes and dried chillies. Stir well and simmer for a few minutes more. Taste the sauce for seasoning.

6 Drain the pasta and transfer it into the frying pan. Add the remaining chopped rosemary and toss to mix the pasta and sauce together. Serve immediately in warmed bowls, garnished with the rosemary sprigs.

COOK'S TIP

The tomatoes look good left whole, but if you prefer you can crush them with the back of a wooden spoon while they are simmering in the pan.

Penne alla Rusticana

Penne with Chicken, Broccoli and Cheese

THE COMBINATION OF BROCCOLI, garlic and Gorgonzola is very good, and goes especially well with chicken.

INGREDIENTS

115g/4oz/scant 1 cup broccoli florets, divided into tiny sprigs
50g/2oz/¼ cup butter
2 skinless chicken breast fillets, cut into thin strips
2 garlic cloves, crushed
400g/14oz/3½ cups dried penne
120ml/4fl oz/½ cup dry white wine
200ml/7fl oz/scant 1 cup panna da cucina or double (heavy) cream
90g/3½oz Gorgonzola cheese, rind removed and diced small
salt and ground black pepper
freshly grated Parmesan cheese, to serve

Serves 4

1 Plunge the broccoli into a pan of boiling salted water. Bring back to the boil and boil for 2 minutes, then drain in a colander and refresh under cold running water. Shake well to remove the surplus water and set aside to drain completely.

2 Melt the butter in a frying pan, add the chicken and garlic, with salt and pepper to taste, and stir well. Fry over a medium heat for 3 minutes or until the chicken becomes white. Meanwhile, start cooking the pasta according to the instructions on the packet.

3 Pour the wine and cream over the chicken mixture in the pan, stir to mix, then simmer, stirring occasionally, for about 5 minutes until the sauce has reduced and thickened. Add the broccoli, increase the heat and toss to heat it through and mix it with the chicken. Taste for seasoning.

4 Drain the pasta and add to the sauce. Add the Gorgonzola and toss well. Serve with grated Parmesan.

VARIATION

Use leeks instead of broccoli if you prefer. Fry them with the chicken.

Pappardelle al Pollo e Porcini

Pappardelle with Chicken and Mushrooms

RICH AND CREAMY, this is a good supper party dish.

INGREDIENTS

15g/½oz dried porcini mushrooms
175ml/6fl oz/¾ cup warm water
25g/1oz/2 tbsp butter
1 garlic clove, crushed
1 small handful fresh flat leaf (Italian) parsley, roughly chopped
1 small leek or 4 spring onions (scallions), chopped
120ml/4fl oz/½ cup dry white wine
250ml/8fl oz/1 cup chicken stock
400g/14oz fresh or dried pappardelle
2 skinless chicken breast fillets, cut into strips
105ml/7 tbsp mascarpone
salt and ground black pepper
fresh basil leaves, shredded, to garnish

Serves 4

1 Put the dried mushrooms in a bowl. Pour in the warm water and leave to soak for 15 minutes. Place in a fine sieve (strainer) set over a bowl and squeeze the mushrooms with your hands to release as much liquid as possible.

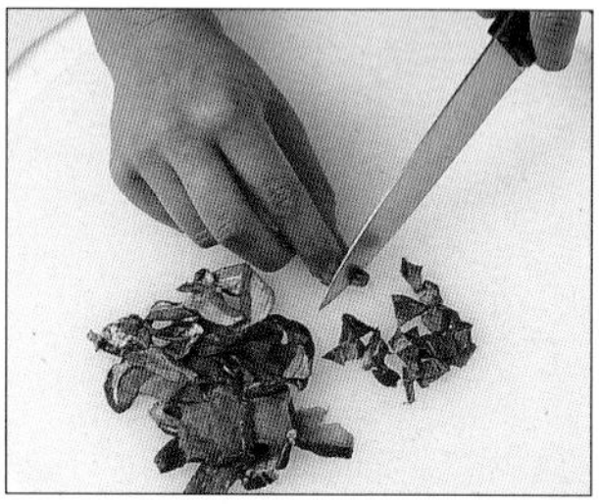

2 Chop the mushrooms finely and set aside the strained soaking liquid until required.

3 Melt the butter in a frying pan, add the chopped mushrooms, garlic, parsley and leek or spring onions, with salt and pepper to taste. Cook over a low heat, stirring frequently, for about 5 minutes, then pour in the wine and stock and bring to the boil. Lower the heat and simmer for about 5 minutes or until the liquid has reduced and is thickened.

4 Meanwhile, start cooking the pasta in salted boiling water according to the packet instructions, adding the reserved soaking liquid from the mushrooms to the water.

5 Add the chicken strips to the sauce and simmer for 5 minutes or until just tender. Add the mascarpone a spoonful at a time, stirring well after each addition, then add one or two spoonfuls of the water used for cooking the pasta. Taste for seasoning.

6 Drain the pasta and transfer it into a warmed large bowl. Add the chicken and sauce and toss well. Serve immediately, topped with the shredded basil leaves.

VARIATIONS

- *Add 115g/4oz/1 cup sliced button (white) mushrooms with the chicken.*
- *Add blanched sprigs of broccoli before the mascarpone in Step 5.*

Conchiglie coi Fegatini alle Erbe

Conchiglie with Chicken Livers and Herbs

FRESH HERBS AND CHICKEN livers are a good combination, often used together on crostini in Tuscany. Here they are tossed with pasta shells to make a very tasty supper dish.

INGREDIENTS

50g/2oz/¼ cup butter

115g/4oz pancetta or rindless streaky (fatty) bacon, diced

250g/9oz frozen chicken livers, thawed, drained and diced

2 garlic cloves, crushed

10ml/2 tsp chopped fresh sage

300g/11oz/2¾ cups dried conchiglie

150ml/¼ pint/⅔ cup dry white wine

4 ripe Italian plum tomatoes, peeled and diced

15ml/1 tbsp chopped fresh flat leaf (Italian) parsley

salt and ground black pepper

Serves 4

1 Melt half the butter in a frying pan, add the pancetta or bacon and fry over a medium heat for a few minutes until it is lightly coloured but not crisp.

2 Add the chicken livers, garlic, half the sage and plenty of pepper. Increase the heat and toss the livers for about 5 minutes, until they change colour all over. Meanwhile, start cooking the pasta according to the instructions on the packet.

3 Pour the wine over the chicken livers in the pan and let it sizzle, then lower the heat and simmer gently for 5 minutes. Add the remaining butter to the pan. As soon as it has melted, add the diced tomatoes, toss to mix, then add the remaining sage and the parsley. Stir well. Taste and add salt if needed.

4 Drain the pasta and transfer it to a warmed bowl. Pour the sauce over and toss well. Serve immediately.

Vegetables and Vegetarian

Pasta really comes into its own when it is served with a vegetable sauce. After all, when pasta was first "invented" it was a food for the poor, and vegetables were often all they could afford.

Vegetable sauces are invariably simple, in fact the simpler the better. Modern recipes often consist of nothing more elaborate than chopped or sliced raw vegetables "cooked" by the heat of freshly drained pasta. Colour, crunch and flavour are all retained, along with maximum nutritive value.

Almost all the recipes in this chapter can be cooked in a very short time, making them perfect for quick after-work suppers. Not all of them contain vegetables; some simply consist of butter and herbs, cheese and pepper, garlic and oil. These are the easiest of all pasta sauces to make, and some of the best.

Traditional vegetable sauces come from the south of Italy, where commercially dried pasta is favoured more than fresh. Generally speaking, dried pasta does seem to be the best choice for serving with vegetables, but for extra nutritional value there is no reason why fresh, egg-enriched pasta cannot be used.

Trenette alla Genovese

Trenette with Pesto, French Beans and Potatoes

In Liguria, it is traditional to serve pesto with trenette, green beans and diced potatoes. The ingredients for making fresh pesto are quite expensive, so the green beans and potatoes are added to help make the pesto go further.

INGREDIENTS

about 40 fresh basil leaves
2 garlic cloves, thinly sliced
25ml/1½ tbsp pine nuts
45ml/3 tbsp freshly grated Parmesan cheese, plus extra to serve
30ml/2 tbsp freshly grated Pecorino cheese, plus extra to serve
60ml/4 tbsp extra virgin olive oil
2 potatoes, total weight about 250g/9oz
100g/3½oz green beans
350g/12oz dried trenette
salt and ground black pepper

Serves 4

1 Put the basil leaves, garlic, pine nuts and cheeses in a blender or food processor and process for about 5 seconds. Add half the olive oil and a pinch of salt and process for 5 seconds more. Stop the machine, remove the lid and scrape down the side of the bowl. Add the remaining oil and process for 5–10 seconds.

2 Cut the potatoes in half lengthways. Slice each half crossways into 5mm/¼in thick slices. Top and tail the beans, then cut them into 2cm/¾in pieces. Plunge the potatoes and beans into a large pan of salted boiling water and boil, uncovered, for about 5 minutes.

3 Add the pasta, bring the water back to the boil, stir well, then cook for 5–7 minutes or until the pasta is *al dente*.

4 Meanwhile, put the pesto in a large bowl and add 45–60ml/3–4 tbsp of the water used for cooking the pasta. Mix well.

5 Drain the pasta and vegetables, add them to the pesto and toss well. Serve immediately on warmed plates, with extra grated Parmesan and Pecorino handed separately.

Cook's Tips

- *Don't worry if the potatoes break up during cooking – this will add to the creaminess of the finished dish.*
- *The pesto can be made up to 2–3 days in advance and kept in a bowl in the refrigerator until needed. Pour a thin film of olive oil over the surface of the pesto and cover the bowl tightly with clear film (plastic wrap) before refrigerating.*
- *Trenette is the traditional Ligurian pasta that is served with pesto, but if you find it difficult to obtain you can use bavette or linguine instead. The two-coloured paglia e fieno would be another good choice.*

Paglia e Fieno con Pomodori Secchi e Radicchio

Paglia e Fieno with Sun-dried Tomatoes and Radicchio

THIS IS A LIGHT, MODERN PASTA dish of the kind served in fashionable restaurants. It is the presentation that sets it apart, not the preparation, which is very quick and easy.

INGREDIENTS

45ml/3 tbsp pine nuts
350g/12oz dried paglia e fieno
45ml/3 tbsp extra virgin olive oil
30ml/2 tbsp sun-dried tomato purée (paste)
2 pieces drained sun-dried tomatoes in olive oil, cut into very thin slivers
40g/1½oz radicchio leaves, finely shredded
4–6 spring onions (scallions), thinly sliced into rings
salt and ground black pepper

Serves 4

1 Put the pine nuts in a frying pan and toss over a low to medium heat for 1–2 minutes or until lightly toasted and golden. Remove and set aside.

2 Cook the pasta according to the packet instructions, keeping the colours separate by using two pans.

3 While the pasta is cooking, heat 15ml/1 tbsp of the oil in a frying pan. Add the sun-dried tomato purée and the sun-dried tomatoes, then stir in two ladlefuls of the water used for cooking the pasta. Simmer until the sauce is slightly reduced, stirring constantly.

4 Mix in the shredded radicchio, then taste and season if necessary. Keep on a low heat. Drain the paglia e fieno, keeping the colours separate, and return the noodles to the pans in which they were cooked. Add about 15ml/1 tbsp oil to each pan and toss over a medium to high heat until the pasta is glistening with the oil.

5 Arrange a portion of green and white pasta in each of four warmed bowls, then spoon the sun-dried tomato and radicchio mixture in the centre. Sprinkle the spring onions and toasted pine nuts decoratively over the top and serve immediately. Before eating, each diner should toss the sauce ingredients with the pasta to mix well.

COOK'S TIP

If you find the presentation too fiddly, you can toss the sun-dried tomato and radicchio mixture with the pasta in one large warmed bowl before serving, then serve it sprinkled with the spring onions and toasted pine nuts.

Penne con Salsa di Carciofi

Penne with Artichokes

ARTICHOKES ARE A VERY popular vegetable in Italy, and are often used in sauces for pasta. This sauce is garlicky and richly flavoured, the perfect dinner party first course during the globe artichoke season.

INGREDIENTS

juice of 1/2–1 lemon
2 globe artichokes
30ml/2 tbsp olive oil
1 small fennel bulb, thinly sliced, with feathery tops reserved
1 onion, finely chopped
4 garlic cloves, finely chopped
1 handful fresh flat leaf (Italian) parsley, roughly chopped
400g/14oz can chopped Italian plum tomatoes
150ml/1/4 pint/2/3 cup dry white wine
350g/12oz/3 cups dried penne
10ml/2 tsp capers, chopped
salt and ground black pepper
freshly grated Parmesan cheese, to serve

Serves 6

1 Have ready a bowl of cold water to which you have added the juice of half a lemon. Cut off the artichoke stalks, then discard the outer leaves until the pale inner leaves that are almost white at the base remain.

2 Cut off the tops of these leaves so that the base remains. Cut the base in half lengthways, then prise the hairy choke out of the centre with the tip of the knife and discard. Cut the artichokes lengthways into 5mm/1/4in slices, adding them immediately to the bowl of acidulated water.

3 Bring a large pan of water to the boil. Add a good pinch of salt, then drain the artichokes and add them immediately to the water. Boil for 5 minutes, drain and set aside.

4 Heat the oil in a frying pan and add the fennel, onion, garlic and parsley. Cook over a low to medium heat, stirring frequently, for about 10 minutes until the fennel has softened and is lightly coloured.

5 Add the tomatoes and wine, with salt and pepper to taste. Bring to the boil, stirring, then lower the heat, cover the pan and simmer for 10–15 minutes. Stir in the artichokes, replace the lid and simmer for 10 minutes more. Meanwhile, cook the pasta in salted boiling water according to the instructions on the packet.

6 Drain the pasta, reserving a little of the cooking water. Stir the capers into the sauce, then taste for seasoning and add the remaining lemon juice if you like.

7 Transfer the pasta into a warmed large bowl, pour the sauce over and toss well to mix, adding a little of the reserved cooking water if you like a runnier sauce. Serve immediately, garnished with the reserved fennel fronds. Hand around a bowl of grated Parmesan separately.

Spaghetti alla Bellini

Spaghetti with Aubergines

THIS FAMOUS DISH IS NAMED after the Sicilian composer. You may also come across it called Spaghetti alla Norma, after Bellini's opera.

INGREDIENTS

60ml/4 tbsp olive oil
1 garlic clove, roughly chopped
450g/1lb ripe Italian plum tomatoes, peeled and chopped
vegetable oil for shallow frying
350g/12oz aubergines (eggplants), diced small
400g/14oz fresh or dried spaghetti
1 handful fresh basil leaves, shredded
115g/4oz ricotta salata cheese, grated
salt and ground black pepper
Serves 4–6

1 Heat the olive oil, add the garlic and cook over a low heat, stirring constantly, for 1–2 minutes. Stir in the tomatoes, then add salt and pepper to taste. Cover and simmer for 20 minutes.

2 Meanwhile, pour oil into a deep frying pan to a depth of about 1cm/½in. Heat the oil until hot but not smoking, then fry the aubergine cubes in batches for 4–5 minutes until tender and lightly browned. Remove the aubergine with a slotted spoon and drain on kitchen paper.

3 Cook the pasta according to the instructions on the packet. Meanwhile, stir the fried aubergines into the tomato sauce and warm through. Taste for seasoning.

4 Drain the pasta and transfer it into a warmed bowl. Add the sauce, with the shredded basil and a generous handful of the grated ricotta salata. Toss well and serve immediately, with the remaining ricotta sprinkled on top.

COOK'S TIP

Some cooks sprinkle aubergines with salt and leave them for 20–30 minutes. This is said to help remove any bitterness, but it is not necessary if the aubergines are young and fresh.

Chiaroscuro

Black Pasta with Ricotta

THIS IS DESIGNER PASTA at its most dramatic, the kind of dish you are most likely to see at a fashionable Italian restaurant. Serve it for a smart dinner party first course – it will be a great talking point.

INGREDIENTS

300g/11oz dried black pasta
60ml/4 tbsp ricotta cheese, as fresh as possible
60ml/4 tbsp extra virgin olive oil
1 small fresh red chilli, seeded and finely chopped
1 small handful fresh basil leaves
salt and ground black pepper
Serves 4

1 Cook the pasta in salted boiling water according to the instructions on the packet. Meanwhile, put the ricotta in a bowl, add salt and pepper to taste and use a little of the hot water from the pasta pan to mix it to a smooth, creamy consistency. Taste for seasoning.

2 Drain the pasta. Heat the oil gently in the clean pan and add the pasta with the chilli and salt and pepper to taste. Toss quickly over a high heat to combine.

3 Divide the pasta equally among four warmed bowls, then top with the ricotta. Sprinkle with the basil leaves and serve immediately. Each diner tosses their own portion of pasta and cheese.

COOK'S TIP

Black pasta is made with squid ink. If you prefer, use green spinach-flavoured pasta or red tomato-flavoured pasta.

Paglia e Fieno alle Noci e Gorgonzola

Paglia e Fieno with Walnuts and Gorgonzola

CHEESE AND NUTS ARE popular ingredients for pasta sauces. The combination is very rich, so reserve this dish for a dinner party starter. It needs no accompaniment other than wine – a dry white would be good.

INGREDIENTS

275g/10oz dried paglia e fieno
25g/1oz/2 tbsp butter
5ml/1 tsp finely chopped fresh sage or 2.5ml/½ tsp dried sage, plus fresh sage leaves, to garnish (optional)
115g/4oz torta di Gorgonzola cheese, diced
45ml/3 tbsp mascarpone
75ml/5 tbsp milk
50g/2oz/½ cup walnut halves, ground
30ml/2 tbsp freshly grated Parmesan cheese
freshly ground black pepper
Serves 4

1 Cook the pasta in a large pan of salted boiling water, according to the instructions on the packet. Meanwhile, melt the butter in a large frying pan over a low heat, add the sage and stir it around. Sprinkle in the diced *torta di Gorgonzola* and then add the mascarpone. Stir the ingredients with a wooden spoon until the cheeses start to melt. Pour in the milk and keep stirring.

2 Sprinkle in the walnuts and grated Parmesan and add plenty of black pepper. Continue to stir over a low heat until the mixture forms a creamy sauce. Do not allow it to boil or the nuts will taste bitter, and do not cook the sauce for longer than a few minutes or the nuts will discolour it.

3 Drain the pasta, transfer it into a warmed bowl, then add the sauce and toss well. Serve immediately, with more black pepper ground on top. Garnish with sage leaves, if you wish.

COOK'S TIP

Ready-ground nuts are sold in packets in supermarkets, but you will get a better flavour if you buy walnut halves and grind them yourself in a food processor.

Conchiglie con Verdure Arrostite

Conchiglie with Roasted Vegetables

Nothing could be simpler – or more delicious – than tossing freshly cooked pasta with roasted vegetables. The flavour is superb.

INGREDIENTS

1 red (bell) pepper, seeded and cut into 1cm/½in squares
1 yellow or orange (bell) pepper, seeded and cut into 1cm/½in squares
1 small aubergine (eggplant), roughly diced
2 courgettes (zucchini), roughly diced
75ml/5 tbsp extra virgin olive oil
15ml/1 tbsp chopped fresh flat leaf (Italian) parsley
5ml/1 tsp dried oregano or marjoram
250g/9oz baby Italian plum tomatoes, hulled and halved lengthways
2 garlic cloves, roughly chopped
350–400g/12–14oz/3–3½ cups dried conchiglie
salt and ground black pepper
4–6 fresh marjoram or oregano flowers, to garnish

Serves 4–6

1 Preheat the oven to 190°C/375°F/Gas 5. Rinse the prepared peppers, aubergine and courgettes in a sieve (strainer) or colander under cold running water, drain, then transfer the vegetables into a large roasting pan.

2 Pour 45ml/3 tbsp of the olive oil over the vegetables and sprinkle with the fresh and dried herbs. Add salt and pepper to taste and stir well. Roast for about 30 minutes, stirring two or three times.

3 Stir the halved tomatoes and chopped garlic into the vegetable mixture, then roast for 20 minutes more, stirring once or twice. Meanwhile, cook the pasta according to the instructions on the packet.

4 Drain the pasta and transfer it into a warmed bowl. Add the roasted vegetables and the remaining oil and toss well. Serve the pasta and vegetables in warmed bowls, sprinkling each portion with a few herb flowers.

Cook's Tip

Pasta and roasted vegetables are very good served cold, so if you have any of this dish left over, cover it tightly with clear film, chill in the refrigerator overnight and serve it the next day as a salad. It would also make a particularly good salad to take on a picnic.

Sugo di Verdure

Green Vegetable Sauce

ALTHOUGH DESCRIBED AS *SUGO* in Italian, this is not a true sauce, because it does not have any liquid apart from the oil and melted butter. It is more a medley of vegetables. Tossed with freshly cooked pasta, it is ideal for a fresh and light lunch or supper. Allow about 450g/1lb dried pasta for this amount of sauce.

INGREDIENTS

2 carrots
1 courgette (zucchini)
75g/3oz green beans
1 small leek
1 handful fresh flat leaf (Italian) parsley
2 ripe Italian plum tomatoes
25g/1oz/2 tbsp butter
45ml/3 tbsp extra virgin olive oil
2.5ml/½ tsp sugar
115g/4oz/1 cup frozen peas
salt and ground black pepper
Serves 4

1 Dice the carrots and the courgette finely. Top and tail the green beans, then cut them into 2cm/¾in lengths. Slice the leek thinly. Peel and dice the tomatoes. Chop the flat leaf parsley and set aside.

2 Melt the butter in the oil in a frying pan. When the mixture sizzles, add the prepared leek and carrots. Sprinkle the sugar over and fry, stirring frequently, for about 5 minutes.

3 Stir in the courgette, green beans, peas and plenty of salt and pepper. Cover and cook over a low to medium heat for 5–8 minutes until the vegetables are tender, stirring occasionally.

4 Stir in the parsley and chopped plum tomatoes and adjust the seasoning to taste. Serve immediately, tossed with freshly cooked pasta of your choice.

Spaghettini all'Aglio Arrostito

Spaghettini with Roasted Garlic

ROASTED GARLIC TASTES sweet and is milder than you would expect.

INGREDIENTS

1 whole head of garlic
400g/14oz fresh or dried spaghettini
120ml/4fl oz/½ cup extra virgin olive oil
salt and ground black pepper
coarsely shaved Parmesan cheese, to serve
Serves 4

1 Preheat the oven to 180°C/350°F/Gas 4. Place the garlic in an oiled roasting pan in the oven for 30 minutes.

2 Cook the pasta in a pan of salted boiling water according to the instructions on the packet.

3 Leave the garlic to cool, then lay it on its side and slice off the top third with a sharp knife.

4 Hold the garlic over a bowl and dig out the flesh from each clove with the point of the knife. When all the flesh has been added to the bowl, pour in the oil and add plenty of black pepper. Mix well.

5 Drain the pasta and return it to the clean pan. Pour in the oil and garlic mixture and toss the pasta vigorously over a medium heat until all the strands are thoroughly coated. Serve immediately, with shavings of Parmesan handed separately.

VARIATION

For a fiery finish, sprinkle crushed, dried red chillies over the pasta when tossing it with the oil and garlic.

COOK'S TIP

Although you can now buy roasted garlic in supermarkets, it is best to roast it yourself for this simple recipe, so that it melts into the olive oil and coats the strands of pasta beautifully.

Elicoidali di Mezzanotte

Elicoidali with Cheese and Cream

MEZZANOTTE MEANS MIDDLE of the night, which is when this rich and filling dish is eaten – after a night on the tiles. When you arrive home hungry from a party, it's just the thing to sober you up.

INGREDIENTS

400g/14oz/3½ cups dried elicoidali
3 egg yolks
105ml/7 tbsp freshly grated Parmesan cheese
200g/7oz/scant 1 cup ricotta cheese
60ml/4 tbsp panna da cucina *or double (heavy) cream*
nutmeg
40g/1½oz/3 tbsp butter
salt and ground black pepper
Serves 4

1 Cook the pasta according to the instructions on the packet.

2 Meanwhile, mix the egg yolks, grated Parmesan and ricotta together in a bowl. Add the cream and mix with a fork.

3 Grate in nutmeg to taste, then season with plenty of black pepper and a little salt. Drain the pasta thoroughly when cooked. Return the clean pan to the heat. Melt the butter, add the drained pasta and toss vigorously over a medium heat.

4 Turn off the heat under the pan and add the ricotta mixture. Stir well with a large spoon for 10–15 seconds until all the pasta is coated in sauce. Serve immediately, in warmed individual bowls.

COOK'S TIP

Elicoidali are a short tubular pasta with curved ridges. If you can't get them, use rigatoni, which have straight ridges.

Spaghetti alla Chitarra con Burro e Erbe

Chitarra Spaghetti with Butter and Herbs

THIS IS A VERSATILE RECIPE. You can use just one favourite herb or several – basil, flat leaf parsley, rosemary, thyme, marjoram or sage would all work well. Square-shaped spaghetti is traditional for this type of sauce, but you can use ordinary spaghetti or spaghettini, or even linguine.

INGREDIENTS

400g/14oz fresh or dried spaghetti alla chitarra
2 good handfuls mixed fresh herbs, plus extra herb leaves and flowers, to garnish
115g/4oz/½ cup butter
salt and ground black pepper
freshly grated Parmesan cheese, to serve
Serves 4

VARIATION

If you like the flavour of garlic with herbs, add 1–2 crushed garlic cloves when melting the butter.

1 Cook the pasta according to the instructions on the packet.

2 Chop the herbs roughly or finely, whichever you prefer.

3 When the pasta is almost *al dente*, melt the butter in a large frying pan. As soon as it sizzles, drain the pasta and add it to the pan, then sprinkle in the herbs and salt and pepper to taste.

4 Toss over a medium heat until the pasta is coated in the oil and herbs. Serve immediately in warmed bowls, sprinkled with extra herb leaves and flowers. Hand around freshly grated Parmesan separately.

Spaghetti Cacio e Pepe

Spaghetti with Cheese and Pepper

THIS IS A ROMAN DISH, always made with spaghetti. It is remarkably easy to cook, and tastes wonderful.

INGREDIENTS

400g/14oz fresh or dried spaghetti
115g/4oz/1⅓ cup freshly grated Pecorino (preferably Pecorino Romano) cheese
5ml/1 tsp coarsely ground black pepper
extra virgin olive oil, to taste
salt
Serves 4

1 Cook the pasta according to the instructions on the packet.

2 As soon as the pasta is *al dente*, drain it, leaving it a little moister than usual, and transfer it into a large warmed bowl.

3 Add the cheese, pepper and salt to taste. Toss well to mix, then moisten with as much olive oil as you like. Serve immediately.

Rigatoni ai Funghi di Bosco

Rigatoni with Wild Mushrooms

THIS IS A GOOD SAUCE to make from storecupboard ingredients because it doesn't rely on anything fresh, apart from the fresh herbs.

INGREDIENTS

2 x 15g/½oz packets dried porcini mushrooms
175ml/6fl oz/¾ cup warm water
30ml/2 tbsp olive oil
2 shallots, finely chopped
2 garlic cloves, crushed
a few sprigs of fresh marjoram, leaves stripped and finely chopped, plus extra to garnish
1 handful fresh flat leaf (Italian) parsley, chopped
25g/1oz/2 tbsp butter, diced
400g/14oz can chopped Italian plum tomatoes
400g/14oz/3½ cups dried rigatoni
25g/1oz/⅓ cup freshly grated Parmesan cheese, plus extra to serve
salt and ground black pepper
Serves 4–6

1 Put the dried mushrooms in a bowl, pour the warm water over and soak for 15–20 minutes. Place into a fine sieve (strainer) set over a bowl and squeeze the mushrooms to release as much liquid as possible. Reserve the mushrooms and the strained liquid.

2 Heat the oil in a frying pan and fry the shallots, garlic and herbs over a low heat, stirring frequently, for about 5 minutes. Add the mushrooms and butter and stir until the butter has melted. Season well.

3 Stir in the tomatoes and the reserved liquid from the soaked mushrooms. Bring to the boil, then cover, lower the heat and simmer for about 20 minutes, stirring occasionally. Meanwhile, cook the pasta according to the instructions on the packet.

4 Taste the sauce for seasoning. Drain the pasta, reserving some of the cooking water, and transfer it into a warmed large bowl. Add the sauce and the grated Parmesan and toss to mix. Add a little cooking water if you prefer a runnier sauce. Serve immediately, garnished with marjoram and with more Parmesan handed separately.

VARIATIONS

- *If you have a bottle of wine open, add a splash with the canned tomatoes.*
- *For a richer sauce, add a few spoonfuls of* panna da cucina, *cream or mascarpone to the sauce just before serving.*

Eliche col Pesto

Eliche with Pesto

BOTTLED PESTO IS a useful stand-by, but if you have a food processor, it is very easy to make your own.

INGREDIENTS

50g/2oz/1 1/3 cups fresh basil leaves, plus fresh basil leaves, to garnish
2–4 garlic cloves
60ml/4 tbsp pine nuts
120ml/4fl oz/1/2 cup extra virgin olive oil
115g/4oz/1 1/3 cups freshly grated Parmesan cheese, plus extra to serve
25g/1oz/1/3 cup freshly grated Pecorino cheese
400g/14oz/3 1/2 cups dried eliche
salt and ground black pepper

Serves 4

1 Put the basil leaves, garlic and pine nuts in a blender or food processor. Add 60ml/4 tbsp of the olive oil. Process until the ingredients are finely chopped, then stop the machine, remove the lid and scrape down the sides of the bowl.

2 Turn the machine on again and slowly pour the remaining oil in a thin, steady stream through the feeder tube. You may need to stop the machine and scrape down the sides of the bowl once or twice to make sure everything is evenly mixed.

3 Scrape the mixture into a large bowl and beat in the cheeses with a wooden spoon. Taste and add salt and pepper if necessary.

4 Cook the pasta according to the instructions on the packet. Drain it well, then add it to the bowl of pesto and toss well. Serve immediately, garnished with the fresh basil leaves. Hand shaved Parmesan separately.

COOK'S TIP

Pesto can be made up to 2–3 days in advance. To store pesto, transfer it to a small bowl and pour a thin film of olive oil over the surface. Cover the bowl tightly with clear film (plastic wrap) and keep it in the refrigerator.

Spaghetti Aglio e Olio

Spaghetti with Garlic and Oil

In Rome they run the words together to pronounce the name of this dish as "spaghetti-ayo-e-oyo" or simply "ayo-e-oyo". Sometimes it is given its full name of *Spaghetti Aglio, Olio e Peperoncino* because chilli – *peperoncino* – is always included to give the dish some bite.

INGREDIENTS

400g/14oz fresh or dried spaghetti
90ml/6 tbsp extra virgin olive oil
2–4 garlic cloves, crushed
1 dried red chilli
1 small handful fresh flat leaf (Italian) parsley, roughly chopped
salt
Serves 4

1 Cook the pasta according to the packet instructions, adding plenty of salt to the water. (See Cook's Tips.)

2 Meanwhile, heat the oil very gently in a frying pan. Add the crushed garlic and whole dried chilli and stir over a low heat until the garlic is just beginning to brown. Remove the chilli and discard.

3 Drain the pasta and transfer it into a warmed large bowl. Pour on the oil and garlic mixture, add the parsley and toss vigorously until the pasta glistens. Serve immediately.

COOK'S TIPS

- *Since the oil is such an important ingredient here, only use the very best cold-pressed extra virgin olive oil.*
- *Don't use salt in the oil and garlic mixture, because it will not dissolve sufficiently. This is why plenty of salt is recommended for cooking the pasta.*
- *In Rome, grated Parmesan is never served with* Spaghetti Aglio e Olio, *nor is the dish seasoned with pepper.*
- *In summer, Romans use fresh chillies, which they grow in pots on their terraces and window ledges.*

Pasta con Funghi

Pasta with Mushrooms

SERVED WITH WARM CIABATTA, this makes an excellent vegetarian supper dish.

INGREDIENTS

15g/½oz dried porcini mushrooms
175ml/6fl oz/¾ cup warm water
45ml/3 tbsp olive oil
2 garlic cloves, finely chopped
1 handful fresh flat leaf (Italian) parsley, roughly chopped
2 large pieces drained sun-dried tomato in olive oil, sliced into thin strips
120ml/4fl oz/½ cup dry white wine
225g/8oz/2 cups chestnut mushrooms, thinly sliced
475ml/16fl oz/2 cups vegetable stock
450g/1lb/4 cups dried short pasta shapes, such as. ruote, penne, fusilli or eliche
salt and ground black pepper
rocket and/or fresh flat leaf (Italian) parsley, to garnish

Serves 4

1 Put the dried porcini mushrooms in a bowl, pour the warm water over and leave to soak for 15–20 minutes. Place into a fine sieve (strainer) set over a bowl and squeeze the porcini with your hands to release as much liquid as possible. Reserve the strained soaking liquid. Chop the porcini finely.

2 Heat the oil and cook the garlic, parsley, sun-dried tomato strips and porcini over a low heat, stirring frequently, for about 5 minutes.

3 Stir in the wine, simmer for a few minutes until reduced, then stir in the chestnut mushrooms. Pour in the stock and simmer, uncovered, for 15–20 minutes more until the liquid has reduced and the sauce is quite thick and rich.

4 Cook the pasta according to the instructions on the packet.

5 Taste the mushroom sauce for seasoning. Drain the pasta, reserving a little of the cooking liquid, and transfer it into a warmed large bowl. Add the mushroom sauce and toss well, thinning the sauce if needed with some of the pasta cooking water. Serve immediately, sprinkled liberally with chopped rocket and/or parsley.

VARIATION

Fresh wild mushrooms can be used instead of chestnut mushrooms, but they are seasonal and often expensive. A cheaper alternative is to use a box of mixed wild mushrooms. These are sold in many supermarkets.

Pizzoccheri della Valtellina

Buckwheat Noodles with Cabbage, Potatoes and Cheese

THIS IS A VERY UNUSUAL PASTA dish from Valtellina in the Italian Alps. The buckwheat noodles are unique to this area, and the dish takes its name from them.

INGREDIENTS

400g/14oz Savoy cabbage, cut into 1cm/½in strips
2 potatoes, total weight about 200g/7oz, cut into 5mm/¼in slices
400g/14oz dried pizzoccheri
75g/3oz/6 tbsp butter
1 generous bunch fresh sage leaves, shredded
2 garlic cloves
200g/7oz Fontina cheese, rind removed and thinly sliced
30–45ml/2–3 tbsp freshly grated Parmesan cheese, plus extra to serve
salt and ground black pepper

Serves 6

1 Bring a very large pan of salted water to the boil. Add the cabbage and potatoes and boil for 5 minutes.

2 Add the pasta, stir well and let the water return to the boil. Lower the heat and simmer for 15 minutes, or according to the instructions on the packet, until the pasta is *al dente*.

3 A few minutes before the pasta is ready, melt the butter in a small pan. Add the sage and whole garlic cloves and fry over a low to medium heat until the garlic is golden and sizzling. Lift the garlic out of the pan and discard it. Set the sage and garlic butter aside.

4 Drain the pasta and vegetables. Pour a quarter of the mixture into a warmed large bowl and arrange about a third of the Fontina slices on top. Repeat these layers until all the ingredients have been used, then sprinkle with the grated Parmesan. Pour the sage and garlic butter over the top and serve immediately, with extra Parmesan handed separately.

COOK'S TIPS

- *Look for packets of dried pizzoccheri pasta in Italian delicatessens.*
- *Fontina is a mountain cheese with a sweet, nutty taste that is quite widely available, but if you cannot get it, look for Taleggio, Gruyère or Emmental – they are all similar cheeses. Cooks in the mountain regions of northern Italy would probably use either* bitto *or* casera *cheese, but these are not so easy to obtain outside the region.*
- *When in season, Swiss chard is used instead of cabbage, as is spinach.*

Fettuccine al Burro e Parmigiano

Fettuccine with Butter and Parmesan

VERY FEW INGREDIENTS are needed to make up this incredibly simple dish. It comes from northern Italy, where butter and cheese are the most popular ingredients to go with pasta.

INGREDIENTS

400g/14oz fresh or dried fettuccine
50g/2oz/¼ cup unsalted (sweet) butter, cubed
115g/4oz/1⅓ cups freshly grated Parmesan cheese
salt and ground black pepper

Serves 4

1 Cook the pasta in a pan of salted boiling water according to the instructions on the packet. Drain, then transfer into a warmed bowl.

2 Add the butter and Parmesan a third at a time, tossing the pasta after each addition until it is evenly coated. Season to taste and serve.

Sugo di Melanzane

Aubergine Sauce

FULL OF FLAVOUR, THIS EXCELLENT vegetarian sauce goes well with any short pasta. It can also be layered with pasta sheets and béchamel sauce to make a vegetarian lasagne.

INGREDIENTS

30ml/2 tbsp olive oil
1 small fresh red chilli
2 garlic cloves
2 handfuls fresh flat leaf (Italian) parsley, roughly chopped
450g/1lb aubergines (eggplants), roughly chopped
1 handful fresh basil leaves
200ml/7fl oz/scant 1 cup water
1 vegetable stock (bouillon) cube
8 ripe Italian plum tomatoes, peeled and finely chopped
60ml/4 tbsp red wine
5ml/1 tsp sugar
1 sachet saffron powder
2.5ml/½ tsp ground paprika
salt and ground black pepper

Serves 4–6

1 Heat the oil in a large frying pan and add the whole chilli, whole garlic cloves and half the chopped parsley. Smash the garlic cloves with a wooden spoon to release their juice, then cover the pan and cook the mixture over a low to medium heat for about 10 minutes, stirring occasionally.

2 Remove and discard the chilli. Add the aubergines to the pan with the rest of the parsley and all the basil. Pour in half the water. Crumble in the stock cube and stir until it is dissolved, then cover and cook, stirring frequently, for about 10 minutes.

3 Add the tomatoes, wine, sugar, saffron and paprika, with salt and pepper to taste, then pour in the remaining water. Stir well, replace the lid and cook for 30–40 minutes more, stirring occasionally. Taste for seasoning and serve with pasta or use as suggested in a baked dish. If you like, garnish with extra chopped parsley.

COOK'S TIP

Italian cooks often sprinkle a little "all-purpose seasoning" into sauces like this one. It is very good for accentuating savoury flavours, and is well worth keeping in the store cupboard.

Orecchiette con la Rucola

Orecchiette with Rocket

THIS HEARTY DISH IS FROM PUGLIA in the south-east of Italy. Serve it as a main course with country bread. Some delicatessens and supermarkets sell a farmhouse-style Italian loaf called *pugliese*, which would be most appropriate.

INGREDIENTS

45ml/3 tbsp olive oil
1 small onion, finely chopped
300g/11oz canned chopped Italian plum tomatoes or passata (bottled strained tomatoes)
2.5ml/½ tsp dried oregano
pinch of chilli powder or cayenne pepper
about 30ml/2 tbsp red or white wine
2 potatoes, total weight about 200g/7oz, diced
300g/11oz/2¾ cups dried orecchiette
2 garlic cloves, finely chopped
150g/5oz rocket (arugula) leaves, stalks removed, shredded
90g/3½oz/scant ½ cup ricotta cheese
salt and ground black pepper
freshly grated Pecorino cheese, to serve

Serves 4–6

1 Heat 15ml/1 tbsp of the olive oil in a medium pan, add half the finely chopped onion and cook gently, stirring frequently, for about 5 minutes until softened. Add the canned tomatoes or passata, oregano and chilli powder or cayenne pepper to the onion. Pour the wine over, if using, and add a little salt and pepper to taste. Cover the pan and simmer for about 15 minutes, stirring occasionally.

2 Bring a large pan of salted water to the boil. Add the potatoes and pasta. Stir well and let the water return to the boil. Lower the heat and simmer for 15 minutes, or according to the instructions on the packet, until the pasta is cooked.

3 Heat the remaining oil in a large frying pan, add the rest of the onion and the garlic and fry for 2–3 minutes, stirring occasionally. Add the rocket, toss over the heat for about 2 minutes until wilted, then stir in the tomato sauce and the ricotta. Mix well.

4 Drain the pasta and potatoes, add both to the pan of sauce and toss to mix. Taste for seasoning and serve immediately in warmed bowls, with grated Pecorino handed separately.

COOK'S TIP

Orecchiette are always slightly chewy. When making this dish it is traditional to cook them in the same pan as the potatoes, but if you are unsure of getting the timing right, cook them separately.

Baked Pasta

Like Bolognese sauce, lasagne, macaroni cheese and cannelloni have become so popular outside Italy that we seldom stop to consider the origins of these delicious pasta dishes. A kind of layered pasta pie was mentioned by the Roman gastronome Apicius in the first century AD, so we know that lasagne, at least, has a very long history. In the Renaissance, sumptuous layered pasta dishes, often moulded into fanciful shapes, were popular with the wealthy. Nowadays, *pasta al forno*, as baked pasta dishes are called in Italy, are more often eaten at family meals, especially on occasions when large numbers must be catered for. Baked dishes can be prepared in advance and are easy to serve.

This chapter introduces classic dishes and regional favourites with modern adaptations. In calculating serving quantities, it is assumed the dish will be a main course, but smaller portions can be served as a first course, which is more traditional in Italy.

Spaghetti Tetrazzini

Spaghetti and Turkey in Cheese Sauce

AN AMERICAN-ITALIAN RECIPE, Spaghetti Tetrazzini makes an excellent family meal. It is quite filling and rich, so serve it with a tossed green salad.

INGREDIENTS

75g/3oz/6 tbsp butter
350g/12oz turkey breast fillet, cut into thin strips
2 pieces bottled roasted (bell) pepper, drained, rinsed, dried and cut into strips
175g/6oz dried spaghetti
50g/2oz/½ cup plain (all-purpose) flour
900ml/1½ pints/3¾ cups hot milk
115g/4oz/1⅓ cups freshly grated Parmesan cheese
1.25–2.5ml/¼–½ tsp mustard powder
salt and ground black pepper

Serves 4–6

1 Melt about a third of the butter in a pan, add the turkey and sprinkle with a little salt and plenty of pepper. Toss the turkey over a medium heat for about 5 minutes until the meat turns white, then add the roasted pepper strips and toss to mix. Remove with a slotted spoon and set aside.

2 Preheat the oven to 180°C/350°F/Gas 4. Cook the pasta according to the instructions on the packet.

3 Meanwhile, melt the remaining butter over a low heat in the pan in which the turkey was cooked. Sprinkle in the flour and cook, stirring, for 1–2 minutes, then increase the heat to medium.

4 Add the hot milk a little at a time, whisking vigorously after each addition. Bring to the boil and cook, stirring, until the sauce is smooth and thick. Add two thirds of the grated Parmesan, then whisk in mustard, salt and pepper to taste. Remove the sauce from the heat.

5 Drain the pasta and return it to the clean pan. Mix in half the cheese sauce, then spoon the mixture around the edge of a baking dish. Stir the turkey mixture into the remaining cheese sauce and spoon into the centre of the dish. Sprinkle the remaining Parmesan evenly over the tetrazzini and bake for 15–20 minutes until the cheese topping is just crisp. Serve hot.

Lasagne di Mare

Shellfish Lasagne

THIS IS A LUXURY LASAGNE suitable for an informal supper or lunch party. It is quite expensive to make, but the flavour is superb, so put it on your list for special occasion meals.

INGREDIENTS

4–6 fresh scallops
450g/1lb peeled raw tiger prawns (shrimp)
1 garlic clove, crushed
75g/3oz/6 tbsp butter
50g/2oz/½ cup plain (all-purpose) flour
600ml/1 pint/2½ cups hot milk
100ml/3½fl oz/scant ½ cup panna da cucina or double (heavy) cream
100ml/3½fl oz/½ cup dry white wine
2 sachets saffron powder
good pinch of cayenne pepper
130g/4½oz Fontina cheese, thinly sliced
75g/3oz/1 cup freshly grated Parmesan cheese
6–8 fresh egg lasagne sheets
salt and ground black pepper

Serves 4–6

1 Preheat the oven to 190°C/375°F/Gas 5. Cut the scallops, corals and prawns into bitesize pieces and spread out in a dish. Sprinkle with the garlic and salt and pepper to taste. Melt about a third of the butter in a medium pan, add the scallops, corals and prawns and toss over a medium heat for 1–2 minutes or just until the prawns turn pink. Remove the shellfish with a slotted spoon and set aside.

2 Add the remaining butter to the pan and melt over a low heat. Sprinkle in the flour and cook, stirring, for 1–2 minutes, then increase the heat to medium and add the hot milk a little at a time, whisking vigorously after each addition. Bring to the boil and cook, stirring, until the sauce is smooth and very thick. Whisk in the cream, wine, saffron powder, cayenne and salt and pepper to taste, then remove the sauce from the heat.

3 Spread about a third of the sauce over the bottom of a baking dish. Arrange half the Fontina slices over the sauce and sprinkle with about a third of the grated Parmesan. Sprinkle about half the shellfish evenly on top, then cover with half the lasagne sheets. Repeat the layers, then cover with the remaining sauce and Parmesan.

4 Bake the lasagne for 30–40 minutes or until the topping is golden brown and bubbling. Allow to stand for 10 minutes before serving.

Lasagne ai Funghi e Zucchine

Mushroom and Courgette Lasagne

THIS IS THE PERFECT main-course lasagne for vegetarians. Adding dried porcini to fresh chestnut mushrooms intensifies the "mushroomy" flavour and gives the whole dish more substance. Serve with crusty Italian bread.

INGREDIENTS

15g/½oz dried porcini mushrooms
175ml/6fl oz/¾ cup warm water
30ml/2 tbsp olive oil
75g/3oz/6 tbsp butter
450g/1lb courgettes (zucchini), thinly sliced
1 onion, finely chopped
450g/1lb/6 cups chestnut mushrooms, thinly sliced
2 garlic cloves, crushed
1 quantity Winter Tomato Sauce
10ml/2 tsp chopped fresh marjoram or 5ml/1 tsp dried marjoram, plus extra fresh leaves, to garnish
6–8 "no-need-to-pre-cook" lasagne sheets
50g/2oz/⅔ cup freshly grated Parmesan cheese
salt and ground black pepper

For the white sauce

40g/1½oz/3 tbsp butter
40g/1½oz/⅓ cup plain (all-purpose) flour
900ml/1½ pints/3¾ cups hot milk
nutmeg

Serves 6

1 Put the dried porcini mushrooms in a bowl. Pour over the warm water and leave to soak for 15–20 minutes. Tip the porcini and liquid into a fine sieve (strainer) set over a bowl and squeeze the mushrooms with your hands to release as much liquid as possible. Chop the mushrooms finely and set aside. Strain the soaking liquid through a fine sieve and reserve half for the sauce.

2 Preheat the oven to 190°C/375°F/Gas 5. Heat the olive oil with 25g/1oz/2 tbsp of the butter in a pan.

3 Add about half the courgette slices to the pan and season with salt and pepper to taste. Cook the courgettes over a medium heat, turning the slices frequently, for 5–8 minutes until they are lightly coloured on both sides. Remove the courgettes from the pan with a slotted spoon and allow to drain on kitchen paper. Repeat with the remaining courgettes.

4 Melt half the remaining butter in the fat remaining in the pan, then cook the finely chopped onion, stirring, for 1–2 minutes. Add half of the fresh mushrooms and the crushed garlic to the pan and sprinkle with a little salt and pepper to taste.

5 Toss the mushrooms over a high heat for 5 minutes or so until the mushrooms are juicy and tender. Transfer to a bowl with a slotted spoon, then repeat with the remaining butter and mushrooms.

6 Make the white sauce. Melt the butter in a large pan, add the flour and cook, stirring, over a medium heat for 1–2 minutes.

7 Add the hot milk a little at a time, whisking well after each addition. Bring to the boil and cook, stirring, until the sauce is smooth and thick. Grate in fresh nutmeg to taste and season with a little salt and pepper. Whisk well, then remove the sauce from the heat.

8 Place the tomato sauce in a blender or food processor with the reserved porcini soaking liquid and blend to a pureé. Add the courgettes to the bowl of fried mushrooms, then stir in the porcini and marjoram.

9 Adjust the seasoning to taste, then spread a third of the tomato sauce in a baking dish. Add half the vegetable mixture, spreading it evenly.

10 Top with about a third of the white sauce, then about half the lasagne sheets. Repeat these layers, then top with the remaining tomato sauce and white sauce and sprinkle with the grated Parmesan cheese.

11 Bake the lasagne for 35–40 minutes, or until the pasta feels tender when pierced with a skewer. Allow to stand for about 10 minutes before serving. If you like, sprinkle each serving with marjoram leaves.

Cook's Tips

- *The amount of pasta will depend on the size and shape of the pasta sheets and your baking dish; you may need to break the pasta to fit.*
- *This dish is time-consuming to prepare, but well worth the effort. You can make the tomato sauce in advance and chill it for up to 2 days until you are ready to assemble the lasagne, or you can freeze it. Make sure that you leave it to thaw completely before using.*

Lasagne con Polpettine

Lasagne with Meatballs

THIS IS AN UNUSUAL RECIPE for lasagne in that there is both a meat sauce and meatballs. The result is very rich and satisfying, making it an ideal dish for an informal winter lunch or supper party. Prepare it the day before and bake it on the day.

INGREDIENTS

300g/11oz minced (ground) beef
300g/11oz minced (ground) pork
1 large egg
50g/2oz/1 cup fresh white breadcrumbs
75ml/5 tbsp freshly grated Parmesan cheese
30ml/2 tbsp chopped fresh flat leaf (Italian) parsley
2 garlic cloves, crushed
60ml/4 tbsp olive oil
1 onion, finely chopped
1 carrot, finely chopped
1 celery stick, finely chopped
2 x 400g/14oz cans chopped Italian plum tomatoes
10ml/2 tsp dried oregano or basil
6–8 fresh lasagne sheets, pre-cooked if necessary
salt and ground black pepper

For the béchamel sauce

750ml/1¼ pints/3 cups milk
1 bay leaf
1 fresh thyme sprig
50g/2oz/¼ cup butter
50g/2oz/½ cup plain (all-purpose) flour
nutmeg

Serves 6–8

1 First make the meatballs. Put 175g/6oz each of the minced beef and pork in a large bowl. Add the egg, breadcrumbs, 30ml/2 tbsp of the grated Parmesan, half the parsley and garlic and plenty of salt and pepper.

2 Mix everything together with a wooden spoon, then use your hands to squeeze and knead the mixture so that it becomes smooth and quite sticky.

3 Wash your hands, rinse under the cold tap, then pick up small pieces of the mixture and roll them between your palms to make about 60 very small balls. Place the balls on a tray and chill for about 30 minutes.

4 Meanwhile, put the milk for the béchamel sauce in a pan. Make a tear in the bay leaf, then add the leaf and thyme sprig to the milk and bring it to the boil. Remove from the heat, cover and leave to infuse.

5 Make the meat sauce. Heat half the oil in a frying pan, add the onion, carrot, celery and remaining garlic and stir over a low heat for about 5 minutes until softened. Add the remaining minced beef and pork and cook gently for 10 minutes, stirring frequently and breaking up any lumps in the meat.

6 Stir in salt and pepper to taste, then add the tomatoes, remaining parsley and the oregano or basil. Stir well, cover and simmer gently for 45 minutes to 1 hour, stirring occasionally.

7 Meanwhile, heat the remaining oil in a large, non-stick frying pan. When hot, cook the meatballs in batches over a medium to high heat for 5–8 minutes until browned on all sides. Shake the pan from time to time so that the meatballs roll around. As they cook, transfer the meatballs to kitchen paper to drain.

8 Preheat the oven to 190°C/375°F/Gas 5. Make the béchamel sauce. Strain the milk to remove the bay leaf and thyme sprig. Melt the butter in a medium pan, add the flour and cook, stirring, for 1–2 minutes.

9 Add the milk a little at a time, whisking vigorously after each addition. Bring to the boil and cook, stirring constantly, until the sauce is smooth and thick. Grate in a little nutmeg to taste and season with salt and pepper. Whisk well, then remove from the heat.

10 Spread about a third of the meat sauce in the bottom of a large, shallow baking dish.

11 Add half the meatballs, spread with a third of the béchamel and cover with half the lasagne sheets. Repeat these layers, then top with the remaining meat sauce and béchamel.

12 Sprinkle the remaining grated Parmesan evenly over the surface and bake for 30–40 minutes or until golden brown and bubbling. Allow the lasagne to stand for 10 minutes before serving. If you like, garnish each serving with extra chopped parsley.

Variation

In the south of Italy, where this type of lasagne is popular, they often add salami, chopped hard-boiled eggs, mozzarella and ricotta cheese to the layers.

Cook's Tips

- *Home-made lasagne does not need pre-cooking, but if you have bought fresh pasta check the instructions on the packet.*
- *To prevent cooked lasagne sheets from sticking together, rinse them under cold running water, then return to the pan with enough cold water to cover. Drain well on kitchen paper before using.*

Frittata di Vermicelli

Vermicelli Omelette

A FRITTATA IS A FLAT BAKED omelette. Here it is made with vegetables and herbs, but you can put anything you fancy in it. Ham, sausage, salami, chicken, mushrooms, courgettes and aubergines are just a few suggestions, or you could simply add mixed herbs. Frittata is absolutely delicious cold. Cut into wedges, it is excellent food for picnics.

INGREDIENTS

50g/2oz dried vermicelli
6 eggs
60ml/4 tbsp panna da cucina or double (heavy) cream
1 handful fresh basil leaves, shredded
1 handful fresh flat leaf (Italian) parsley, chopped
75g/3oz/1 cup freshly grated Parmesan cheese
25g/1oz/2 tbsp butter
15ml/1 tbsp olive oil
1 onion, finely sliced
3 pieces bottled roasted red (bell) pepper, drained, rinsed, dried and cut into strips
1 garlic clove, crushed
salt and ground black pepper
rocket (arugula) leaves, to serve

Serves 4–6

1 Preheat the oven to 190°C/375°F/Gas 5. Cook the pasta in a pan of salted boiling water for 8 minutes.

2 Meanwhile, break the eggs into a bowl and add the cream and herbs. Whisk in about two-thirds of the grated Parmesan and add salt and pepper to taste.

3 Drain the pasta well and allow to cool; snip it into short lengths with scissors. Add to the egg mixture and whisk again. Set aside.

4 Melt the butter in the oil in a large, ovenproof non-stick frying pan. Add the onion and cook gently, stirring frequently, for 5 minutes until softened. Add the peppers and garlic.

5 Pour the egg and pasta mixture into the pan and stir well. Cook over a low to medium heat, without stirring, for 3–5 minutes or until the frittata is just set underneath. Sprinkle over the remaining Parmesan and bake in the oven for 5 minutes or until set. Before serving, leave to stand for at least 5 minutes. Cut into wedges and serve warm or cold, with rocket.

Lasagne Bolognesi

Lasagne from Bologna

THIS IS THE CLASSIC *lasagne al forno*. It is based on a rich, meaty filling, as you would expect from an authentic Bolognese recipe.

INGREDIENTS

1 quantity Bolognese Meat Sauce
150–250ml/5–8fl oz/2/3–1 cup hot beef stock
12 "no-need-to-pre-cook" dried lasagne sheets
50g/2oz/2/3 cup freshly grated Parmesan cheese

For the white sauce
50g/2oz/1/4 cup butter
50g/2oz/1/2 cup plain (all-purpose) flour
900ml/1 1/2 pints/3 3/4 cups hot milk
salt and ground black pepper
Serves 6

1 Preheat the oven to 190°C/375°F/Gas 5. If the Bolognese sauce is cold, reheat it. Once it is hot, stir in enough stock to make it quite runny.

2 Make the white sauce. Melt the butter in a medium pan, add the flour and cook, stirring, for about 1–2 minutes. Add the milk a little at a time, whisking vigorously after each addition. Bring to the boil and cook, stirring, until the sauce is smooth and thick. Add salt and pepper to taste, whisk well, then remove from the heat.

3 Spread about a third of the Bolognese sauce over the bottom of a baking dish.

4 Cover the Bolognese sauce in the bottom of the dish with about a quarter of the white sauce, followed by four sheets of lasagne. Repeat the layers twice more, then cover the top layer of lasagne with the remaining white sauce and sprinkle the grated Parmesan evenly over the top.

5 Bake for 40–45 minutes or until the pasta feels tender when pierced with a skewer. Allow to stand for about 10 minutes before serving.

COOK'S TIPS

- *The Bolognese sauce can be made up to 3 days in advance and kept in a covered container in the refrigerator.*
- *The lasagne is best baked straight after layering or the pasta will begin to absorb the sauces and dry out.*
- *To reheat leftover lasagne, prick it all over with a skewer, then slowly pour a little milk over to moisten. Cover with foil and reheat in a 190°C/375°F/Gas 5 oven for 20 minutes, or until bubbling.*

Cannelloni alla Sorrentina

Cannelloni Sorrentina-style

THERE'S MORE THAN ONE way of making cannelloni. For this fresh-tasting dish, sheets of cooked lasagne are rolled around a tomato filling to make a delicious main course for a summer dinner party. The ingredients are similar to those used on a Neapolitan pizza.

INGREDIENTS

60ml/4 tbsp olive oil
1 small onion, finely chopped
900g/2lb ripe Italian plum tomatoes, peeled and finely chopped
2 garlic cloves, crushed
1 large handful fresh basil leaves, shredded, plus extra basil leaves, to garnish
250ml/8fl oz/1 cup vegetable stock
250ml/8fl oz/1 cup dry white wine
30ml/2 tbsp sun-dried tomato purée (paste)
2.5ml/½ tsp sugar
16–18 fresh or dried lasagne sheets
250g/9oz/generous 1 cup ricotta cheese
130g/4½oz packet mozzarella cheese, drained and diced small
8 bottled anchovy fillets in olive oil, drained and halved lengthways
50g/2oz/⅔ cup freshly grated Parmesan cheese
salt and ground black pepper

Serves 4–6

1 Heat the oil in a medium pan, add the onion and cook gently, stirring frequently, for about 5 minutes until softened. Stir in the tomatoes, garlic and half the basil. Season with salt and pepper to taste and toss over a medium to high heat for 5 minutes.

2 Scoop about half the tomato mixture out of the pan, place in a bowl and set it aside to cool.

3 Stir the vegetable stock, white wine, tomato purée and sugar into the tomato mixture remaining in the pan and simmer for about 20 minutes, stirring occasionally.

4 Meanwhile, cook the lasagne sheets in batches in a pan of salted boiling water, according to the instructions on the packet. Drain and separate the sheets of lasagne and lay them out flat on a clean dish towel.

VARIATION

For vegetarians, use 8 pitted black olives instead of the anchovies. Chop them roughly and sprinkle them in a line along the length of the cannelloni filling.

5 Preheat the oven to 190°C/375°F/Gas 5. Add the ricotta and mozzarella to the tomato mixture in the bowl. Stir in the remaining basil and season to taste with salt and pepper.

6 Spread a little of the mixture over each lasagne sheet. Place an anchovy fillet across the width of each sheet, close to one of the short ends. Starting from the end with the anchovy, roll each lasagne sheet up like a Swiss roll (jelly roll).

7 Purée the tomato sauce in a blender or food processor. Spread a little of the tomato sauce over the bottom of a large baking dish. Arrange the cannelloni seam side down in a single layer in the dish and spoon the remaining sauce over them.

8 Sprinkle the Parmesan over the top and bake for 20 minutes or until the topping is golden brown and bubbling. Serve hot, garnished with basil leaves.

Lasagne ai Tre Formaggi

Lasagne with Three Cheeses

RICH AND FILLING, this is the type of lasagne that is popular in America. It was invented by Italian immigrants who made full use of the abundant ingredients available to them.

INGREDIENTS

25g/1oz/2 tbsp butter
15ml/1 tbsp olive oil
225–250g/8–9oz/2–2¼ cups button (white) mushrooms, quartered lengthways
30ml/2 tbsp chopped fresh flat leaf (Italian) parsley
1 quantity Bolognese Sauce with Red Wine
250–350ml/8–12fl oz/1–1½ cups hot beef stock
9–12 fresh lasagne sheets, pre-cooked if necessary
450g/1lb/2 cups ricotta cheese
1 large egg
3 x 130g/4½oz packets mozzarella cheese, drained and thinly sliced
115g/4oz/1⅓ cups freshly grated Parmesan cheese
salt and ground black pepper
Serves 6–8

1 Preheat the oven to 190°C/375°F/Gas 5. Melt the butter in the oil in a frying pan. Add the mushrooms, with salt and pepper to taste, and toss over a medium to high heat for about 5–8 minutes until the mushrooms are tender and quite dry. Remove the pan from the heat and stir in the parsley.

2 Make the Bolognese sauce or, if it is cold, reheat it. Once it is hot, stir in enough hot beef stock to make the sauce quite runny.

3 Stir in the mushroom and parsley mixture, then spread about a quarter of this sauce over the bottom of a baking dish. Cover with three or four sheets of lasagne.

4 Beat together the ricotta and egg in a bowl, with salt and pepper to taste, then spread about a third of the mixture over the lasagne sheets. Cover with a third of the mozzarella slices, then sprinkle with about a quarter of the grated Parmesan.

5 Repeat these layers twice, using half the remaining Bolognese sauce each time, and finishing with the remaining Parmesan.

6 Bake the lasagne for 30–40 minutes or until the cheese topping is golden brown and bubbling. Allow to stand for about 10 minutes before serving.

VARIATIONS

- *For a spicier alternative version of this recipe, replace the meat sauce with the sauce used for Spaghetti with Minced Beef Sauce.*
- *Grated mature (sharp) Cheddar cheese is very good in lasagne. Use it instead of some, or all, of the grated Parmesan. It is a good deal less expensive than Parmesan.*

COOK'S TIP

If you have made the lasagne yourself, there is no need to pre-cook it, but if you have bought fresh lasagne, check whether it needs to be boiled briefly before being layered. Packets of fresh lasagne from the supermarket usually need to be boiled for 2 minutes before use.

Conchiglie Ripiene

Stuffed Shells

THIS MAKES AN EXCELLENT dinner party starter for six, or a vegetarian main course for four, in which case you should fill 20 shells, rather than 18; there will be more than enough filling.

INGREDIENTS

18 large pasta shells for stuffing
25g/1oz/2 tbsp butter
1 small onion, finely chopped
275g/10oz fresh spinach leaves, trimmed, washed and shredded
1 garlic clove, crushed
1 sachet of saffron powder
nutmeg
250g/9oz/generous 1 cup ricotta cheese
1 egg
1 quantity Winter Tomato Sauce
about 150ml/¼ pint/⅔ cup dry white wine, vegetable stock or water
100ml/3½fl oz/scant ½ cup panna da cucina or double (heavy) cream
50g/2oz/⅔ cup freshly grated Parmesan cheese
salt and ground black pepper

Serves 6

1 Preheat the oven to 190°C/375°F/Gas 5. Bring a large pan of salted water to the boil. Add the pasta shells and cook for 10 minutes. Drain the shells, half fill the pan with cold water and place the shells in the water.

2 Melt the butter in a pan, add the onion and cook gently, stirring, for about 5 minutes until softened. Add the spinach, garlic and saffron, then grate in plenty of nutmeg and add salt and pepper to taste. Stir well, increase the heat to medium and cook for 5–8 minutes, stirring frequently, until the spinach is wilted and tender.

3 Increase the heat to high and stir until the water is driven off and the spinach is quite dry. Place the spinach into a bowl, add the ricotta and beat well to mix. Taste for seasoning, then add the egg and beat well again.

4 Purée the tomato sauce in a blender or food processor, pour it into a measuring jug (cup) and make it up to 750ml/1¼ pints/3 cups with wine, stock or water. Add the cream, stir well to mix and taste for seasoning.

5 Spread about half the sauce over the bottom of six individual gratin dishes. Remove the pasta shells one at a time from the water, shake them well and fill them with the spinach and ricotta mixture, using a teaspoon. Arrange three shells in the centre of each dish, spoon the remaining sauce over them, then cover with the grated Parmesan. Bake in the oven for 10–12 minutes or until hot. Leave to stand for about 5 minutes before serving.

Cannelloni di Carne Mista

Mixed Meat Cannelloni

A CREAMY, RICH FILLING and sauce make this an unusual cannelloni.

INGREDIENTS

60ml/4 tbsp olive oil
1 onion, finely chopped
1 carrot, finely chopped
2 garlic cloves, crushed
2 ripe Italian plum tomatoes, peeled and finely chopped
130g/4½oz minced (ground) beef
130g/4½oz minced (ground) pork
250g/9oz minced (ground) chicken
30ml/2 tbsp brandy
25g/1oz/2 tbsp butter
90ml/6 tbsp panna da cucina or double (heavy) cream
16 dried cannelloni tubes
75g/3oz/1 cup freshly grated Parmesan cheese
salt and ground black pepper
green salad, to serve

For the white sauce
50g/2oz/¼ cup butter
50g/2oz/½ cup plain (all-purpose) flour
900ml/1½ pints/3¾ cups milk
nutmeg

Serves 4

1 Heat the oil in a frying pan, add the onion, carrot, garlic and tomatoes and cook over a low heat, stirring, for about 10 minutes or until very soft.

COOK'S TIP

Instead of pasta tubes you could roll fresh lasagne sheets around the filling.

2 Add all the minced meats to the pan and cook gently for about 10 minutes, stirring frequently to break up any lumps. Add the brandy, increase the heat and stir until it has reduced, then add the butter and cream and cook gently, stirring occasionally, for about 10 minutes. Allow to cool.

3 Preheat the oven to 190°C/375°F/Gas 5. Make the white sauce. Melt the butter in a medium pan, add the flour and cook, stirring, for 1–2 minutes. Add the milk a little at a time, whisking vigorously after each addition. Bring to the boil and cook, stirring, until the sauce is smooth and thick. Grate in fresh nutmeg to taste, then season with salt and pepper and whisk well. Remove the pan from the heat.

4 Spoon a little of the white sauce into a baking dish. Fill the cannelloni tubes with the meat mixture and place in a single layer in the dish. Pour the remaining white sauce over them, then sprinkle with the Parmesan. Bake for 35–40 minutes or until the pasta feels tender when pierced with a skewer. Allow to stand for 10 minutes before serving with green salad.

Cannelloni con Ripieno di Carne

Cannelloni Stuffed with Meat

THIS IS A RICH AND SUBSTANTIAL dish, which takes quite a long time to prepare. Serve it for a party – it can be made a day ahead up to the baking stage. Your guests are bound to appreciate your efforts, because the cannelloni tastes so good.

INGREDIENTS

15ml/1 tbsp olive oil
1 small onion, finely chopped
450g/1lb minced (ground) beef
1 garlic clove, finely chopped
5ml/1 tsp dried mixed herbs
120ml/4fl oz/½ cup beef stock
1 egg
75g/3oz cooked ham or mortadella sausage, finely chopped
45ml/3 tbsp fine fresh white breadcrumbs
150g/5oz/1⅔ cups freshly grated Parmesan cheese
18 "no-need-to-pre-cook" cannelloni tubes
salt and ground black pepper

For the tomato sauce

30ml/2 tbsp olive oil
1 small onion, finely chopped
½ carrot, finely chopped
1 celery stick, finely chopped
1 garlic clove, crushed
400g/14oz can chopped Italian plum tomatoes
a few sprigs of fresh basil
2.5ml/½ tsp dried oregano

For the white sauce

50g/2oz/¼ cup butter
50g/2oz/½ cup plain (all-purpose) flour
900ml/1½ pints/3¾ cups milk
nutmeg

Serves 6

1 Heat the olive oil in a frying pan and cook the finely chopped onion over a gentle heat, stirring occasionally, for about 5 minutes until softened.

2 Add the minced beef and garlic and cook gently for 10 minutes, stirring and breaking up any lumps with a wooden spoon. Add the mixed herbs, and salt and pepper to taste, then moisten with half the stock. Cover the pan and simmer for 25 minutes, stirring from time to time and adding more stock as the mixture reduces. Spoon into a bowl and leave to cool.

3 Meanwhile, make the tomato sauce. Heat the olive oil in a medium pan, add the vegetables and garlic and cook over a medium heat, stirring frequently, for about 10 minutes. Add the canned tomatoes. Fill the empty can with water, pour it into the pan, then stir in the herbs, with salt and pepper to taste. Bring to the boil, lower the heat, cover and simmer for about 25–30 minutes, stirring occasionally. Purée the tomato sauce in a blender or food processor.

4 Add the egg, ham or mortadella, breadcrumbs and 90ml/6 tbsp of the grated Parmesan to the meat and stir well to mix. Taste for seasoning.

5 Spread a little of the tomato sauce over the bottom of a baking dish. Using a teaspoon, fill the cannelloni tubes with the meat mixture and place them in a single layer in the dish on top of the tomato sauce. Pour the remaining tomato sauce over the top.

6 Preheat the oven to 190°C/375°F/Gas 5. Make the white sauce. Melt the butter in a pan, add the flour and cook, stirring, for 1–2 minutes. Add the milk a little at a time, whisking vigorously after each addition.

7 Bring to the boil and cook, stirring, until the sauce is smooth and thick. Grate in fresh nutmeg to taste and season with a little salt and pepper. Whisk well, then remove from the heat.

8 Pour the white sauce over the stuffed cannelloni, then sprinkle with the remaining Parmesan. Place in the oven and bake for 40–45 minutes or until the cannelloni tubes feel tender when pierced with a skewer. Allow the cannelloni to stand for about 10 minutes before serving.

Maccheroni ai Quattro Formaggi

Macaroni with Four Cheeses

RICH AND CREAMY, this is a deluxe macaroni cheese that can be served for an informal lunch or supper party. It goes well with both a tomato and basil salad or a leafy green salad.

INGREDIENTS

250g/9oz/2¼ cups short-cut macaroni
50g/2oz/¼ cup butter
50g/2oz/½ cup plain (all-purpose) flour
600ml/1 pint/2½ cups milk
100ml/3½ fl oz/scant ½ cup panna da cucina *or double (heavy) cream*
100ml/3½ fl oz/scant ½ cup dry white wine
50g/2oz/½ cup grated Gruyère or Emmenthal cheese
50g/2oz Fontina cheese, diced small
50g/2oz Gorgonzola cheese, crumbled
75g/3oz/1 cup freshly grated Parmesan cheese
salt and ground black pepper

Serves 4

1 Preheat the oven to 180°C/350°F/Gas 4. Cook the pasta according to the instructions on the packet.

2 Meanwhile, gently melt the butter in a medium pan, add the flour and cook, stirring, for about 1–2 minutes. Add the milk a little at a time, whisking vigorously after each addition. Stir in the cream, followed by the dry white wine. Bring to the boil. Cook, stirring continuously, until the sauce thickens, then remove the sauce from the heat.

3 Add the Gruyère or Emmental, Fontina, Gorgonzola and about a third of the grated Parmesan to the sauce. Stir well to mix in the cheeses, then taste for seasoning and add salt and pepper if necessary.

4 Drain the pasta well and transfer it into a baking dish. Pour the sauce over the pasta and mix well, then sprinkle the remaining Parmesan over the top. Bake for 25–30 minutes or until golden brown. Serve hot.

Lasagne alla Siciliana

Sicilian Lasagne

LASAGNE IS NOT TRADITIONAL in Sicily as it is in northern Italy, but the Sicilians have their own version.

INGREDIENTS

1 small onion
1/2 carrot
1/2 celery stick
45ml/3 tbsp olive oil
250g/9oz diced boneless pork
60ml/4 tbsp dry white wine
400g/14oz can chopped Italian plum tomatoes or 400ml/14fl oz/1 2/3 cups passata (bottled strained tomatoes)
200ml/7fl oz/scant 1 cup chicken stock
15ml/1 tbsp tomato purée (paste)
2 bay leaves
15ml/1 tbsp chopped fresh flat leaf (Italian) parsley
250g/9oz fresh lasagne sheets, pre-cooked if necessary
2 hard-boiled eggs, sliced
125g/4 1/2oz packet mozzarella cheese, drained and sliced
60ml/4 tbsp freshly grated Pecorino cheese
salt and ground black pepper

Serves 6

1 Chop the fresh vegetables finely, either in a food processor or by hand. Heat 30ml/2 tbsp of the oil in a frying pan, add the chopped vegetables and cook over a medium heat, stirring frequently, for about 10 minutes.

2 Add the pork and fry for about 5 minutes, stirring occasionally, until well browned on all sides. Pour in the wine and let it bubble and reduce for a few minutes, then add the tomatoes or passata, the stock and the tomato purée. Make a tear in each bay leaf to release the flavour, then add to the pan with the parsley and salt and pepper to taste, mixing well. Cover and cook for 30–40 minutes until the pork is tender, stirring from time to time. Take the pan off the heat and remove and discard the bay leaves from the sauce.

3 Using a slotted spoon, lift the pieces of meat out of the sauce. Chop them roughly, then return them to the sauce. Stir well.

4 Preheat the oven to 190°C/375°F/Gas 5. Bring a pan of salted water to the boil. Cut the lasagne sheets into 2.5cm/1in strips and add them to the boiling water. Cook for 3–4 minutes until just *al dente*. Drain well, then stir the strips into the sauce.

5 Spread out half the pasta and sauce mixture in a shallow baking dish and cover with half the egg and mozzarella slices and half the grated Pecorino. Repeat the layers, then drizzle the remaining oil over the top. Bake for 30–35 minutes until golden brown and bubbling. Allow to stand for about 10 minutes before serving.

Pasticcio di Fusilli

Fusilli with Ham and Cheese

WITH ITS CRISPY CRUST and moist and creamy centre, this quick and easy pasta bake is both filling and nutritious. Serve it for a winter supper, with a salad on the side.

INGREDIENTS

300g/11oz/2¾ cups dried fusilli, eliche or other short pasta shapes
3 eggs
200ml/7fl oz/scant 1 cup milk
150ml/¼ pint/⅔ cup single (light) cream
150g/5oz Gruyère cheese, grated
nutmeg
115g/4oz cooked ham, cut into strips
30ml/2 tbsp freshly grated Parmesan cheese
salt and ground black pepper

Serves 4

1 Preheat the oven to 190°C/375°F/Gas 5. Bring a large pan of salted water to the boil. Add the pasta and cook for 5 minutes.

2 Meanwhile, beat the eggs in a jug with the milk, cream and half the grated Gruyère. Grate in a little fresh nutmeg and season to taste.

3 Drain the pasta and transfer half of it into a buttered baking dish. Arrange half the strips of ham on top, then follow with the remaining pasta and ham. Pour the egg and cream mixture into the dish, stir to mix a little, then sprinkle the remaining Gruyère and the Parmesan over the top. Bake for 30 minutes or until golden brown.

Lasagne al Ragù d'Agnello

Lasagne with Lamb

IT IS UNUSUAL TO MAKE lasagne with lamb, but the flavour is excellent.

INGREDIENTS

15ml/1 tbsp olive oil
1 small onion, finely chopped
450g/1lb minced (ground) lamb
1 garlic clove, crushed
45ml/3 tbsp dry white wine
5ml/1 tsp dried mixed herbs
5ml/1 tsp dried oregano
450ml/¾ pint/scant 2 cups passata (bottled strained tomatoes)
12–16 fresh lasagne sheets
30ml/2 tbsp freshly grated Parmesan cheese
salt and ground black pepper

For the white sauce
50g/2oz/½ cup butter
50g/2oz/½ cup plain (all-purpose) flour
900ml/1½ pints/3¾ cups hot milk
30ml/2 tbsp freshly grated Parmesan cheese
nutmeg

Serves 4–6

1 Heat the oil in a pan and cook the onion over a gentle heat, stirring frequently, for about 5 minutes until softened. Add the minced lamb and garlic and cook gently for 10 minutes, stirring frequently. Stir in salt and pepper to taste, then add the wine and cook rapidly for about 2 minutes, stirring constantly. Stir in the herbs and passata. Simmer gently for 45 minutes to 1 hour, stirring occasionally.

2 Preheat the oven to 190°C/375°F/Gas 5. Make the white sauce. Melt the butter in a pan, add the flour and cook, stirring, for 1–2 minutes. Add the milk a little at a time, whisking vigorously after each addition. Bring to the boil and cook, stirring, until the sauce is smooth and thick. Add the Parmesan, grate in fresh nutmeg to taste, season with a little salt and pepper and whisk well. Remove the pan from the heat.

3 Spread a few spoonfuls of meat sauce over the bottom of a baking dish and cover with three or four sheets of lasagne. Spread a quarter of the remaining meat sauce over the lasagne, then a quarter of the white sauce. Repeat the layers three times, finishing with white sauce.

4 Sprinkle the Parmesan over the surface and bake for 30–40 minutes or until the topping is golden brown and bubbling. Allow to stand for about 10 minutes before serving.

Pasticciata

Pasta Pie

THIS IS AN EXCELLENT SUPPER dish for vegetarians, and children absolutely love it. All the ingredients will probably already be in your store cupboard or refrigerator, so it makes a good "standby" meal if you have guests at short notice.

INGREDIENTS

30ml/2 tbsp olive oil
1 small onion, finely chopped
400g/14oz can chopped Italian plum tomatoes
15ml/1 tbsp sun-dried tomato purée (paste)
5ml/1 tsp dried mixed herbs
5ml/1 tsp dried oregano or basil
5ml/1 tsp sugar
175g/6oz/1 1/2 cups dried conchiglie or rigatoni
30ml/2 tbsp freshly grated Parmesan cheese
30ml/2 tbsp dried breadcrumbs
salt and ground black pepper

For the white sauce
25g/1oz/2 tbsp butter
25g/1oz/1/4 cup plain (all-purpose) flour
600ml/1 pint/2 1/2 cups milk
1 egg

Serves 4

1 Heat the olive oil in a large frying pan and cook the finely chopped onion over a gentle heat, stirring frequently, for about 5 minutes until softened. Stir in the tomatoes. Fill the empty can with water and add it to the tomato mixture, with the tomato purée, herbs and sugar.

2 Add salt and pepper to taste and bring to the boil, stirring. Cover the pan, lower the heat and simmer, stirring occasionally, for 10–15 minutes.

3 Meanwhile, preheat the oven to 190°C/375°F/Gas 5. Cook the pasta according to the instructions on the packet.

4 Meanwhile, make the white sauce. Melt the butter in a pan, add the flour and cook, stirring, for 1 minute.

5 Add the milk a little at a time, whisking well after each addition. Bring to the boil and cook, stirring, until the sauce is smooth and thick. Season, then remove the pan from the heat.

6 Drain the pasta and transfer it into a baking dish. Taste the tomato sauce and add salt and pepper. Pour the sauce into the dish and stir well to mix with the pasta.

7 Beat the egg into the white sauce, then pour the sauce over the pasta mixture. Separate the pasta, with a fork, in several places so that the white sauce fills the gaps.

8 Level the surface, sprinkle it with grated Parmesan and breadcrumbs and bake for 15–20 minutes or until the topping is golden brown and the cheese is bubbling. Allow to stand for about 10 minutes before serving.

VARIATIONS

- *If you don't have any dried breadcrumbs, you can cheat by crushing a packet of crisps and sprinkling them over the pasticciata instead. Children love this crisp topping, especially if you use their favourite flavour.*
- *You could add chunks of roasted vegetables, such as courgettes (zucchini), bell peppers or aubergines (eggplants) to the tomato sauce if you like. This will add extra flavour and make a more substantial meal.*
- *For meat eaters, Bolognese sauce can be used instead of the tomato sauce.*

Stuffed Pasta

Making your own pasta is easier than you think, especially if you have a pasta machine. You can make pasta by hand, but the machine will save you time and effort, and make the whole process much more interesting and fun.

The recipes in this chapter are for a variety of different shapes, but they all use the same basic pasta dough. For stuffing, the pasta is always made with eggs, which strengthens the dough. This helps to hold the filling in during cooking.

Stuffed pasta originated in the north of Italy, but now every Italian town seems to have its own speciality, often associated with a particular day in the calendar, like a feast day or New Year. Home-made stuffed pasta is therefore a special occasion dish, and it is usually served very simply, either drizzled with melted butter or oil, or floating in *brodo*.

If you are going to try your hand at making your own stuffed pasta, it is the ideal dinner party starter. Practice makes perfect when it comes to making anything by hand, but much of the charm of home-made pasta lies in its imperfections, so don't try too hard to make every shape precisely the same size. After all, you want your guests to know you have made it yourself. See page 42 for the recipe to make home-made pasta (Pasta with Eggs).

Ravioli alla Romagnola

Ravioli with Pork and Turkey

THIS ROMAN-STYLE RAVIOLI stuffed with minced meat and cheese is scented with fresh herbs. It makes a substantial first course.

INGREDIENTS

1 quantity Pasta with Eggs
50g/2oz/¼ cup butter
a large bunch of fresh sage, leaves removed and roughly chopped
60ml/4 tbsp freshly grated Parmesan cheese
extra sage leaves and freshly grated Parmesan cheese, to serve

For the filling

25g/1oz/2 tbsp butter
150g/5oz minced (ground) pork
115g/4oz minced (ground) turkey
4 fresh sage leaves, finely chopped
1 sprig of fresh rosemary, leaves removed and finely chopped
30ml/2 tbsp dry white wine
65g/2½oz/generous ¼ cup ricotta cheese
45ml/3 tbsp freshly grated Parmesan cheese
1 egg
nutmeg
salt and ground black pepper

Serves 8

1 Make the filling. Melt the butter in a medium pan, add the minced pork and turkey and the herbs and cook gently for 5–6 minutes, stirring frequently and breaking up any lumps in the meat with a wooden spoon. Add salt and pepper to taste and stir well to mix thoroughly.

2 Add the wine to the pan and stir again. Simmer for 1–2 minutes until reduced slightly, then cover the pan and simmer gently for about 20 minutes, stirring occasionally. With a slotted spoon, transfer the meat to a bowl and leave to cool.

3 Add the ricotta and Parmesan cheeses to the bowl with the egg and freshly grated nutmeg to taste. Stir well to mix the ingredients thoroughly.

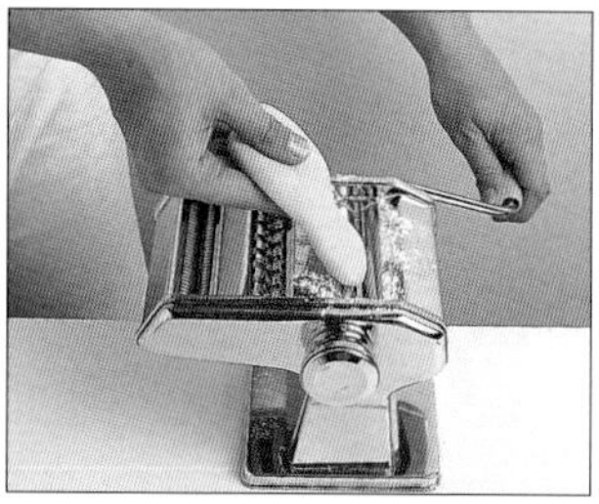

4 Using a pasta machine, roll out one-quarter of the pasta into a 90cm–1 metre/35in–3 foot strip. Cut the strip with a sharp knife into two 45–50cm/18–20in lengths (you can do this during rolling if the strip gets too long to manage).

5 Using a teaspoon, put 10–12 little mounds of the filling along one side of one of the pasta strips, spacing them evenly. Brush a little water on to the pasta strip around each mound, then fold the plain side of the pasta strip over the filling.

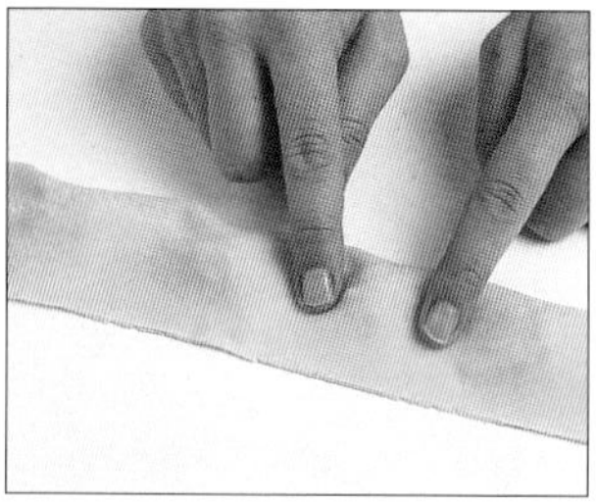

6 Starting from the folded edge, press down gently with your fingertips around each mound of filling, pushing the air out at the unfolded edge. Sprinkle lightly with flour.

7 With a fluted pasta wheel, cut along each long side, then in between each mound to make small square shapes. Dust lightly with flour.

8 Put the ravioli in a single layer on floured dish towels and leave to dry while repeating the process with the remaining pasta to make 80–96 ravioli altogether.

9 Drop the ravioli into a large pan of salted boiling water, bring back to the boil and boil for 4–5 minutes.

COOK'S TIP

Minced (ground) pork and turkey are widely available at supermarkets, but if you cannot get one or the other you can use just one type of meat, or substitute minced veal, beef or lamb to use in the ravioli filling.

10 While the ravioli are cooking, melt the butter in a small saucepan, add the fresh sage leaves and stir over a medium to high heat until the sage leaves are sizzling in the butter.

11 Drain the ravioli and pour half into a warmed large bowl. Sprinkle with half the grated Parmesan, then half the sage butter. Repeat with the remaining ravioli, Parmesan and sage butter. Serve immediately, garnished with fresh sage leaves. Hand more grated Parmesan separately.

Agnolotti alla Salsa di Vodka

Meat-filled Agnolotti with Vodka Sauce

DAINTY HALF MOON SHAPES are filled with spiced meat and bacon and served with a cream and blue-cheese sauce spiked with vodka. This is a special first course for a dinner party.

INGREDIENTS

1 quantity Pasta with Eggs
freshly grated Parmesan cheese, to serve

For the filling

15ml/1 tbsp olive oil
75g/3oz pancetta, streaky (fatty) bacon or ham, finely diced
250g/9oz minced (ground) pork or veal
2 garlic cloves, crushed
good pinch of ground cinnamon
120ml/4fl oz/½ cup red wine
60ml/4 tbsp chopped fresh flat leaf (Italian) parsley
1 small egg
salt and ground black pepper

For the sauce

50g/2oz/¼ cup butter
250ml/8fl oz/1 cup panna da cucina or double (heavy) cream
115g/4oz Gorgonzola cheese, diced
45ml/3 tbsp vodka

Serves 6–8

1 Make the filling. Heat the oil in a medium pan, add the pancetta, bacon or ham and stir-fry for a few minutes until lightly coloured. Add the minced pork, the garlic, cinnamon and salt and pepper to taste and cook gently for 5–6 minutes, stirring frequently and breaking up any lumps.

2 Pour in the wine and stir well to mix, then simmer gently, stirring occasionally, for 15–20 minutes until the meat is cooked and quite dry. Transfer the meat to a bowl with a slotted spoon and leave to cool.

3 Add the parsley and egg to the meat mixture and stir well to mix.

4 Using a pasta machine, roll out one-quarter of the pasta into a 90cm–1 metre/36in–3 foot strip. Cut the strip with a sharp knife into two 45–50cm/18–20in lengths (you can do this during rolling if the strip gets too long to manage).

5 Using a teaspoon, put 8–10 little mounds of the filling along one side of one of the pasta strips, spacing them evenly. Brush a little water around each mound, then fold the plain side of the pasta strip over the filling.

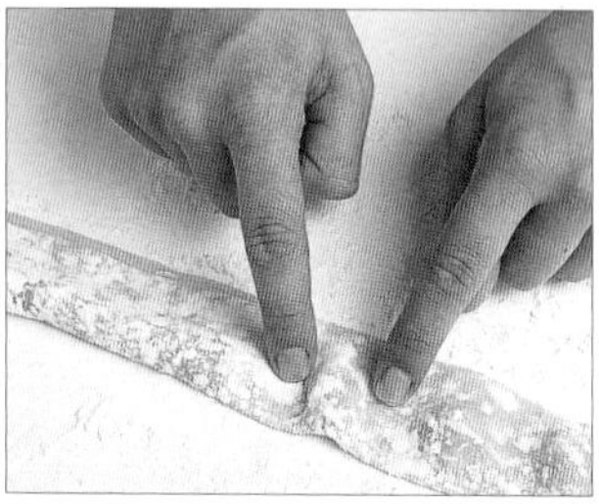

6 Starting from the folded edge, press down gently with your fingertips around each mound, pushing the air out at the unfolded edge.

7 Using only half of a 5cm/2in fluted round ravioli or biscuit (cookie) cutter, cut around each mound of filling to make a half-moon shape. The folded edge should be the straight edge. If you like, press the cut edges of the agnolotti with the tines of a fork to give a decorative effect.

8 Put the agnolotti on floured dish towels, spreading them out in a single layer, so that they don't stick together. Sprinkle them lightly with flour and leave to dry while repeating the process with the remaining pasta to get 64–80 agnolotti altogether.

9 Drop the agnolotti into a large pan of salted boiling water, bring back to the boil and boil for 4–5 minutes.

10 Meanwhile, make the sauce. Melt the butter in a medium pan, add the cream and cheese and heat through, stirring, until the cheese has melted. Add the vodka, season to taste with black pepper and stir well to mix.

11 Drain the agnolotti and divide them among six or eight warmed bowls. Spoon the sauce over them and sprinkle liberally with grated Parmesan. Serve immediately.

Variation

- *Instead of the pancetta, bacon or ham, you could use a spicy salami for the agnolotti filling. Buy the salami in one very thick piece, peel off the skin, then chop the salami finely.*
- *Agnolotti are also often made with prosciutto crudo (Parma ham), which gives them a more delicate flavour than the streaky (fatty) pancetta.*

Cook's Tip

Gorgonzola is a sharp-tasting blue Italian cheese with a soft and creamy consistency. Gorgonzola piccante *is a particularly strong variety, while gorgonzola* dolce *– better known as dolcelatte – is creamier and less sharp in flavour. Supermarkets, specialist cheese shops and delicatessens usually sell both types of Gorgonzola.*

Ravioli con la Zucca

Ravioli with Pumpkin

THIS IS A VERY SIMPLE VERSION of a Christmas Eve speciality from Lombardy. In traditional recipes the pumpkin filling is flavoured with *mostarda di frutta* (a kind of sweet fruit pickle), crushed amaretti biscuits and sugar. Here the pumpkin is seasoned with Parmesan and nutmeg. It is quite sweet enough for most tastes.

INGREDIENTS

1 quantity Pasta with Eggs
115g/4oz/½ cup butter
freshly grated Parmesan cheese, to serve

For the filling

450g/1lb piece of pumpkin
15ml/1 tbsp olive oil
40g/1½oz/scant ¼ cup freshly grated Parmesan cheese
nutmeg
salt and ground black pepper

Serves 8

1 Make the filling. Preheat the oven to 220°C/425°F/Gas 7. Cut the piece of pumpkin into chunks and remove the seeds and fibres. Put the chunks, skin side down, in a roasting pan and drizzle the oil over the pumpkin flesh. Roast in the oven for 30 minutes, turning the pieces over once or twice.

2 Leave the roasted pumpkin until it is cool enough to handle, then scrape the flesh out into a bowl and discard the pumpkin skin.

3 Mash the roasted pumpkin flesh with a fork, then add the grated Parmesan and freshly grated nutmeg and salt and pepper to taste. Stir well to mix, then set aside until cold.

4 Using a pasta machine, roll out one-quarter of the pasta into a 90cm–1 metre/35in–3 foot strip. Cut the strip with a sharp knife into two 45–50cm/18–20in lengths (you can do this during rolling if the strip gets too long to manage).

5 Using a teaspoon, put 10–12 little mounds of the filling along one side of one of the pasta strips, spacing them evenly.

6 Brush a little water around each mound, then fold the plain side of the pasta strip over the mounds of filling. Starting from the folded edge, press down gently with your fingertips around each mound, pushing the air out at the unfolded edge. Sprinkle lightly with flour.

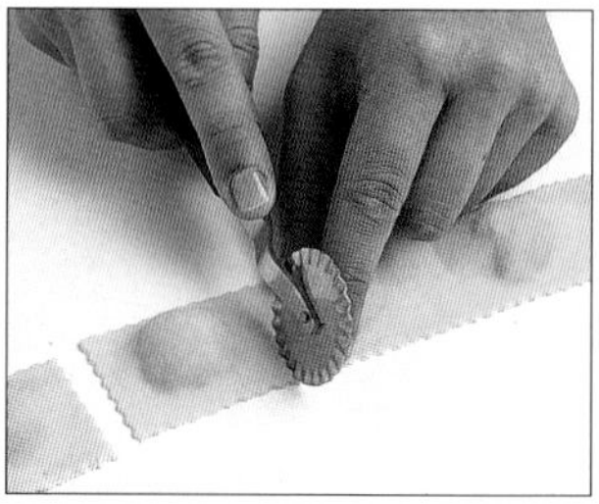

7 With a fluted pasta wheel, cut along each long side, then in between each mound to make small square shapes. Put the ravioli on floured dish towels, sprinkle lightly with flour and leave to dry, while repeating the process with the remaining pasta to get 80–96 ravioli altogether.

8 Drop the ravioli into a large pan of salted boiling water, bring back to the boil and boil for 4–5 minutes. Meanwhile, melt the butter in a small pan until it is sizzling.

9 Drain the ravioli and divide them equally among eight warmed dinner plates or large bowls. Drizzle the sizzling butter over the ravioli and serve immediately, sprinkled with grated Parmesan. Hand more grated Parmesan separately.

VARIATION

You can buy mostarda di frutta *at Italian delicatessens, especially at Christmas time. If you would like to try some in the filling, add about 45ml/3 tbsp, together with a few crushed amaretti.*

Ravioli di Magro

Spinach and Ricotta Ravioli

THE LITERAL TRANSLATION OF *ravioli di magro* is lean ravioli. It is used to describe meat-less ravioli, usually those with a spinach and ricotta filling. *Ravioli di magro* are served on Christmas Eve, a time when meat-filled pasta should not be eaten.

INGREDIENTS

1 quantity Pasta with Eggs
freshly grated Parmesan cheese, to serve

For the filling

40g/1 1/2oz/3 tbsp butter
175g/6oz fresh spinach leaves, trimmed, washed and shredded
200g/7oz/scant 1 cup ricotta cheese
25g/1oz/1/3 cup freshly grated Parmesan cheese
nutmeg
1 small egg
salt and ground black pepper

For the sauce

50g/2oz/1/4 cup butter
250ml/8fl oz/1 cup panna da cucina or double (heavy) cream
50g/2oz/2/3 cup freshly grated Parmesan cheese

Serves 8

1 Make the filling. Melt the butter in a medium pan, add the spinach and salt and pepper to taste and cook over a medium heat for 5–8 minutes, stirring frequently, until the spinach is wilted and tender. Increase the heat to high and stir until the water is driven off and the spinach is quite dry.

2 Place the spinach into a bowl and leave until cold, then add the ricotta, grated Parmesan and freshly grated nutmeg to taste. Beat well to mix, taste for seasoning, then add the egg and beat well again.

3 Using a pasta machine, roll out one-quarter of the pasta into a 90cm–1 metre/36in–3 foot strip. Cut the strip with a sharp knife into two 45–50cm/18–20in lengths (you can do this during rolling if the strip gets too long to manage).

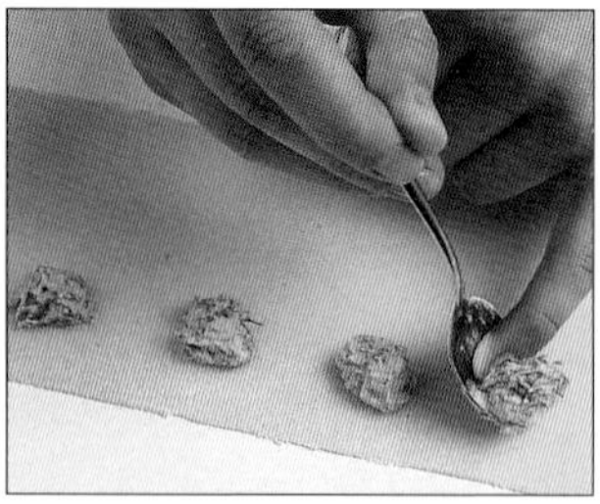

4 Using a teaspoon, put 10–12 little mounds of the filling along one side of one of the pasta strips, spacing them evenly. Brush a little water around each mound, then fold the plain side of the pasta strip over the filling.

5 Starting from the folded edge, press down gently with your fingertips around each mound of filling, pushing the air out at the unfolded edge. Sprinkle lightly with flour.

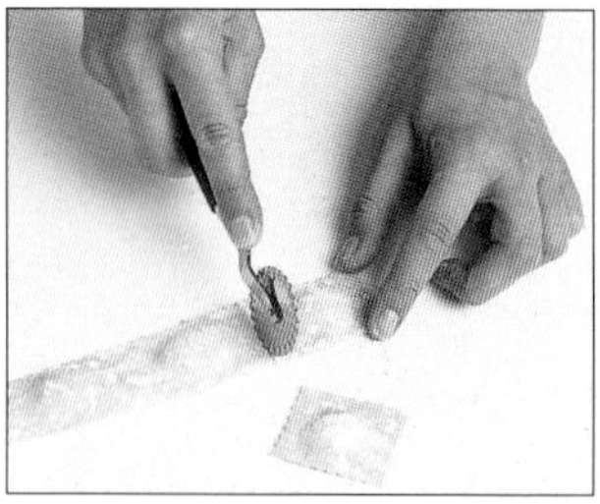

6 With a fluted pasta wheel, cut along each long side, then in between each mound to make small square shapes.

7 Put the ravioli on floured dish towels, sprinkle lightly with flour and leave to dry while repeating the process with the remaining pasta to get 80–96 ravioli altogether.

8 Drop the ravioli into a large pan of salted boiling water, bring back to the boil and boil for 4–5 minutes.

9 Meanwhile, make the sauce. Gently heat the butter, cream and Parmesan in a medium pan until the butter and Parmesan have melted.

10 Increase the heat and simmer for a minute or two until the sauce is slightly reduced, then add salt and pepper to taste.

11 Drain the ravioli and divide them equally among eight warmed large bowls. Drizzle the sauce over them and serve immediately, sprinkled with grated Parmesan.

Variation

If you prefer, serve the ravioli with sizzling sage butter. Melt 50g/2oz/ 1/4 cup butter in a small pan, add a handful of fresh sage leaves and stir constantly over a medium to high heat until sizzling. This will be slightly less rich than the cream sauce suggested here.

Cook's Tip

To prevent the pasta sticking when working with it, lightly flour the work surface and your cutting tools and use more flour as necessary.

Ravioli al Granchio

Ravioli with Crab

THIS MODERN RECIPE for a dinner party starter uses chilli-flavoured pasta, which looks and tastes good with crab, but you can use plain pasta if you prefer.

INGREDIENTS

1 quantity Chilli-flavoured Pasta with Eggs
90g/3½oz/ 6 tbsp butter
juice of 1 lemon

For the filling

175g/6oz/¾ cup mascarpone
175g/6oz/¾ cup crabmeat
30ml/2 tbsp finely chopped fresh flat leaf (Italian) parsley
finely grated rind of 1 lemon
pinch of crushed dried chillies (optional)
salt and ground black pepper

Serves 4

COOK'S TIP

You can use all white crabmeat or a mixture of white and dark. If you use dark meat, the flavour will be stronger.

1 Make the filling. Put the mascarpone in a bowl and mash it with a fork. Add the crabmeat, parsley, lemon rind, crushed dried chillies (if using) and salt and pepper to taste. Stir well.

2 Using a pasta machine, roll out one-quarter of the pasta into a 90cm–1 metre/36in–3 foot strip. Cut the strip with a sharp knife into two 45–50cm/18–20in lengths (you can do this during rolling if the strip gets too long to manage).

3 With a 6cm/2½in fluted biscuit (cookie) cutter, cut out eight squares from each pasta strip.

4 Using a teaspoon, put a mound of filling in the centre of half the discs. Brush a little water around the edge of the filled discs, then top with the plain discs and press the edges to seal. For a decorative finish, press the edges with the tines of a fork.

5 Put the ravioli on floured dish towels, sprinkle lightly with flour and leave to dry while repeating the process with the remaining dough to make 32 ravioli altogether. If you have any stuffing left, you can re-roll the pasta trimmings and make more ravioli.

6 Cook the ravioli in a large pan of salted boiling water for 4–5 minutes. Meanwhile, melt the butter and lemon juice in a small pan until sizzling.

7 Drain the ravioli and divide them equally among four warmed bowls. Drizzle the lemon butter over the ravioli and serve immediately.

Culurgiones

Sardinian Ravioli

THESE RAVIOLI, with their unusual mashed potato and mint filling, are from northern Sardinia. Here they are gratinéed in the oven with butter and cheese, but they are often served dressed with a tomato sauce.

INGREDIENTS

1 quantity Pasta with Eggs
50g/2oz/¼ cup butter
50g/2oz/⅔ cup freshly grated Pecorino cheese

For the filling

2 potatoes, each about 200g/7oz, diced
65g/2½oz/generous ⅔ cup freshly grated hard salty Pecorino cheese
75g/3oz soft fresh Pecorino cheese
1 egg yolk
1 large bunch fresh mint, leaves removed and chopped
good pinch of saffron powder
salt and ground black pepper

Serves 4–6

1 Make the filling. Cook the diced potatoes in salted boiling water for 15–20 minutes or until soft. Drain the potatoes and transfer into a bowl, then mash until smooth. Leave until cold. Add the cheeses, egg yolk, mint, saffron and salt and pepper to taste and stir well to mix.

2 Using a pasta machine, roll out one-quarter of the pasta into a 90cm–1 metre/36in–3 foot strip. Cut the strip with a sharp knife into two 45–50cm/18–20in lengths.

3 With a fluted 10cm/4in biscuit (cookie) cutter, cut out 4–5 discs from one of the pasta strips. Using a heaped teaspoon, put a mound of filling on one side of each disc. Brush a little water around the edge of each disc, then fold the plain side of the disc over the filling to make a half-moon shape. Pleat the curved edge to seal.

4 Put the *culurgiones* on floured dish towels, sprinkle with flour and leave to dry. Repeat the process with the remaining dough to make 32–40 *culurgiones* altogether. If you have any stuffing left, re-roll the pasta trimmings and make more *culurgiones*.

5 Preheat the oven to 190°C/375°F/ Gas 5. Cook the *culurgiones* in a large pan of salted boiling water for 4–5 minutes. Meanwhile, melt the butter in a small pan.

6 Drain the *culurgiones*, turn them into a large baking dish and pour the melted butter over them. Sprinkle with the grated Pecorino and bake in the oven for 10–15 minutes until golden and bubbly. Allow to stand for 5 minutes before serving.

COOK'S TIP

There is quite an art to pleating the curved edge of culurgiones*, but each cook has his or her own way of doing it, so don't worry about getting a precise finish. Do whatever you think looks best – some* culurgiones *look like miniature Cornish pasties, others more like Chinese wontons. If you prefer, simply make square or round ravioli, or plain half-moons.*

Rotolo di Pasta Farcita

Stuffed Pasta Roll

THIS IS A DINNER PARTY first course to impress. It takes quite a long time to make, but it can be made up to the baking stage the day before.

INGREDIENTS

75g/3oz/6 tbsp butter
1 small onion, finely chopped
150g/5oz fresh spinach leaves, washed and trimmed
250g/9oz/generous 1 cup ricotta cheese
1 egg
60ml/4 tbsp freshly grated Parmesan cheese
60ml/4 tbsp freshly grated Pecorino cheese
nutmeg
2/3 quantity Pasta with Eggs
salt and ground black pepper

For the tomato sauce

60ml/4 tbsp olive oil
1 onion, finely chopped
1 carrot, finely chopped
1 celery stick, finely chopped
1 garlic clove, thinly sliced
a few leaves each fresh basil, thyme and oregano or marjoram, plus extra basil leaves, to garnish
2 x 400g/14oz cans chopped Italian plum tomatoes
15ml/1 tbsp sun-dried tomato purée (paste)
5ml/1 tsp sugar
75–105ml/5–7 tbsp dry white wine

Serves 6

1 Melt 25g/1oz/2 tbsp of the butter in a medium pan, add the finely chopped onion and cook gently, stirring frequently, for about 5 minutes until softened.

2 Add the spinach and salt and pepper to taste and cook over a medium heat for 5–8 minutes, stirring frequently, until the spinach is wilted and tender. Increase the heat to high and stir until the water is driven off and the spinach is quite dry.

3 Finely chop the spinach mixture in a food processor or by hand. Transfer to a bowl and add the ricotta, egg and half the grated Parmesan and Pecorino. Season to taste with freshly grated nutmeg and salt, and add plenty of pepper. Beat well to mix.

4 Roll out the pasta dough to a 50 x 40cm/20 x 16in rectangle. Place the rectangle on a large piece of muslin (cheesecloth), with one of the short sides nearest you.

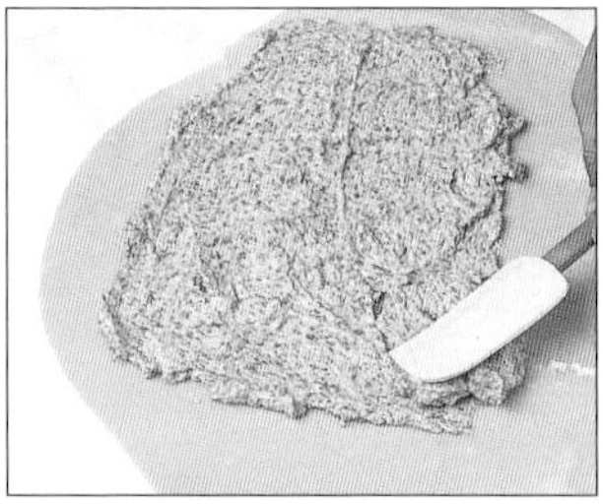

5 Spread the spinach mixture thinly over the pasta, leaving a 2cm/3/4in margin along the two long sides and a 5cm/2in margin along the short side that is furthest away from you. Moisten the two long sides with water.

6 Starting from the short side that is nearest you, pick up the muslin and roll the pasta away from you as you would a Swiss roll (jelly roll). Don't press it, just let it roll until you have a 40cm/16in long "sausage". Press the two open ends to seal the pasta, then roll the muslin around the *rotolo* a couple of times and tie the two ends tightly with string.

7 Half fill a fish kettle or large oval flameproof casserole with water and bring it to the boil. Add a large pinch of salt, then the *rotolo*. Half cover with a lid and simmer for 45 minutes, turning the *rotolo* over twice. Remove the *rotolo* from the water and place it on a board near the sink. Prop the board up at one end to allow the excess water to drain away from the *rotolo*, then leave to cool.

8 Make the tomato sauce. Chop the onion, carrot and celery finely, either in a food processor or by hand. Heat the oil in a pan, add the garlic slices and stir over a very low heat for 1–2 minutes. Add the chopped vegetables and the fresh herbs. Cook over a low heat, stirring for 5–7 minutes until the vegetables have softened and are lightly coloured.

9 Add the tomatoes, tomato purée and sugar, then add salt and pepper to taste. Bring to the boil, stirring all the time, then lower the heat and simmer gently, uncovered, for about 45 minutes, stirring occasionally.

10 Preheat the oven to 200°C/ 400°F/ Gas 6. Unwrap the *rotolo* and cut it into 12 thick slices. Melt the remaining butter and brush a little of it over the inside of six individual ovenproof dishes or a large shallow baking dish.

11 Arrange the *rotolo* slices slightly overlapping in the dishes or dish and drizzle the remaining butter over them. Sprinkle with the remaining Parmesan and Pecorino and bake in the oven for 10–15 minutes or until golden brown.

12 Meanwhile, blend the tomato sauce in a food processor until smooth. Transfer the sauce to a pan and add enough wine to thin it down to a pouring consistency, then heat until bubbling. Serve the *rotolo* slices on individual plates, on a pool of tomato sauce, sprinkled with basil leaves.

Cook's Tip

If you have a pasta machine, roll out half the dough into a 90cm–1 metre/ 36in–3 foot strip. Cut the strip with a sharp knife into two 50cm/20in lengths (you can do this during rolling if the strip gets too long to manage). Brush the long edge of one of the strips with water, then overlap the other strip on top by about 1cm/½in. Dust lightly with flour and press together, then seal the join by rolling over it with a rolling pin. Repeat with the remaining dough, then join the two pieces of pasta together in the same way so that you have a large rectangle.

Cappellacci alla Bolognese

Cheese Cappellacci with Bolognese Sauce

IN EMILIA-ROMAGNA it is traditional to serve these *cappellacci* with a rich meat sauce, but if you prefer you can serve them with a tomato sauce, or just melted butter.

INGREDIENTS

1 quantity Pasta with Eggs
2 litres/3 1/2 pints/8 cups beef stock made with stock (bouillon) cubes or diluted canned consommé
freshly grated Parmesan cheese, to serve
basil leaves, to garnish

For the filling

250g/9oz/generous 1 cup ricotta cheese
90g/3 1/2oz taleggio cheese, rind removed, diced very small
60ml/4 tbsp freshly grated Parmesan cheese
1 small egg
nutmeg
salt and ground black pepper

For the Bolognese meat sauce

25g/1oz/2 tbsp butter
15ml/1 tbsp olive oil
1 onion
2 carrots
2 celery sticks
2 garlic cloves
130g/4 1/2oz pancetta or rindless streaky (fatty) bacon, diced
250g/9oz lean minced (ground) beef
250g/9oz lean minced (ground) pork
120ml/4fl oz/1/2 cup dry white wine
2 x 400g/14oz cans crushed Italian plum tomatoes
475–750ml/16fl oz–1 1/4 pints/2–3 cups beef stock
100ml/3 1/2fl oz/scant 1/2 cup panna da cucina or double (heavy) cream

Serves 6

1 Make the filling. Put the ricotta, taleggio and grated Parmesan in a bowl and mash together with a fork.

2 Add the egg and freshly grated nutmeg and salt and pepper to taste and stir well to mix.

3 Using a pasta machine, roll out one-quarter of the pasta into a 90cm–1 metre/36in–3 foot strip. Cut the strip with a sharp knife into two 45–50cm/18–20in lengths (you can do this during rolling if the strip gets too long to manage).

4 Using a 6–7.5cm/2 1/2–3in square ravioli cutter, cut 6–7 squares from one of the pasta strips. Using a teaspoon, put a mound of filling in the centre of each square. Brush a little water around the edge of each square, then fold the square diagonally in half over the filling to make a triangular shape. Press to seal.

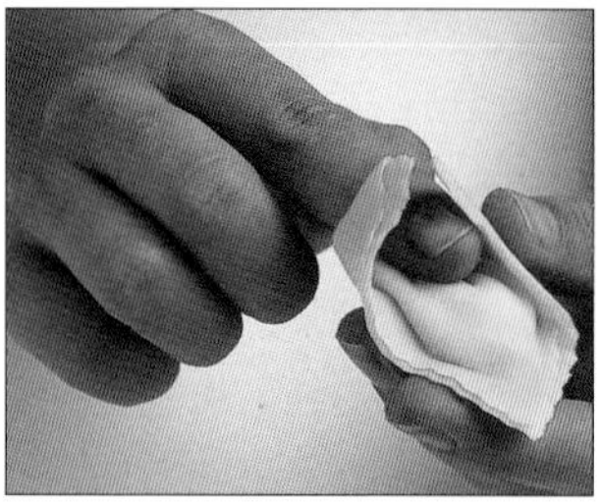

5 Wrap the triangle around one of your index fingers, bringing the bottom two corners together. Pinch the ends together to seal, then press with your fingertip around the top edge of the filling to make an indentation so that the "hat" looks like a bishop's mitre.

6 Place the *cappellacci* on floured dish towels, sprinkle them lightly with flour and leave to dry while repeating the process with the remaining dough to make 48–56 *cappellacci* altogether.

7 Make the meat sauce. Heat the butter and oil in a frying pan until sizzling. Add the vegetables, garlic, and the pancetta or bacon and cook over a medium heat, stirring frequently, for 10 minutes or until the vegetables have softened.

8 Add the minced beef and pork, lower the heat and cook gently for 10 minutes, stirring frequently and breaking up any lumps in the meat with a wooden spoon. Stir in salt and pepper to taste, then add the wine and stir again. Simmer for about 5 minutes, or until reduced.

9 Add the tomatoes and 250ml/8fl oz/1 cup of the stock and bring to the boil. Stir well, then lower the heat, half cover the pan with a lid and leave to simmer very gently for 2 hours. Stir occasionally during this time and add more stock as it becomes absorbed.

10 Add the *panna da cucina* or double cream to the meat sauce. Stir well to mix, then simmer the sauce, without a lid, for another 30 minutes, stirring frequently.

11 Bring the stock to the boil in a large pan.

12 Drop the *cappellacci* into the stock, bring back to the boil and boil for 4–5 minutes; drain the *cappellacci* and divide them among six warmed bowls. Spoon the hot Bolognese sauce over the *cappellacci* and sprinkle with grated Parmesan and basil leaves. Serve immediately.

Cook's Tip

The exact shape of cappellacci *varies from one cook to another. Some are made from discs rather than squares of pasta, although these are more often called* tortellini *or* tortelloni*. It all depends on the region in which they are made. If you prefer a party-hat shape to a bishop's mitre, don't make an indentation above the filling in Step 5, but instead turn up the bottom edge of each "hat" so that they have brims.* Cappelletti *are the same shape as* cappellacci *but are made from smaller squares of pasta (about 5cm/2in square). Not surprisingly, because of their size,* cappelletti *are very fiddly to make.*

Ravioli alla Napoletana

Cheese and Ham Ravioli with Tomato Sauce

TYPICAL OF SOUTHERN ITALIAN cuisine, these ravioli are very tasty. They are substantial enough for a main course, served with a green or mixed salad. If you prefer them as a first course, there are enough ravioli for 8 servings.

INGREDIENTS

1 quantity Pasta with Eggs
60ml/4 tbsp freshly grated Pecorino cheese, plus extra to serve

For the filling

175g/6oz/¾ cup ricotta cheese
30ml/2 tbsp freshly grated Parmesan cheese
115g/4oz prosciutto, finely chopped
150g/5oz packet mozzarella cheese, drained and finely chopped
1 small egg
15ml/1 tbsp chopped fresh flat leaf (Italian) parsley, plus extra to garnish

For the tomato sauce

30ml/2 tbsp olive oil
1 onion, finely chopped
400g/14oz can chopped Italian plum tomatoes
15ml/1 tbsp sun-dried tomato purée (paste)
5–10ml/1–2 tsp dried oregano, to taste
salt and ground black pepper

Serves 4–6

1 Make the sauce. Heat the oil in a medium pan, add the onion and cook gently, stirring frequently, for about 5 minutes until softened.

2 Add the tomatoes. Fill the empty can with water, pour it into the pan, then stir in the tomato purée, oregano and salt and pepper to taste. Bring to the boil and stir well, then cover the pan and simmer gently for 30 minutes, stirring occasionally and adding more water if the sauce becomes too thick.

3 Meanwhile, make the filling and the ravioli. Put all the filling ingredients in a bowl with salt and pepper to taste. Mix well with a fork, breaking up any lumps in the ricotta.

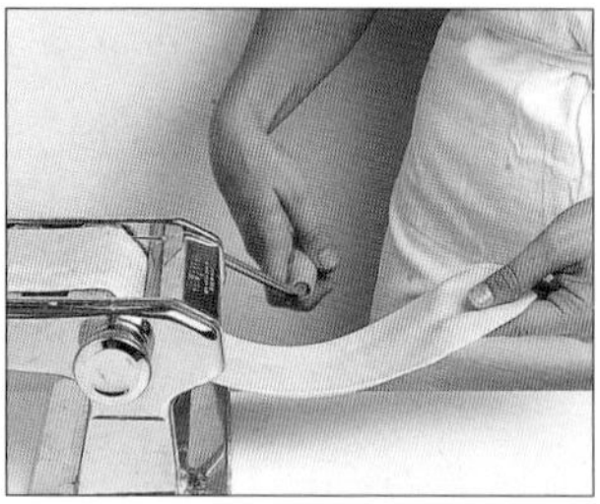

4 Using a pasta machine, roll out one-quarter of the pasta into a 90cm–1 metre/36in–3 foot strip. Cut the strip with a sharp knife into two 45–50cm/18–20in lengths (you can do this during rolling if the strip gets too long to manage).

5 Using 2 teaspoons, put 10–12 little mounds of the filling along one side of one of the pasta strips, spacing them evenly. The filling will be quite moist. Brush a little water around each mound, then fold the plain side of the pasta strip over the filling.

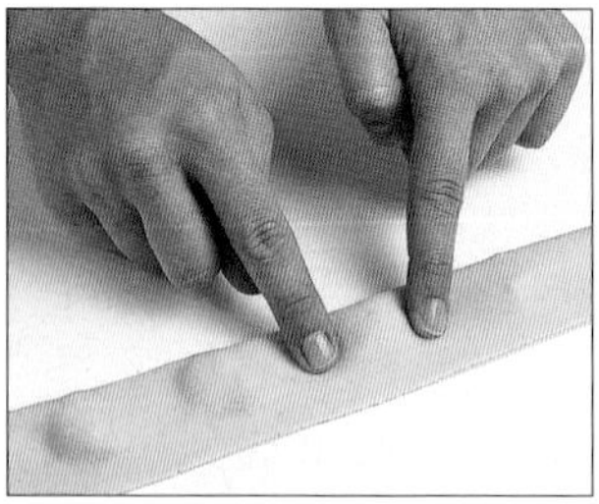

6 Starting from the folded edge, press down gently with your fingertips around each mound, pushing the air out at the unfolded edge.

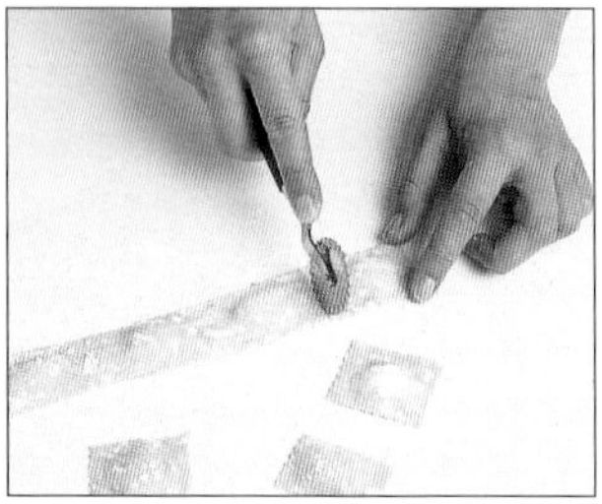

7 Sprinkle lightly with flour. With a fluted pasta wheel, cut along each long side, then in between each mound to make small square shapes.

8 Put the ravioli on floured dish towels; sprinkle lightly with flour.

9 Leave the ravioli to dry while repeating the process with the remaining pasta to get 80–96 ravioli altogether. Drop the ravioli into a large pan of salted boiling water, bring back to the boil and boil for 4–5 minutes.

10 Drain the ravioli well and pour about a third of them into a warmed bowl. Sprinkle 15ml/1 tbsp freshly grated Pecorino over the ravioli. Pour over a third of the tomato sauce.

11 Repeat the layers twice, then top with the remaining grated Pecorino. Serve immediately, garnished with chopped parsley. Hand around more grated Pecorino separately.

Variation

If you like the flavour of garlic with tomatoes, gently cook 1–2 crushed garlic cloves, with the onion when making the tomato sauce.

Agnolotti di Taleggio e Maggiorama

Agnolotti with Taleggio and Marjoram

THE FILLING FOR THESE LITTLE half-moons is very simple – only two ingredients – but the combination of flavours is absolutely delicious.

INGREDIENTS

1 quantity Pasta with Eggs
350–400g/12–14oz taleggio cheese
about 30ml/2 tbsp finely chopped fresh marjoram, plus extra to garnish
115g/4oz/½ cup butter
salt and ground black pepper
freshly grated Parmesan cheese, to serve

Serves 6–8

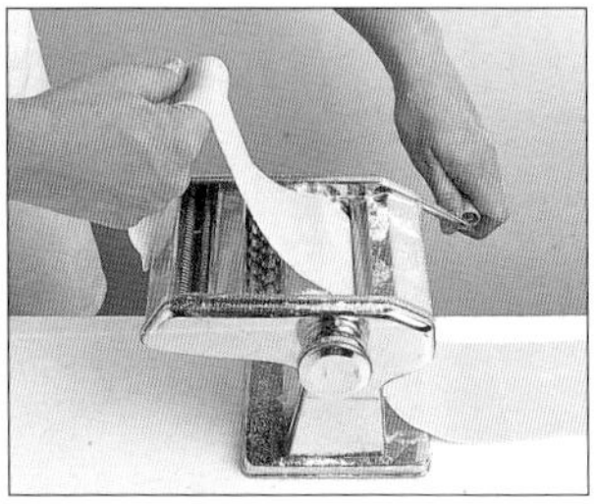

1 Using a pasta machine, roll out a quarter of the pasta into a 90cm–1 metre/36in–3 foot strip. Cut the strip with a sharp knife into two 45–50cm/18–20in lengths (you can do this during rolling if the strip gets too long to manage).

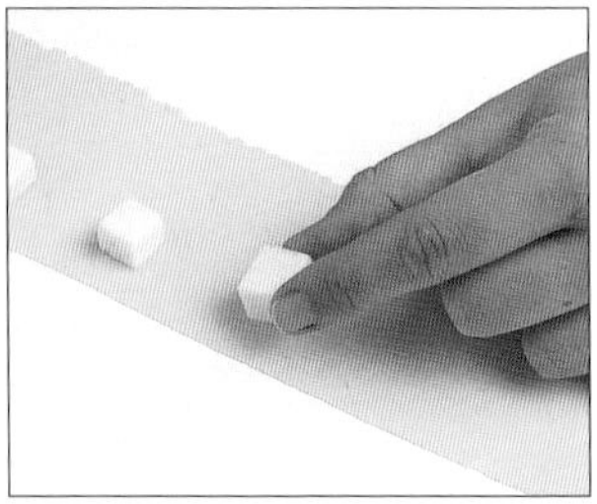

2 Cut 8–10 little cubes of taleggio and place them along one side of one of the pasta strips, spacing them evenly. Sprinkle each taleggio cube with a little chopped marjoram and pepper to taste.

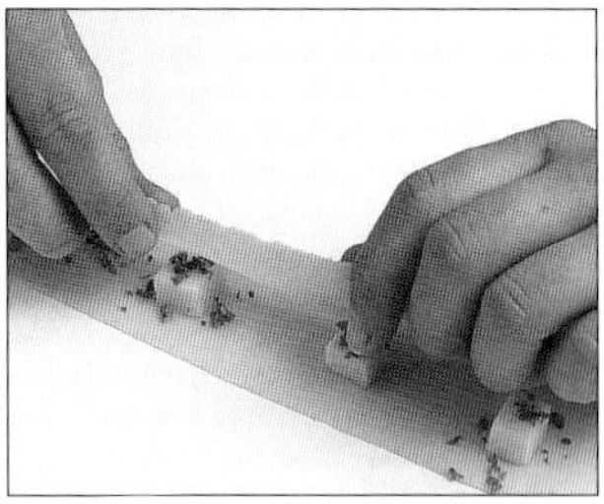

3 Brush a little water around each cube of cheese, then fold the plain side of the pasta strip over them.

4 Starting from the folded edge, press down gently with your fingertips around each cube, pushing the air out at the unfolded edge. Sprinkle lightly with flour.

5 Using only half of a 5cm/2in fluted round ravioli or biscuit (cookie) cutter, cut around each cube of cheese to make a half-moon shape. The folded edge should be the straight edge.

6 If you like, press the cut edges of the agnolotti with the tines of a fork to give a decorative effect.

7 Put the agnolotti on floured dish towels, sprinkle lightly with flour and leave to dry while repeating the process with the remaining pasta, cheese, marjoram and pepper to get 64–80 agnolotti altogether.

8 Drop the agnolotti into a large pan of salted boiling water, bring back to the boil and boil for 4–5 minutes until *al dente*.

9 Meanwhile, melt the butter in a small pan until it is sizzling.

10 Drain the agnolotti and divide them equally among six or eight warmed large bowls. Drizzle the sizzling butter over them and serve immediately, sprinkled with freshly grated Parmesan and chopped fresh marjoram. Hand around more grated Parmesan separately.

COOK'S TIPS

- *Taleggio is a square-shaped, semi-soft cheese from Lombardy. It is quite easy to get in large supermarkets, or any Italian delicatessen. It has a mild, slightly nutty flavour and good melting qualities. For this recipe, make sure that you remove the rind, which tends to be quite tough and salty.*
- *If you are unable to get taleggio, use fontina cheese instead, or a strongly flavoured blue cheese, such as Gorgonzola. If you use a blue cheese, substitute sage for the marjoram.*

VARIATION

Marjoram is traditional with the taleggio cheese in this recipe, both for the filling and the sizzling butter, but you can use other fresh herbs, such as sage, basil or flat leaf (Italian) parsley.

Pansotti con Erbe e Formaggi

Pansotti with Herbs and Cheese

IN LIGURIA, THE DOUGH for *pansotti* is flavoured with white wine, and the stuffing is made of cheese and *preboggion*, a mixture of many different types of fresh herbs and wild leaves. The dish is traditionally served with a kind of pesto made from walnuts, making it very rich and quite complex. The recipe given here is a simple version.

INGREDIENTS

1 quantity Herb-flavoured Pasta with Eggs
50g/2oz/¼ cup butter
freshly grated Parmesan cheese, to serve

For the filling

250g/9oz/generous 1 cup ricotta cheese
150g/5oz/1⅔ cups freshly grated Parmesan cheese
1 large handful fresh basil leaves, finely chopped
1 large handful fresh flat leaf parsley, finely chopped
a few sprigs fresh marjoram or oregano, leaves removed and finely chopped
1 garlic clove, crushed
1 small egg
salt and ground black pepper

For the sauce

90g/3½oz shelled walnuts
1 garlic clove
60ml/4 tbsp extra virgin olive oil
125ml/4fl oz/½ cup panna da cucina or double (heavy) cream

Serves 6–8

1 First make the filling and sauce. Put the ricotta, Parmesan, herbs, garlic and egg in a bowl with salt and pepper to taste and beat well to mix.

2 To make the sauce, put the walnuts, garlic clove and oil in a food processor and process to a paste, adding up to 125ml/4fl oz/½ cup warm water through the feeder tube to slacken the consistency. Spoon the mixture into a large bowl and add the cream. Beat well to mix, then add salt and pepper to taste.

3 Using a pasta machine, roll out one-quarter of the pasta into a 90cm–1 metre/36in–3 foot strip. Cut the strip with a sharp knife into two 45–50cm/18–20in lengths (you can do this during rolling if the strip gets too long to manage).

4 Using a 5cm/2in square ravioli cutter, cut 8–10 squares from one of the pasta strips. Using a teaspoon, put a mound of filling in the centre of each square.

5 Brush a little water around the edge of each square, then fold the square diagonally in half over the filling to make a triangular shape. Press gently to seal.

6 Spread out the *pansotti* on clean floured dish towels, sprinkle lightly with flour and leave to dry, while repeating the process with the remaining dough to make 64–80 *pansotti* altogether.

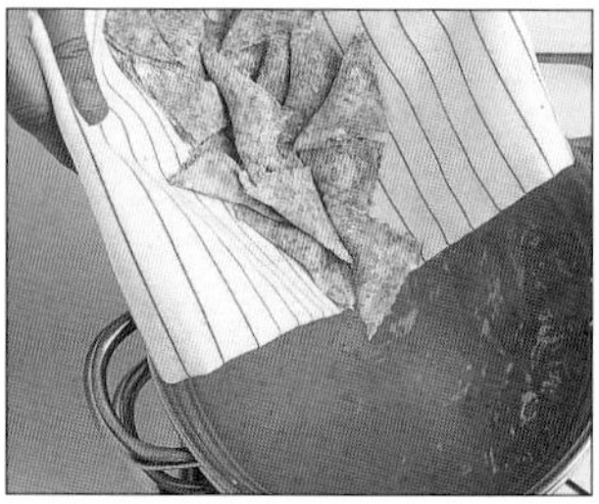

7 Cook the *pansotti* in a large pan of salted boiling water for 4–5 minutes. Meanwhile, put the walnut sauce in a large warmed bowl and add a ladleful of the pasta cooking water to thin it down. Melt the butter in a small pan until sizzling.

8 Drain the *pansotti* and transfer into the bowl of walnut sauce. Drizzle the butter over them, toss well, then sprinkle with grated Parmesan. Alternatively, toss the pansotti in the melted butter, spoon into warmed individual bowls and drizzle over the sauce. Serve immediately, with more grated Parmesan handed separately.

COOK'S TIP

Try not to overfill the pansotti, or they will burst open during cooking.

Tortellini Romagnoli

Tortellini from Emilia-Romagna

THESE ARE THE TORTELLINI that are served on the day after Christmas in Emilia-Romagna. Traditionally they were made with minced leftover capon from Christmas Day, but nowadays turkey or chicken is often used.

INGREDIENTS

1 quantity Pasta with Eggs
2 litres/3½ pints/8 cups beef stock made with stock (bouillon) cubes or diluted canned consommé
freshly grated Parmesan cheese, to serve

For the filling

25g/1oz/2 tbsp butter
250g/9oz minced (ground) turkey or chicken
5ml/1 tsp chopped fresh rosemary
5ml/1 tsp chopped fresh sage
nutmeg
250ml/8fl oz/1 cup chicken stock
60ml/4tbsp freshly grated Parmesan cheese
90g/3½oz mortadella sausage, very finely chopped
1 small egg
salt and ground black pepper

Serves 6–8

1 Make the filling. Melt the butter in a frying pan, then add the minced turkey or chicken and chopped herbs.

2 Grate in a little nutmeg and add salt and pepper to taste. Cook gently for 5–6 minutes, stirring frequently and breaking up any lumps in the meat with a wooden spoon.

3 Add the stock and stir well to mix, then simmer gently, uncovered, for 15–20 minutes until the meat is cooked and quite dry. Transfer the meat to a bowl with a slotted spoon and leave to cool. Add the grated Parmesan, mortadella and egg to the meat and stir well to mix.

4 Using a pasta machine, roll out one-quarter of the pasta into a 90cm–1 metre/36in–3 foot strip. Cut the strip with a sharp knife into two 45–50cm/18–20in lengths (you can do this during rolling if the strip gets too long to manage).

5 With a 5cm/2in fluted ravioli or biscuit (cookie) cutter, cut out 8–10 discs from one of the pasta strips. Using a teaspoon, put a little mound of filling in the centre of each disc, then brush a little water around the edge.

6 Fold the disc in half over the filling so that the edges do not quite meet. Press to seal. Wrap the tortellini shape around your index finger and pinch the bottom corners together to seal.

7 Put the tortellini in a single layer on floured dish towels, sprinkle lightly with flour and leave to dry while repeating the process with the remaining dough to make 64–80 tortellini altogether. If you have any stuffing left, re-roll the pasta trimmings and make more tortellini.

8 Bring the beef stock to the boil in a large pan. Drop in the tortellini, then bring back to the boil and boil for 4–5 minutes. Taste the stock and season with salt and pepper if necessary.

9 Pour the tortellini and stock into a warmed large soup tureen, sprinkle with a little grated Parmesan and serve immediately. Hand more Parmesan separately.

COOK'S TIP

In Emilia-Romagna, cooked leftover meat is minced by hand for these tortellini, or raw meat is cooked in the piece and then minced. For speed and convenience in this recipe, raw minced (ground) poultry is cooked with herbs and seasonings before being used in the filling.

Fresh and Healthy

Chargrilled vegetables, designer salad leaves and pesto made with rocket are just a few of the new ingredients being introduced to pasta by today's chefs. To call these sauces is stretching the point a little: many of them consist of little more than a handful of fresh ingredients tossed with hot pasta, but the results are simply sensational.

These are not traditional pasta dishes. Many of them originated in restaurants, in response to the current taste for lighter, healthier food, but they are so quick and easy to make at home that you will find there's no need to go out to eat them.

The recipes in this chapter are tried and tested, but there are no hard-and-fast rules. Half the fun is in inventing your own combinations, using fresh vegetables and herbs according to the season. The key to success lies in the quality of these ingredients, and only the best will do. This goes for the pasta as much as anything else. Buy Italian brands of pasta to be sure of good texture and taste or, if you have the inclination and time, make your own fresh egg pasta.

Pasta is a natural, additive-free food, packed with protein, vitamins and minerals – the perfect partner for other healthy ingredients to make a high-energy meal.

Penne con la Rucola e la Mozzarella

Penne with Rocket and Mozzarella

LIKE A WARM SALAD, this pasta dish is very quick and easy to make – perfect for an *al fresco* summer lunch. Its success depends on the very best Italian ingredients, so make sure they are as fresh as possible and in tip-top condition.

INGREDIENTS

400g/14oz/3½ cups fresh or dried penne
6 ripe Italian plum tomatoes, peeled, seeded and diced
2 x 150g/5oz packets mozzarella cheese, drained and diced
2 large handfuls of rocket (arugula), total weight about 150g/5oz
75ml/5 tbsp extra virgin olive oil
salt and ground black pepper
Serves 4

1 Cook the pasta in a large pan of salted boiling water according to the packet instructions.

2 Meanwhile, put the tomatoes, mozzarella, rocket and olive oil into a large bowl with a little salt and pepper to taste and toss well to mix.

3 Drain the cooked pasta and transfer it into the bowl. Toss well to mix and serve immediately.

VARIATION

For a less peppery taste, use basil leaves instead of rocket, or a mixture of the two.

Eliche ai Peperoni Arrostiti

Eliche with Chargrilled Peppers

CHARGRILLED PEPPERS ARE GOOD with pasta because they have a soft juicy texture and a wonderful smoky flavour. This is a dish for high summer when peppers and tomatoes are plentiful and ripe. It is equally good cold as a salad.

INGREDIENTS

3 large (bell) peppers, red, yellow and orange
350g/12oz/3 cups fresh or dried eliche or fusilli
1–2 garlic cloves, to taste, finely chopped
60ml/4 tbsp extra virgin olive oil
4 ripe Italian plum tomatoes, peeled, seeded and diced
50g/2oz/½ cup pitted black olives, halved or quartered lengthways
1 handful of fresh basil leaves
salt and ground black pepper
Serves 4

1 Put the whole peppers under a hot grill (broiler) and cook them for about 10 minutes, turning them frequently until they are charred on all sides. Put the hot peppers in a plastic bag, seal the bag and set aside until the peppers are cold.

2 Remove the peppers from the bag and hold them one at a time under cold running water. Peel off the charred skins with your fingers, split the peppers open and pull out the cores. Rub off all the seeds under the running water, then pat the peppers dry on kitchen paper.

3 Cook the pasta in a large pan of salted boiling water according to the instructions on the packet until *al dente*.

4 Meanwhile, thinly slice the peppers and place them in a large bowl with the remaining ingredients and salt and pepper to taste.

5 Drain the cooked pasta and transfer it into the bowl. Toss well to mix and serve immediately.

VARIATION

Add a few slivers of bottled or canned anchovy fillets in Step 4.

Tagliatelle Verdissime

Tagliatelle with Broccoli and Spinach

THIS IS AN EXCELLENT vegetarian supper dish. It is nutritious and filling, and needs no accompaniment. If you like, you can use tagliatelle flecked with herbs.

INGREDIENTS

2 heads of broccoli
450g/1lb fresh spinach, stalks removed
nutmeg
450g/1lb fresh or dried egg tagliatelle
about 45ml/3 tbsp extra virgin olive oil
juice of 1/2 lemon, or to taste
salt and ground black pepper
freshly grated Parmesan cheese, to serve

Serves 4

1 Put the broccoli in the basket of a steamer, cover and steam over boiling water for 10 minutes. Add the spinach to the broccoli, cover and steam for 4–5 minutes or until both are tender. Towards the end of the cooking time, sprinkle the vegetables with freshly grated nutmeg and salt and pepper to taste. Transfer the vegetables to a colander.

2 Add salt to the water in the steamer and fill the steamer pan with boiling water, then add the pasta and cook according to the instructions on the packet. Meanwhile, chop the broccoli and spinach in the colander.

3 Drain the pasta. Heat 45ml/3tbsp oil in the pasta pan, add the pasta and chopped vegetables and toss over a medium heat until evenly mixed. Sprinkle in the lemon juice and plenty of black pepper, then taste and add more lemon juice, oil, salt and nutmeg if you like. Serve immediately, sprinkled liberally with freshly grated Parmesan and black pepper.

VARIATIONS

- *If you like, add a sprinkling of crushed dried chillies with the black pepper in Step 3.*
- *To add both texture and protein, garnish the finished dish with one or two handfuls of toasted pine nuts. They are often served with broccoli and spinach in Italy.*

Conchiglie di Pisa

Conchiglie from Pisa

NOTHING COULD BE MORE simple than hot pasta tossed with fresh ripe tomatoes, ricotta and sweet basil. Serve it on hot summer days – it is surprisingly cool and refreshing.

INGREDIENTS

350g/12oz/3 cups dried conchiglie
125g/4½oz/generous ½ cup ricotta cheese
6 ripe Italian plum tomatoes, diced
2 garlic cloves, crushed
1 handful fresh basil leaves, shredded, plus extra basil leaves to garnish
60ml/4 tbsp extra virgin olive oil
salt and ground black pepper
Serves 4–6

1 Cook the pasta in salted boiling water according to the instructions on the packet.

COOK'S TIP

If you like, peel the tomatoes before you dice them. It won't take long if the tomatoes are ripe.

2 Meanwhile, put the ricotta in a large bowl and mash with a fork.

3 Add the tomatoes, garlic and basil, with salt and pepper to taste, and mix well. Add the olive oil and whisk thoroughly. Taste for seasoning.

4 Drain the cooked pasta, transfer it into the ricotta mixture and toss well to mix. Garnish with basil leaves and serve immediately.

VARIATIONS

- *You can use diced mozzarella instead of ricotta cheese and call the dish* Conchiglie Caprese, *after the salad of tomatoes, mozzarella and basil known as* Caprese.
- *An avocado is the ideal ingredient for adding extra colour and flavour to this pasta dish. Halve, stone (pit) and peel, then dice the flesh. Toss it with the hot pasta at the last minute.*

Tagliatelle alle Erbe

Tagliatelle with Herbs

THIS IS A LOVELY dish for summer when fresh herbs are plentiful. It is quick and ideal for vegetarians.

INGREDIENTS

3 rosemary sprigs
1 handful fresh flat leaf (Italian) parsley
5–6 fresh mint leaves
5–6 fresh sage leaves
8–10 large fresh basil leaves
30ml/2 tbsp extra virgin olive oil
50g/2oz/¼ cup butter
1 shallot, finely chopped
2 garlic cloves, finely chopped
pinch of chilli powder, to taste
400g/14oz fresh egg tagliatelle
1 bay leaf
120ml/4fl oz/½ cup dry white wine
90–120ml/6–8 tbsp vegetable stock
salt and ground black pepper
Serves 4

1 Strip the rosemary and parsley leaves from their stalks and chop them together with the fresh mint, sage and basil.

2 Heat the olive oil and half the butter in a large frying pan. Add the shallot and garlic and the chilli powder, and cook over a very low heat, stirring frequently, for 2–3 minutes.

3 Cook the pasta in salted boiling water according to the packet instructions.

4 Add the chopped herbs and the bay leaf to the shallot mixture and stir for 2–3 minutes, then add the wine and increase the heat. Boil rapidly for 1–2 minutes until the wine reduces. Lower the heat, add the stock and simmer gently for 1–2 minutes.

5 Drain the pasta and add it to the herb mixture. Toss well to mix and remove and discard the bay leaf.

6 Put the remaining butter in a warmed large bowl, transfer the dressed pasta into it and toss well to mix. Serve immediately.

Garganelli Primavera

Garganelli with Spring Vegetables

YOUNG FRESH VEGETABLES both look and taste good with pasta. Butter is used to marry the two together, but you can use extra virgin olive oil if you prefer.

INGREDIENTS

1 bunch asparagus, about 350g/12oz
4 young carrots
1 bunch spring onions (scallions)
130g/4½oz shelled fresh peas
350g/12oz/3 cups dried garganelli
60ml/4 tbsp dry white wine
75g/3oz/6 tbsp unsalted (sweet) butter, diced
a few sprigs each fresh flat leaf (Italian) parsley, mint and basil, leaves stripped and chopped
salt and ground black pepper
freshly grated Parmesan cheese, to serve
Serves 4

1 Trim off and discard the woody part of each asparagus stem, then cut off the tips on the diagonal. Cut the stems on the diagonal into 4cm/1½in pieces. Cut the carrots and spring onions on the diagonal into similar pieces.

2 Plunge the asparagus stems, carrots and peas into a pan of salted boiling water. Bring back to the boil and simmer for 5–8 minutes, adding the asparagus tips for the last 3 minutes.

3 Meanwhile, cook the pasta in salted boiling water according to the instructions on the packet.

4 Drain the vegetables and return them to the pan. Add the wine, butter and salt and pepper to taste, then toss over a medium to high heat until the wine has reduced and the vegetables glisten with melted butter.

5 Drain the pasta and transfer it into a warmed large bowl. Add the vegetables, spring onions and herbs and toss well. Serve immediately, with freshly grated Parmesan.

COOK'S TIP

Garganelli are rolled short pasta shapes made with egg. If you can't get garganelli, use another short shape made with egg.

Spaghetti al Pesto di Rucola

Spaghetti with Rocket Pesto

THIS IS THE PESTO for real rocket lovers. It is sharp and peppery, and delicious for a summer pasta meal with a glass of chilled dry white wine.

INGREDIENTS

4 garlic cloves
90ml/6 tbsp pine nuts
2 large handfuls rocket (arugula), total weight about 150g/5oz, stalks removed
50g/2oz/2/3 cup Parmesan cheese, freshly grated
50g/2oz/2/3 cup Pecorino cheese, freshly grated
90ml/6 tbsp extra virgin olive oil
400g/14oz fresh or dried spaghetti
salt and ground black pepper
freshly grated Parmesan and Pecorino cheese, to serve

Serves 4

1 Put the garlic and pine nuts in a blender or food processor and process until finely chopped.

2 Add the rocket, Parmesan and Pecorino, oil and salt and pepper to taste and process for 5 seconds. Stop and scrape down the side of the bowl. Process for 5–10 seconds more until a smooth paste is formed.

3 Cook the spaghetti in a pan of salted boiling water according to the packet instructions.

4 Turn the pesto into a large bowl. Just before the pasta is ready, add 1–2 ladlefuls of the cooking water to the pesto and stir well to mix.

5 Drain the pasta, transfer it into the bowl of pesto and toss well to mix. Serve immediately, with the grated cheeses handed separately.

VARIATION

To temper the flavour of the rocket and make the pesto milder, add 115g/4oz/1/2 cup ricotta or mascarpone cheese to the pesto in Step 4 and mix well before adding the water.

Spaghetti al Limone

Spaghetti with Lemon

THIS IS THE DISH TO MAKE when you get home and find there's nothing to eat. If you keep spaghetti and olive oil in the store cupboard and garlic and lemons in the vegetable rack, you can prepare the most delicious meal in minutes.

INGREDIENTS

350g/12oz dried spaghetti
90ml/6 tbsp extra virgin olive oil
juice of 1 large lemon
2 garlic cloves, cut into very thin slivers
salt and ground black pepper
freshly grated Parmesan cheese, to serve
Serves 4

1 Cook the pasta in a pan of salted boiling water according to the instructions on the packet, then drain well and return to the pan.

2 Pour the olive oil and lemon juice over the cooked pasta, sprinkle in the slivers of garlic and add salt and pepper to taste.

3 Toss the pasta over a medium to high heat for 1–2 minutes. Serve immediately in four warmed bowls, with freshly grated Parmesan.

COOK'S TIP

Spaghetti is the best type of pasta for this recipe, because the olive oil and lemon juice cling to its long thin strands – even more so if you serve it with freshly grated Parmesan. If you are out of spaghetti, use another dried long pasta shape instead, such as spaghettini, linguine or tagliatelle.

Pipe con Ricotta e Spinaci

Pipe with Ricotta, Saffron and Spinach

TOSSING PASTA IN RICOTTA is popular in Sicily and Sardinia, where this cheese is widely used in cooking. For best results, use fresh white ricotta, which is sold by weight in Italian delicatessens. Serve this fairly rich dish in small quantities. Omit the saffron, with its quite strong flavour, if liked.

INGREDIENTS

1 small pinch of saffron threads
300g/11oz/2¾ cups dried pipe
300–350g/11–12oz fresh spinach, stalks removed
nutmeg
250g/9oz/generous 1 cup ricotta cheese
salt and ground black pepper
freshly grated Pecorino cheese, to serve

Serves 4–6

1 Soak the saffron threads in 60ml/4 tbsp warm water. Cook the pasta according to the packet instructions.

2 Meanwhile, wash the spinach and put the leaves in a pan with only the water clinging to the leaves. Season with freshly grated nutmeg, salt and pepper to taste,

3 Cover the pan and cook over a medium to high heat for about 5 minutes, shaking the pan occasionally, until the spinach is wilted and tender. Transfer into a colander, press it to extract as much liquid as possible, then chop it, letting the water drain through.

4 Put the ricotta in a large bowl. Strain in the saffron water. Add the spinach, beat well to mix, then add a ladleful or two of the pasta cooking water to loosen the mixture. Season.

5 Drain the pasta, reserving some of the cooking water. Add the pasta to the ricotta mixture and toss well, adding a little water if necessary. Serve immediarely, sprinkled with Pecorino.

Tagliarini al Tartufo Bianco

Tagliarini with White Truffle

THERE IS NOTHING QUITE like the fragrance and flavour of the Italian white truffle. It is one of the rarest and therefore most expensive of truffles, which comes from around the towns of Alba and Asti in Piedmont. This simple style of serving it is one of the best ways to enjoy it.

INGREDIENTS

350g/12oz fresh tagliarini
75g/3oz/6 tbsp unsalted (sweet) butter, diced
60ml/4 tbsp freshly grated Parmesan cheese
nutmeg
1 small white truffle, about 25–40g/1–1½oz
salt and ground black pepper

Serves 4

1 Cook the pasta in salted boiling water according to the instructions on the packet.

2 Drain the cooked pasta thoroughly and transfer it into a warmed large bowl. Add the diced butter, grated Parmesan, freshly grated nutmeg and a little salt and pepper to taste. Toss well until the pasta is coated in melted butter.

3 Divide the pasta equally among four warmed bowls and shave paper-thin slivers of the white truffle on top. Serve immediately.

COOK'S TIPS

- *White Italian truffles can be bought during the months of September and October from specialist food shops and delicatessens. They are very expensive, however, and there are some alternative ways of getting the flavour of truffles without the expense. Some Italian delicatessens sell "truffle cheese", which is a mountain cheese with shavings of truffle in it, and this can be used instead of the Parmesan and truffle in this recipe. Another alternative is to toss hot pasta in truffle oil and serve it with freshly grated Parmesan.*
- *In Piedmont a very thin home-made egg pasta called* tagliarin *or* tajarin *is used for this dish. Tagliarini are the nearest equivalent, or you could use tagliatellini or tagliolini instead, or even fettuccine if you like.*

Linguine con la Rucola

Linguine with Rocket

THIS IS A FIRST COURSE THAT you will find in many a fashionable restaurant in Italy. It is very quick and easy to make at home and is worth trying for yourself.

INGREDIENTS

350g/12oz fresh or dried linguine
120ml/4fl oz/½ cup extra virgin olive oil
1 large bunch rocket (arugula), about 150g/5oz, stalks removed, shredded or torn
75g/3oz/1 cup freshly grated Parmesan cheese
salt and ground black pepper
Serves 4

1 Cook the pasta in a large pan of salted boiling water according to the instructions on the packet, then drain thoroughly.

2 Heat about 60ml/4 tbsp of the olive oil in the pasta pan, then add the drained pasta, followed by the rocket. Toss over a medium to high heat for 1–2 minutes or until the rocket is just wilted, then remove the pan from the heat.

3 Transfer the pasta and rocket into a warmed large bowl. Add half the freshly grated Parmesan and the remaining olive oil. Add a little salt and black pepper to taste.

4 Toss the mixture quickly to mix. Serve immediately, sprinkled with the remaining Parmesan.

COOK'S TIP

Buy rocket by the bunch from the greengrocer. The type sold in small cellophane packets in supermarkets is very expensive for this kind of dish. Always check when buying rocket that all the leaves are bright green. In hot weather, rocket leaves quickly turn yellow.

Strozzapreti ai Fiori di Zucca

Strozzapreti with Courgette Flowers

THIS PRETTY, SUMMERY DISH is strewn with courgette flowers, but you can make it even if you don't have the flowers. In Italy, bunches of courgette flowers are a common sight on vegetable stalls in summer, and are frequently used for stuffing and cooking.

INGREDIENTS

50g/2oz/¼ cup butter
30ml/2 tbsp extra virgin olive oil
1 small onion, thinly sliced
200g/7oz small courgettes (zucchini), cut into thin julienne
1 garlic clove, crushed
10ml/2 tsp finely chopped fresh marjoram
350g/12oz/3 cups dried strozzapreti
1 large handful courgette (zucchini) flowers, thoroughly washed and dried
salt and ground black pepper
thin shavings of Parmesan cheese, to serve

Serves 4

1 Heat the butter and half the olive oil in a medium pan, add the sliced onion and cook gently, stirring frequently, for about 5 minutes until softened. Add the courgettes to the pan and sprinkle with the crushed garlic, chopped marjoram and salt and pepper to taste. Cook for 5–8 minutes until the courgettes have softened but are not coloured, turning them over from time to time.

2 Meanwhile, cook the pasta in a pan of salted boiling water according to the packet instructions.

3 Set aside a few whole courgette flowers for the garnish, then roughly shred the rest and add them to the courgette mixture. Stir to mix and taste for seasoning.

4 Drain the pasta, transfer it into a warmed large bowl and add the remaining oil. Toss, add the courgette mixture and toss again. Top with Parmesan and the reserved flowers.

COOK'S TIP

Strozzapreti or "priest stranglers" are a special kind of short pasta shape from Modena. You can buy packets of them in Italian delicatessens, or use gemelli, a similar kind of twisted pasta.

Tagliatelle Tricolore

Three-colour Tagliatelle

COURGETTES AND CARROTS are cut into delicate ribbons so that when they are cooked and tossed with tagliatelle they look like coloured pasta. Serve as a side dish, or sprinkle with freshly grated Parmesan cheese for a light starter or vegetarian main course.

INGREDIENTS

2 large courgettes (zucchini)
2 large carrots
250g/9oz fresh egg tagliatelle
60ml/4 tbsp extra virgin olive oil
flesh of 2 roasted garlic cloves, plus extra roasted garlic cloves, to serve (optional)
salt and ground black pepper

Serves 4

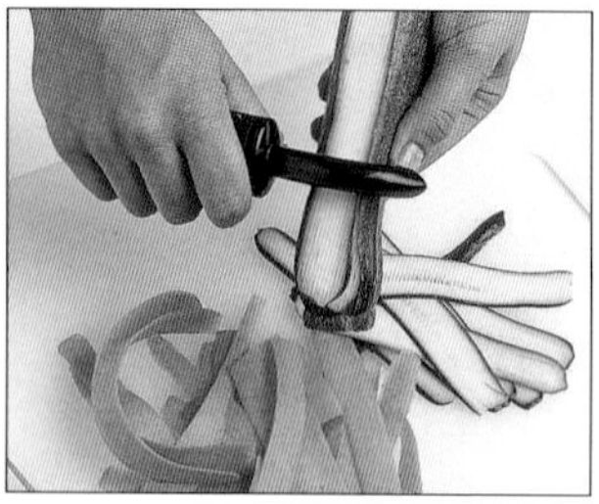

1 With a vegetable peeler, cut the courgettes and carrots into long thin ribbons. Bring a large pan of salted water to the boil, then add the courgette and carrot ribbons. Bring the water back to the boil and boil for 30 seconds, then drain and set aside.

2 Cook the pasta according to the instructions on the packet.

3 Drain the pasta and return it to the pan. Add the vegetable ribbons, oil, garlic and salt and pepper and toss over a medium to high heat until the pasta and vegetables are glistening with oil. Serve immediately, with extra roasted garlic, if you like.

COOK'S TIP

To roast garlic, put a whole head of garlic on a lightly oiled baking sheet. Place in a 180°C/350°F/Gas 4 oven and roast for about 30 minutes. Remove the garlic from the oven and set aside. When cool enough to handle, dig out the flesh from the cloves with the point of a knife. If you don't want to go to the trouble of roasting garlic, you can use crushed raw garlic but the flavour will be stronger.

Maccheroni con i Broccoli in Tegame

Macaroni with Broccoli and Cauliflower

THIS IS A SOUTHERN ITALIAN DISH, full of flavour. Without the anchovies, it can be served to vegetarians.

INGREDIENTS

175g/6oz cauliflower florets, cut into small sprigs
175g/6oz broccoli florets, cut into small sprigs
350g/12oz/3 cups short-cut macaroni
45ml/3 tbsp extra virgin olive oil
1 onion, finely chopped
45ml/3 tbsp pine nuts
1 sachet of saffron powder, dissolved in 15ml/1 tbsp warm water
15–30ml/1–2 tbsp raisins, to taste
30ml/2 tbsp sun-dried tomato purée (paste)
4 bottled or canned anchovies in olive oil, drained and chopped, plus extra anchovies to serve (optional)
salt and ground black pepper
freshly grated Pecorino cheese, to serve

Serves 4

1 Cook the cauliflower sprigs in a large pan of salted boiling water for 3 minutes. Add the broccoli and boil for another 2 minutes. Remove the vegetables from the pan with a large slotted spoon and set aside.

2 Add the pasta to the vegetable cooking water and bring the water back to the boil. Cook the pasta according to the instructions on the packet until it is *al dente*.

3 Meanwhile, heat the olive oil in a frying pan, add the finely chopped onion and cook over a low to medium heat, stirring frequently, for about 2–3 minutes or until golden. Add the pine nuts, the cooked broccoli and cauliflower, and the saffron water. Add the raisins, sun-dried tomato purée and a couple of ladlefuls of the pasta cooking water until the vegetable mixture has the consistency of a sauce. Finally, add plenty of pepper.

4 Stir well, cook for 1–2 minutes, then add the chopped anchovies. Drain the pasta and transfer it into the vegetable mixture. Toss well, then taste for seasoning and add salt if necessary. Serve the pasta immediately in four warmed bowls, sprinkled with freshly grated Pecorino. If you like the flavour of anchovies, add 1–2 whole anchovies to each serving.

Pasta Salads

Although not traditionally Italian, pasta salads have earned their place in the Italian cook's repertoire. They are extremely versatile in that they can be served as part of an antipasto, as a first course or a main course. Salads can be prepared well in advance, so make marvellous party food, and are popular for picnics, because they are so easy to transport.

Freshly cooked pasta soaks up oil, lemon juice, vinegar and seasonings so that when the pasta cools down, the shapes are separate, moist and full of flavour. Never soak pasta in cold water after cooking; this makes the pasta waterlogged and soggy, especially with shapes like shells and tubes that trap liquid. Simply cook the pasta until it is *al dente*, then drain it thoroughly and toss it in extra virgin olive oil or dressing until it glistens. This method works well for any vinaigrette-type dressing, but if you are using mayonnaise it is best to wait until the pasta has cooled down before tossing, or the mayonnaise may spoil.

Any pasta shape can be used in a salad, although shells and tubes are particularly good, because they trap the dressing so well. Many Italians prefer egg pasta to plain durum wheat pasta, because it has a good colour, holds its shape well and does not stick.

Insalata Nizzarda

Pasta Salade Niçoise

ALONG THE MEDITERRANEAN coast, where Italy meets France, the cuisines of both countries have many similarities. In this salad the ingredients of a classic French *salade niçoise* are given a modern Italian twist.

INGREDIENTS

115g/4oz green beans, topped and tailed and cut into 5cm/2in lengths
250g/9oz/2 1/4 cups dried penne rigate
105ml/7 tbsp extra virgin olive oil
2 fresh tuna steaks, total weight 350–450g/12oz–1lb
6 baby Italian plum tomatoes, quartered lengthways
50g/2oz/1/2 cup pitted black olives, halved lengthways
6 bottled or canned anchovies in olive oil, drained and chopped
30–45ml/2–3 tbsp chopped fresh flat leaf (Italian) parsley, to taste
juice of 1/2–1 lemon, to taste
2 heads of chicory, leaves separated
salt and ground black pepper
lemon wedges, to serve

Serves 4

1 Cook the beans in a large pan of salted boiling water for 5–6 minutes. Remove the beans with a large slotted spoon and refresh under the cold tap.

2 Add the pasta to the pan of bean cooking water, bring back to the boil and cook according to the instructions on the packet.

3 Meanwhile, heat a ridged cast-iron pan over a low heat. Dip a wad of kitchen paper in the oil, wipe it over the surface of the pan and heat gently. Brush the tuna steaks on both sides with oil and sprinkle liberally with pepper; add to the pan and cook over a medium to high heat for 1–2 minutes on each side. Remove and set aside.

4 Drain the cooked pasta well and transfer into a large bowl. Add the remaining oil, the beans, tomato quarters, black olives, anchovies, parsley, lemon juice and salt and pepper to taste. Toss well to mix, then leave to cool.

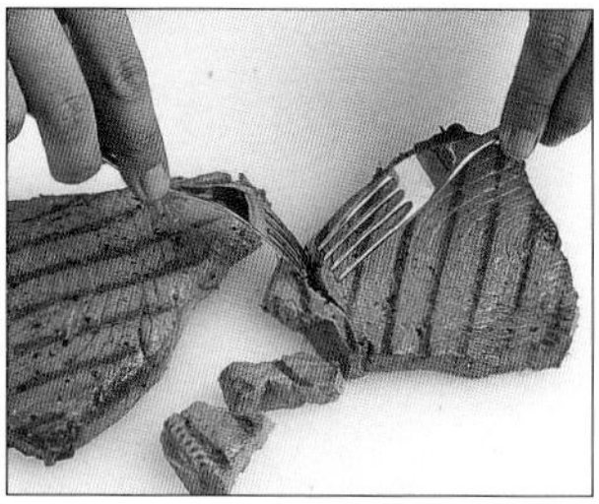

5 Flake or slice the tuna into large pieces, discarding the skin, then fold it into the salad. Taste the salad for seasoning. Arrange the chicory leaves around the insides of a large shallow bowl. Spoon the pasta salad into the centre and serve with lemon wedges.

Insalata ai Peperoni Arrostiti

Chargrilled Pepper Salad

THIS IS A GOOD SIDE SALAD to serve with plain grilled or barbecued chicken or fish. The ingredients are simple and few, but the overall flavour is quite intense.

INGREDIENTS

2 large peppers (red and green)
250g/9oz/2 1/4 cups dried fusilli tricolore
1 handful fresh basil leaves
1 handful fresh coriander (cilantro) leaves
1 garlic clove
salt and ground black pepper

For the dressing

30ml/2 tbsp bottled pesto
juice of 1/2 lemon
60ml/4 tbsp extra virgin olive oil

Serves 4

1 Put the peppers under a hot grill (broiler) and cook for 10 minutes, turning them frequently until they are charred on all sides. Put the hot peppers in a plastic bag, seal the bag and set aside until the peppers are cool. Meanwhile, cook the pasta according to the instructions on the packet.

2 Whisk all the dressing ingredients together in a large bowl. Drain the cooked pasta well and transfer it into the bowl of dressing. Toss well to mix and set aside to cool.

3 Remove the peppers from the bag and hold them one at a time under cold running water. Peel off the charred skins with your fingers, split the peppers open and pull out the cores. Rub off all the seeds under the running water, then pat the peppers dry on kitchen paper.

4 Chop the peppers and add them to the pasta. Put the basil, coriander and garlic on a board and chop them all together. Add to the pasta and toss to mix, then taste for seasoning and serve.

COOK'S TIP

Serve the salad at room temperature or chilled, whichever you prefer.

Insalata con Tonno e Mais

Tuna and Sweetcorn Salad

THIS IS AN EXCELLENT main course salad for a summer lunch outside. It travels very well, so it is good for picnics, too.

INGREDIENTS

175g/6oz/1 ½ cups dried conchiglie
175g/6oz can tuna in olive oil, drained and flaked
175g/6oz can corn, drained
75g/3oz bottled roasted red (bell) pepper, rinsed, dried and finely chopped
1 handful of fresh basil leaves, chopped
salt and ground black pepper

For the dressing

60ml/4 tbsp extra virgin olive oil
15ml/1 tbsp balsamic vinegar
5ml/1 tsp red wine vinegar
5ml/1 tsp Dijon mustard
5–10ml/1–2 tsp honey, to taste

Serves 4

1 Cook the pasta according to packet instructions. Drain it into a colander, and rinse under cold running water. Leave to drain until cold and dry, shaking the colander occasionally.

2 Make the dressing. Put the oil in a large bowl, add the two kinds of vinegar and whisk well together until emulsified. Add the mustard, honey and salt and pepper to taste and whisk again until thick.

3 Add the pasta to the dressing and toss well to mix, then add the tuna, corn and roasted pepper and toss again. Mix in about half the basil and taste for seasoning. Serve at room temperature or chilled, with the remaining basil sprinkled on top.

VARIATION

To save time, you could use canned sweetcorn with peppers.

Insalata Rosa e Verde

Pink and Green Salad

SPIKED WITH A LITTLE fresh chilli, this pretty salad makes a delicious light lunch served with hot ciabatta rolls and a bottle of sparkling dry Italian white wine.

INGREDIENTS

225g/8oz/2 cups dried farfalle
juice of ½ lemon
1 small fresh red chilli, seeded and very finely chopped
60ml/4 tbsp chopped fresh basil
30ml/2 tbsp chopped fresh coriander (cilantro)
60ml/4 tbsp extra virgin olive oil
15ml/1 tbsp mayonnaise
250g/9oz/1 ½ cups peeled cooked prawns (shrimp)
1 avocado
salt and ground black pepper

Serves 4

1 Cook the pasta in a large pan of salted boiling water according to the packet instructions.

2 Meanwhile, put the lemon juice and chilli in a bowl with half the basil and coriander and salt and pepper to taste. Whisk well to mix, then whisk in the oil and mayonnaise until thick. Add the prawns and gently stir to coat in the dressing.

3 Drain the pasta into a colander, and rinse under cold running water until cold. Leave to drain and dry, shaking the colander occasionally.

4 Halve, stone and peel the avocado, then cut the flesh into neat dice. Add to the prawns and dressing with the pasta, toss well to mix and taste for seasoning. Serve immediately, sprinkled with the remaining basil and coriander.

COOK'S TIP

This pasta salad can be made several hours ahead of time, without the avocado. Cover with clear film (plastic wrap) and chill in the refrigerator. Prepare the avocado and add it to the salad just before serving or it will discolour.

Insalata di Mare

Seafood Salad

THIS IS A VERY SPECIAL SALAD which can be served as a first course or main meal. One of the unusual "designer" pasta shapes would suit it well.

INGREDIENTS

450g/1lb mussels
250ml/8fl oz/1 cup dry white wine
2 garlic cloves, roughly chopped
1 handful of fresh flat leaf (Italian) parsley
175g/6oz/1 cup prepared squid rings
175g/6oz/1½ cups small dried pasta shapes
175g/6oz/1 cup peeled cooked prawns (shrimp)

For the dressing

90ml/6 tbsp extra virgin olive oil
juice of 1 lemon
5–10ml/1–2 tsp capers, to taste, roughly chopped
1 garlic clove, crushed
1 small handful fresh flat leaf (Italian) parsley, finely chopped
salt and ground black pepper

Serves 4–6

1 Scrub the mussels under cold running water to remove the beards. Discard any that are open or that do not close when sharply tapped against the work surface.

2 Pour half the wine into a large pan, add the garlic, parsley and mussels. Cover the pan tightly and bring to the boil over a high heat. Cook for about 5 minutes, shaking the pan frequently, until the mussels are open.

3 Place the mussels and their liquid into a colander set over a bowl . Leave the mussels until cool enough to handle. Reserve a few mussels for garnishing, then remove the rest from their shells, tipping the liquid from the mussels into the bowl of cooking liquid. Discard any closed mussels.

4 Return the mussel cooking liquid to the pan and add the remaining wine and the squid rings. Bring to the boil, cover and simmer gently, stirring occasionally, for 30 minutes or until the squid is tender. Leave the squid to cool in the cooking liquid.

5 Meanwhile, cook the pasta according to packet instructions and whisk all the dressing ingredients in a large bowl, adding a little salt and pepper to taste.

6 Drain the cooked pasta well, add it to the bowl of dressing and toss well to mix. Leave to cool.

7 Place the cooled squid into a sieve (strainer) and drain well, then rinse it lightly under the cold tap. Add the squid, mussels and prawns to the dressed pasta and toss well to mix. Cover the bowl with clear film (plastic wrap) and chill in the refrigerator for about 4 hours. Toss well and adjust the seasoning to taste before serving.

COOK'S TIP

For a quick and easy short cut, buy ready-prepared seafood salad from an Italian delicatessen and toss it with the pasta and dressing.

Insalata con Pomodori Arrostiti e Rucola

Roasted Cherry Tomato and Rocket Salad

THIS IS A GOOD SIDE SALAD to accompany barbecued chicken, steaks or chops. Roasted tomatoes are very juicy, with an intense, smoky-sweet flavour.

INGREDIENTS

225g/8oz/2 cups dried chifferini or pipe
450g/1lb ripe baby Italian plum tomatoes, halved lengthways
75ml/5 tbsp extra virgin olive oil
2 garlic cloves, cut into thin slivers
30ml/2 tbsp balsamic vinegar
2 pieces sun-dried tomato in olive oil, drained and chopped
large pinch of sugar, to taste
1 handful rocket (arugula), about 65g/2½oz
salt and ground black pepper

Serves 4

1 Preheat the oven to 190°C/375°F/Gas 5. Meanwhile, cook the pasta in salted boiling water according to the instructions on the packet.

2 Arrange the halved tomatoes cut side up in a roasting pan, drizzle 30ml/2tbsp of the oil over them and sprinkle with the slivers of garlic and salt and pepper to taste. Roast in the oven for 20 minutes, turning once.

3 Put the remaining oil in a large bowl with the vinegar, sun-dried tomatoes, sugar and a little salt and pepper to taste. Stir well to mix. Drain the pasta, add it to the bowl of dressing and toss to mix. Add the roasted tomatoes and mix gently.

4 Before serving, add the chopped rocket, toss lightly and taste for seasoning. Serve either at room temperature or chilled.

VARIATIONS

- *If you are in a hurry and don't have time to roast the tomatoes, you can make the salad with halved raw tomatoes instead.*
- *If you like, add 150g/5oz mozzarella cheese, drained and diced, with the rocket in Step 4.*

Insalata Estiva

Summer Salad

RIPE RED TOMATOES, mozzarella and olives make a good base for a fresh and tangy salad for a summer lunch.

INGREDIENTS

350g/12oz/3 cups dried penne
3 ripe tomatoes, diced
150g/5oz packet mozzarella di bufala, drained and diced
10 pitted black olives, sliced
10 pitted green olives, sliced
1 spring onion (scallion), thinly sliced on the diagonal
1 handful fresh basil leaves

For the dressing

90ml/6 tbsp extra virgin olive oil
15ml/1 tbsp balsamic vinegar or lemon juice
salt and ground black pepper

Serves 4

1 Cook the pasta according to the instructions on the packet. Transfer it into a colander and rinse under cold running water, then shake the colander to remove as much water as possible. Leave the pasta to drain.

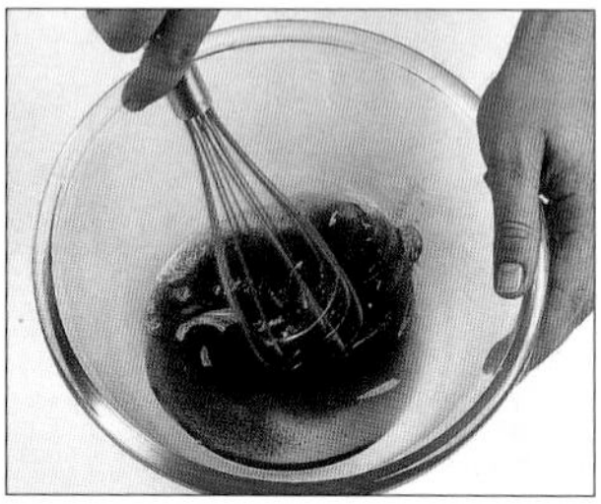

2 Make the dressing. Whisk the olive oil and balsamic vinegar or lemon juice in a large bowl with a little salt and pepper to taste.

3 Add the pasta, mozzarella, tomatoes, olives and spring onion to the dressing and toss together well. Taste for seasoning before serving, sprinkled with basil leaves.

COOK'S TIP

Mozzarella made from buffalo milk has more flavour than the type made with cow's milk. It is sold in most delicatessens and supermarkets.

VARIATION

Make the salad more substantial by adding other ingredients, such as sliced peppers, flaked tuna, bottled or canned anchovy fillets or diced ham.

Fusilli Campagnoli

Country Pasta Salad

COLOURFUL, TASTY and nutritious, this is the ideal pasta salad for a summer picnic.

INGREDIENTS

300g/11oz/2¾ cups dried fusilli
150g/5oz green beans, topped and tailed and cut into 5cm/2in lengths
1 potato, about 150g/5oz, diced
200g/7oz baby tomatoes, hulled and halved
2 spring onions, finely chopped
90g/3½oz Parmesan cheese, diced or shaved
6–8 pitted black olives, cut into rings
15–30ml/1–2 tbsp capers, to taste

For the dressing

90ml/6 tbsp extra virgin olive oil
15ml/1 tbsp balsamic vinegar
15ml/1 tbsp chopped fresh flat leaf (Italian) parsley
salt and ground black pepper

Serves 6

1 Cook the pasta according to the instructions on the packet. Drain it into a colander, rinse under cold running water until cold, then shake the colander to remove as much water as possible. Leave to drain and dry, shaking the colander occasionally.

2 Cook the beans and diced potato in a pan of salted boiling water for 5–6 minutes or until tender. Drain and leave to cool.

3 Make the dressing. Put all the ingredients in a large bowl with salt and pepper to taste and whisk well to mix.

4 Add the baby tomatoes, spring onions, Parmesan, olive rings and capers to the dressing, then the cold pasta, beans and potato. Toss well to mix. Cover and leave to stand for about 30 minutes. Taste for seasoning before serving.

COOK'S TIP

Buy a piece of fresh Parmesan from the delicatessen. This is the less mature (sharp), softer type, which is sold as a table cheese, rather than the hard, mature Parmesan used for grating.

Insalata di Pollo e Broccoli

Chicken and Broccoli Salad

GORGONZOLA MAKES A tangy dressing that goes well with both chicken and broccoli. Serve for a lunch or supper dish, with crusty Italian bread.

INGREDIENTS

175g/6oz broccoli florets, divided into small sprigs
225g/8oz/2 cups dried farfalle
2 large cooked chicken breast fillets

For the dressing

90g/3½oz Gorgonzola cheese
15ml/1 tbsp white wine vinegar
60ml/4 tbsp extra virgin olive oil
2.5–5ml/½–1 tsp finely chopped fresh sage, plus extra sage sprigs to garnish
salt and ground black pepper

Serves 4

1 Cook the broccoli florets in a large pan of salted boiling water for 3 minutes. Remove with a slotted spoon and rinse under cold running water, then spread out on kitchen towels to drain and dry.

2 Add the pasta to the broccoli cooking water, then bring back to the boil and cook according to the packet instructions. When cooked, drain the pasta into a colander, rinse under cold running water until cold, then leave to drain and dry, shaking the colander occasionally.

3 Remove the skin from the cooked chicken breasts and cut the meat into bitesize pieces.

4 Make the dressing. Put the cheese in a large bowl and mash with a fork, then whisk in the wine vinegar followed by the oil and sage and salt and pepper to taste.

5 Add the pasta, chicken and broccoli. Toss well, then season to taste and serve, garnished with sage.

Insalata Saporita

Pasta Salad with Salami and Olives

GARLIC AND HERB DRESSING gives a Mediterranean flavour to a handful of ingredients from the store cupboard and refrigerator, making this an excellent salad for winter. There are many different types of Italian salami that can be used. *Salame napoletano* is coarse cut and peppery, while *salame milanese* is fine cut and mild in flavour.

INGREDIENTS

225g/8oz/2 cups dried gnocchi or conchiglie
50g/2oz/½ cup pitted black olives, quartered lengthways
75g/3oz thinly sliced salami, any skin removed, diced
½ small red onion, finely chopped
1 large handful fresh basil leaves

For the dressing

60ml/4 tbsp extra virgin olive oil
good pinch of sugar, to taste
juice of ½ lemon
5ml/1 tsp Dijon mustard
10ml/2 tsp dried oregano
1 garlic clove, crushed
salt and ground black pepper

Serves 4

1 Cook the pasta in a pan of salted boiling water according to the packet instructions.

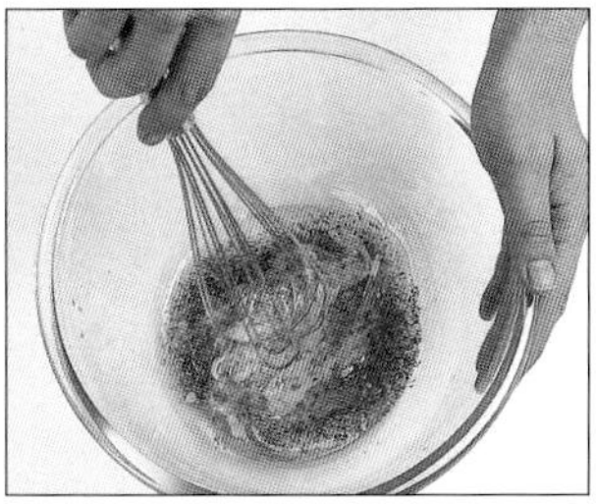

2 Meanwhile, make the dressing for the pasta. Put all the ingredients for the dressing in a large bowl with a little salt and pepper to taste, and whisk well to mix.

3 Drain the pasta thoroughly, add it to the bowl of dressing and toss well to mix. Leave the dressed pasta to cool, stirring occasionally.

4 When the pasta is cold, add the remaining ingredients and toss well to mix again. Taste for seasoning, then serve immediately.

Index

Author's Acknowledgements

I am indebted most of all to Elisa Surini, for her invaluable assistance with this book, and also to Roberta Mitchell in Rome, for her up-to-the-minute knowledge and advice. I would also like to thank my daughter Sophie and the following friends, each of whom has given me some of her favourite recipes: Alessia Ferretti, Silvana Hobcraft-Capraro, Isabella Medri, Stefania Spiga and Karin Trczka. Last, but by no means least, I would like to thank Liz Mizon, for her unstinting administrative and technological support.

Publisher's Acknowledgements

The publishers would like to thank Jenni Fleetwood for her skilful editing, Annabel Ford for tracking down the pasta shapes for photography, photographers William Lingwood (recipes) and Janine Hosegood (cut-outs), props stylist Helen Trent, Lucy McKelvie and Kate Jay, who prepared the food for photography, Elisa Surini for checking the Italian terms, and Giuseppe Tranchina of Italbrokers Foodservice, who supplied egg pasta for recipe testing and photography.